Rocking in the Free World

Rocking in the Free World

*Popular Music and the Politics of Freedom
in Postwar America*

Nicholas Tochka

OXFORD
UNIVERSITY PRESS

Oxford University Press is a department of the University of Oxford. It furthers
the University's objective of excellence in research, scholarship, and education
by publishing worldwide. Oxford is a registered trade mark of Oxford University
Press in the UK and certain other countries.

Published in the United States of America by Oxford University Press
198 Madison Avenue, New York, NY 10016, United States of America.

© Oxford University Press 2023

All rights reserved. No part of this publication may be reproduced, stored in
a retrieval system, or transmitted, in any form or by any means, without the
prior permission in writing of Oxford University Press, or as expressly permitted
by law, by license, or under terms agreed with the appropriate reproduction
rights organization. Inquiries concerning reproduction outside the scope of the
above should be sent to the Rights Department, Oxford University Press, at the
address above.

You must not circulate this work in any other form
and you must impose this same condition on any acquirer.

Library of Congress Cataloging-in-Publication Data
Names: Tochka, Nicholas, author.
Title: Rocking in the free world : popular music and the politics of
freedom in postwar America / Nicholas Tochka.
Description: [1.] | New York : Oxford University Press, 2023. |
Includes bibliographical references and index.
Identifiers: LCCN 2023004634 (print) | LCCN 2023004635 (ebook) |
ISBN 9780197566510 (hardback) | ISBN 9780197566534 (epub)
Subjects: LCSH: Rock music—Political aspects—United States—History—20th century.
Classification: LCC ML3918.R63 T63 2023 (print) | LCC ML3918.R63 (ebook) |
DDC 781.660973—dc23/eng/20230131
LC record available at https://lccn.loc.gov/2023004634
LC ebook record available at https://lccn.loc.gov/2023004635

DOI: 10.1093/oso/9780197566510.001.0001

Printed by Sheridan Books, Inc., United States of America

. . . a history of rock cannot help but violate the music's essence. As quick kicks, rock should be as disposable as a paper plate. That it isn't may reflect the kind of ersatz historical tug that masks America's empty sense of tradition; then again, it may be that rock really does represent a lasting cultural statement, a popular expression that will survive its moment, either as artifact or artwork.

    Jim Miller, *Rolling Stone Illustrated History of Rock 'n' Roll***, 1977**

Make no mistake about it: only America, the greatest social laboratory in the history of the planet, could have produced a cultural phenomenon as singularly violent, plaintive, reckless, tender, risky, lurid, threatening, heart-wrenching, grotesque, corruptible, and vital as rock and roll. It took a land where every soul had a fairly decent shot at the awesome state of freedom *with* license to hatch an art form so triumphantly incendiary.

    Timothy White, *Rock Stars***, 1984**

Contents

List of Illustrations   ix
Preface and Acknowledgments   xi

    Prologue: Popular Music as Political Theory   1

1. How Rock 'n' Roll Invented the Teenager   7
2. How Americans Rocked Cairo (and London, and Moscow, and Tehran, and . . .)   29
3. How Trash Became Art   54
4. How the Counterculture Dug Deeper   77
5. How Songwriters Revealed Our Inner Truth   107
6. How Rock Got Real Again   131
7. How We Taught the World to Sing   156

    Epilogue: Rocking in the Free World   182

Notes   189
References   209
Index   219

List of Illustrations

Figure 1   "Good Clubs Are Democratic," *Planning for Fun: How to Organize a Teen-Age Night Club* (1944). Written and published for Boys and Girls of America by Bottlers of Royal Crown Cola   12

Figure 2   "A Reporter Attempts to Explain What It All Means," a photo-essay by Gertrude Samuels, "Why They Rock 'n' Roll—and Should They?," in *New York Times* (12 January 1958)   16

Figure 3   "President Eisenhower's Middle East Policies Are Being Called the Rock 'n' Roll Doctrine," by Osgood Carruthers, "Rock 'n' Roll Cuts Swath in Egypt," in *New York Times* (23 June 1957)   30

Figure 4   "Rock 'n' Roll is a Controversial Subject in the World," photo collage from a "Global Report on Rock 'n' Roll," in *New York Times* (20 April 1958)   44

Figure 5   "If Ravi Shankar is *the* classical music guy of India, then the Bauls are the Muddy Waters," Bob Dylans's manager, Albert Grossman. Album cover, *The Bengali Bauls . . . at Big Pink* (1969) Buddha Records BDS 5050   87

Figure 6   "Three rock-n-roll bands were in the center of the gymnasium playing simultaneously all during the dance, and all during the dance, movies were shown on two screens at the opposite ends of the gymnasium," from the Burns Report, released by the California State Senate's Subcommittee on Un-American Activities (June 1965). Collage "Hippies," the Group Image c. 1967, National Portrait Gallery, Smithsonian Institution   98

Figure 7   "Of course, don't ever tell anybody that they're not free, 'cause then they're gonna get real busy killin' and maimin' to prove to you that they are. Oh, yeah, they gonna talk to you, and talk to you, and talk to you about individual freedom. But they see a free individual, it's gonna scare 'em.'" Lobby card, *Easy Rider*. Copyright 1969, renewed 1997 Columbia Pictures Industries, Inc. All rights reserved. Courtesy of Columbia Pictures   117

Figure 8   "Good ole George, honest and bland, is being transformed into sexy George, George the Hip, George the Magnetic, all because of a powerful new magic weapon in his campaign," according to Maureen Orth in the *Village Voice*. Concert poster *McGovern: Carole King- Barbara Streisand- James Taylor: In Concert* (1972)   120

Figure 9   "We gots just one thing to say to you fuckin' hippies, and that is: 'Rock 'n' Roll Is Here To Stay!'" Sha Na Na's Bowser, introducing track D2, "Rock 'n' Roll Is Here To Stay." Album cover, *The Golden Age of Rock 'n' Roll* (1973) Kama Sutra KSBS 2073-2   135

x List of Illustrations

Figure 10   "And there was a seven-hour punk concert, 'Rock against Reagan,' featuring such artists as The Dead Kennedys. *I left my heart in San Francisco* ... But that was the kind of effluvium that is to be found, in more diluted form perhaps, in half a dozen other large American cities," in *National Review* (10 August 1984). Concert bill, *Rock Against Reagan* (1984)   152

Figure 11   "They're talking about, 'Oh there's no spirit—it's not like Woodstock.' Well, I say screw them—Woodstock's over, the Sixties are finished, and I say: Good riddance!" Danny Elfman, on stage at the US Festival '83. Photograph by Bev Davies   167

Figure 12   "I'm not here for any government. I've come to play rock 'n' roll for you in the hope that one day all the barriers will be torn down," Bruce Springsteen in East Germany (1988). Photograph by Sandra Tiger   177

Preface and Acknowledgments

I'm sitting in the reading room at the National Library in Tirana, Albania, flipping through decades-old communist-era newspapers and journals. For the last few months, I had been reading chronologically, beginning in the 1950s. But as I reach the late 1980s, something strange happens. A few stories about American rock 'n' roll, translated from English into Albanian, appear in the back pages of a few journals. The author by-lines seem familiar, and suddenly I am struck by a sense of déjà vu.

These are the same kind of stories I had eagerly consumed in magazines like *Rolling Stone* or *Guitar Player* as an American teenager in the 1990s. But I am reading them out of context, through the eyes of the pro-Western intellectuals self-appointed to oversee Albanians' transition from state socialism to market capitalism. Many of these people believed rock to be an important political symbol. For them, it represented a constellation of values related to "freedom." And to these intellectuals, I would come to realize, the stories that American journalists told about rock's political power provided a privileged lens for understanding their own communist past—and democratic future. While that insight shaped my academic writing about how Albanians experienced postsocialism, my initial sense of disorientation remained. Because as I began pondering how American narratives about rock 'n' roll had, in this case quite literally, been translated half a world away, I suddenly realized how little I understood about where these stories had come from in the first place.

It seemed obvious to me that the stories Albanians were telling about rock and its politics of freedom explained more about the political situation in Albania than about a quality inherent in the music itself. So why hadn't I considered the opposite—that the stories *Americans* invented about rock 'n' roll revealed equally significant insights about the United States? Like many fans, I had taken rock's self-mythologizing at face value. But where did these stories come from? And just how deeply had they shaped my own beliefs about freedom, democracy, even the very idea of "America" itself?

* * *

If today I am a rock 'n' roll skeptic, I once was a true believer. As a white teenager playing bass in garage bands during the 1990s, I acquired a basic musical grammar that emphasized simplicity, rawness, authenticity, honesty. My friends and I learned a particular story about the political significance of rock music, from its riotous origins in the 1950s, to its countercultural roots in the 1960s, to its antiestablishment challenge in the 1970s, to its corporate subversion in the 1980s. Guitar magazines, trade paperbacks, classic concert films, and television documentaries guided our political maturation. We learned to appreciate the classics, groups such as the Beatles, the Doors, and Jimi Hendrix, and to recognize the genius of Bob Dylan, Lou Reed, and Frank Zappa. We came to value punk and hardcore groups such as the Ramones, Dead Kennedys, and Black Flag, and we discovered less commonly known (at least for suburban Massachusetts) critical darlings such as the Fugs, MC5, or Flipper. Above all, we learned to separate the real from the fake, artful self-expression from the soul-deadening commercial stuff. We even learned to play for real, expressing our own personal truths by imitating the sincerity we knew to listen for on record.

Self-expression, individualism, the grit to speak truth to power: I am sketching with broad strokes the kinds of taken-for-granted, common-sense assumptions we held. For a long time, I held such truths to be self-evident, proof of the cultural and political significance of the music my friends and I esteemed. And we were not outliers. By the 2000s, the term rockism became a popular way to label this stance. "A rockist," Kelefa Sanneh wrote in the *New York Times*, "isn't just someone who loves rock 'n' roll, who goes on and on about Bruce Springsteen, who champions ragged-voiced singer-songwriters no one has ever heard of. A rockist is someone who reduces rock 'n' roll to a caricature, then uses that caricature as a weapon. Rockism means idolizing the authentic old legend (or underground hero) while mocking the latest pop star; lionizing punk while barely tolerating disco; loving the live show and hating the music video; extolling the growling performer while hating the lip-syncher."[1] Counter-perspectives emerged to nuance this critique, but on the whole, it rings true to me. For sure, I suffered from what Saul Austerlitz once called "*Rolling Stone* disease."[2]

This syndrome has prompted two main responses. Criticism conducted under the label "poptimism" or "popism" aims to take seriously the kinds of commercial music formerly denied serious critical consideration. Poptimists institutionalize a more diverse array of musicians, mounting campaigns to induct hip hop or pop artists into the Rock and Roll Hall of Fame, ensuring their annual year-end "Best Album" lists include artists from diverse demographic backgrounds, curating and archiving non-rock styles at their institutions, and broadening the purview of popular music history surveys at their universities. And to this compensatory work has been joined a new strain of revisionist historiography. The revisionist historians often eschew major styles, artists, and trends; they instead seek out the untapped margins of popular music's "forgotten" or "silenced" histories, choosing topics, styles, or locations that allow them to foreground the contributions of a more diverse cast of characters.[3]

And so, by and large, much writing about the heyday of rock 'n' roll (let's say, the period between the 1950s and the 1980s) now begins from a position of mistrust. On closer examination, that ineffable essence that rock's chroniclers had for so long taken for granted—its rebelliousness, its potentials for resistance, its sheer political power—"seems to float in the air, unsupported by any edifice."[4] Authors inevitably must tell the "secret" or "untold" or "shadow" histories of rock, uncovering its hidden figures, performances, and stories.

* * *

This book takes the opposite tack. It revisits major figures, albums, and performances composing rock 'n' roll's mainstream, not-so-hidden narratives. In the following chapters, I examine how dominant stories about the political significance of rock music *could* emerge—that is, I sketch the *conditions of possibility* in which rock acquired political meanings between the 1950s and the 1980s. Recent reappraisals of that era have helped explain the erasure from rockist narratives of people who were not white, male, or heterosexual. But we still need to parse the basis on which so many critics and fans argued for rock's significance in the first place: its purported political power in general, as well as its imagined relationship to a collection of American cultural values in particular.

As my own political commitments evolve, I'm finding myself questioning certain longstanding claims about the "power" of music to effect change. My coursework in graduate school taught me to identify how popular music gives voice to the voiceless, how it enables the politically disenfranchised to imagine new political futures for themselves, how it challenges illiberalism, and resists or even subverts authoritarian political structures. As I'm writing these words today, liberals in the United States are making similar claims with renewed urgency. That's one reason why, I think, we need to understand where these ideas came from in the first place. Because knowing the genesis of these stories, and how they spread so widely, might allow us to see more clearly the potentials—but also the limits—of music as a political force in the United States today.

* * *

I'm grateful to the very many people who have contributed to this project over the past few years. Thanks to my former students at Tufts University and Northern Arizona University, where I first posed some of the ideas in this book, and to my former colleagues Barbara Haggh-Huglo, Olga Haldey, Richard King, Fernando Rios, Pat Warfield, and Larry Witzleben at the University of Maryland for their feedback and support during the project's early stages. Will Robin read several chapter drafts at the proposal stage, and I'm especially grateful to him for his advice and friendship.

This project has benefited from feedback I've received at conferences organized by the Society for Ethnomusicology, IASPM, and IASPM-ANZ since 2016. I'd especially like to acknowledge the larger community of popular music scholars here in Australia and New Zealand. Financial support from the University of Maryland and the University of Melbourne allowed me to present at these conferences and conduct archival research; a grant from the Rock and Roll Hall of Fame enabled me to visit their archives and library. A huge thanks to the librarians and staff members at the Rock and Roll Hall of Fame Library and Archives, the New York Public Library Special Collections, the New York Public Library for the Performing Arts at Lincoln Center Archives, and the University of Melbourne. Thanks also to my editors at Oxford University Press, Suzanne Ryan and then Norm Hirschy, as well as the anonymous reviewers who read my work so carefully and generously.

Parts of this book have received helpful feedback at presentations here in Melbourne. Thanks to participants at the Conservatorium's Postgraduate Seminar and the Melbourne Eurasianist Seminar Series. For their support and comments, thanks also to my colleagues here, past and present: Carla Blackwood, Julie Fedor, John Gabriel, Tami Gadir, Erin Helyard, David Irving, Linda Kouvaras, Richard Kurth, Paul Long, Una McIlvenna, Ken Murray, Melanie Plesch, Cath Strong, and Paul Watt. Without the skillful and good-humored help of several research assistants, this book would've taken a lot longer and included even more mistakes. Thank you Alex Hedt, Krishan Meepe, and Stephanie Shon. And a very special thanks to Liz Kertesz and Michael Christoforidis for their ongoing encouragement, advice, and friendship.

Thanks and much love to Dave, my first bandmate. Thanks to my beautiful children, B, Sot, and Nita, who have suffered through years of dad rock over the course of this project. And my last thank you goes to my father: for filling the home I grew up in with records and books, and for giving me the care and support that allowed me so many opportunities to make music, read, and think. This book is dedicated to him.

Prologue: Popular Music as Political Theory

It is late January of 1988, and rock royalty packs the grand ballroom at the Waldorf-Astoria in Manhattan for the Rock and Roll Hall of Fame's induction ceremony. Rock 'n' roll screamer Little Richard laughs with *Rolling Stone* founder Jann Wenner and famed label boss Ahmet Ertegun, as these and other major figures carve out places for themselves in the history of this distinctly American art form. Bruce Springsteen is on hand to introduce Bob Dylan, honored this year along with the Beatles, the Beach Boys, the Drifters, and the Supremes as a foundational voice in the tradition. Stepping on stage, he delivers what the amused critic at the *Washington Post* calls a "Bruce Springsteen Memorial Induction Anecdote."[1]

"The first time that I heard Bob Dylan," Springsteen begins, "I was in the car with my mother and we were listening to maybe WMCA. And on came that snare shot that sounded like somebody kicked open the door to your mind, from 'Like a Rolling Stone.' I ran out and I bought the single and ran home and I put on the 45. But they must have made a mistake at the factory because a Lenny Welch song came on. The label was wrong. So I ran back, got [the Dylan record], and I came back and I played it."

The audience claps and laughs. The single might have been Welch's "Since I Fell for You," a hit by the schmaltzy, middle-of-the-road crooner that reached #4 on the Billboard Charts in 1963. (Or "A Taste of Honey," released the previous year? The cameras do not pan to Paul, George, and Ringo, who included a saccharine cover of that song on *Please Please Me*.) The audience is laughing in recognition. They understand that a teenaged Springsteen needed something *real*: that voice that "thrilled and scared" him, those lyrics that raised the hairs on the back of his neck. He needed that snare shot. Not syrupy, commercial Lenny Welch.

Back to the podium.

"Dylan was a revolutionary," Springsteen concludes. "The way that Elvis freed your body, Bob freed your mind. He showed us that just because the music was innately physical did not mean that it was anti-intellect. He had the vision and the talent to expand a pop song until it could contain the whole world."[2]

Six months later, Springsteen brought the E Street Band to East Berlin on their Tunnel of Love Express Tour. "I'm not here for any government," Springsteen tells the Berlin audience in halting German, reading from a scrap of paper words rendered phonetically by his taxi driver just an hour before. "I've come to play rock 'n' roll for you in the hope that one day all the barriers will be torn down." The E Street Band launches into the opening chords of "Chimes of Freedom" (1964), Dylan's psalm to the marginalized and the downtrodden, here ringing out against a Berlin Wall soon to crumble, then fall.

Six weeks after East Berlin, Springsteen headed back out on the road to headline Amnesty International's Human Rights Now! Tour. Organized by legendary rock promoter Bill Graham, this latest iteration in a string of charity mega-events sought to raise money and awareness about political prisoners. ("Feel as if the collective spirit of rock has suddenly been hot-wired for social activism?" *Time* magazine asked.[3]) Ticket purchases included a pocket edition of the United Nations Declaration of Human Rights; T-shirts emblazoned with the tour logo, a dynamic human figure crashing through a wall, could be bought separately. And the all-star line-up's encore? A massive sing-along to Dylan's 1967 song, "I Shall Be Released."

Though each musician appears at different points, this book is not about Springsteen or Dylan. Rather, it seeks to explain how political labels related to an abstract, US-invented notion of "freedom" became affixed to rock music, and certain kinds of rock musicians, between the 1950s and the 1980s. Springsteen provides a useful example of this phenomenon as it reached its mature form. Consider how both liberal Walter Mondale and conservative Ronald Reagan sought his endorsement during their 1984 presidential campaigns. (Though Springsteen disavowed each: "I'm not registered as one party or another," he told *Rolling Stone*'s Kurt Loder. "I don't generally think along those lines.")[4] Or consider how rock's meaning had become so elastic that America's longest-standing liberal outlet, *The Nation*, could laud Springsteen for having "brought an unmistakable progressive political message to his concerts"—and this in describing a tour supporting an album the conservative *National Review* praised for songs whose "heroes are invested with a cowboy libertarianism."[5]

* * *

We are beginning at the end, at the culmination of a grand narrative about the political significance of rock music in the United States. The story explained the music's revolutionary potential. Rock hit you in the gut; it taught you to liberate yourself, body and mind; it freed you from the social mores and structures that tried to make you unfree. The rock gospel—the revelation of that first snare hit—divided your life into two distinct periods: before rock, and after. Its ambassadors promoted rock's message globally; publishers and critics helped theorize its contours in the mainstream press; a body of albums, songs, and performances authored by figures such as Springsteen and Dylan comprised its canon.

This kind of music, it seemed, could only have originated in the United States. After all, the conditions that produced rock had also forged the national temperament of the American people, maybe even the democratic nature of the First World itself. Nowhere would the American character of rock music emerge quite so distinctly than when exported outside this free world. Electric guitars feeding back up and over the Berlin Wall, power chords ringing out to shred the Iron Curtain, rock musicians helped teach the captive peoples of the Second World the meaning of freedom. Coming together in song, these same musicians expressed in one voice the imperative to emancipate the developing peoples of the Third World from their bonds of poverty and backwardness. For ultimately, rock's message had revealed itself to be universal, capable of addressing the human condition itself.

Or at least, that's the story.

But we can unbundle the threads making up this larger narrative, tracing each constituent strand's history to its first emergence, stripping away its assumptions about the nature of the postwar world, its inhabitants, and the power of popular music. Because rock 'n' roll had to *become* enmeshed with an entire constellation of political values that, at least initially in the 1950s, seemed entirely at odds with this new style. Radical conservatives wove conspiracy theories about rock 'n' roll's Communist origins, while racists damned the "jungle rhythms" of this "Mau Mau" music as not just black, but backwards. Liberals worried about the dehumanizing effects of this textbook example of "mass culture," as social scientists predicted dire political consequences for young consumers, cataloguing the music's deleterious effects alongside the maleficent specters of Second World brainwashing and Third World trancing practices.

From a plot to promote unthinking conformism to a vehicle for authentic self-expression, from a technique for social control to a means of radical political liberation, from a declaration of barbarism to an expression of universal transcendence: Americans would learn the truth about rock 'n' roll and its politics of freedom.

* * *

There exists in the United States a long tradition of narrating the relationship between rock music and liberation. "This is a kind of freedom we are learning about," American rock critic Greil Marcus wrote in "Who Put the Bomp?," from his important early collection of essays, *Rock and Roll Will Stand* (1969). "Affecting our own perspectives—artistic, social, and personal—it makes the tangible and the factual that much more reprehensible, that much more deadening. The intellectual leap, the habit of free association, the facility of making a single rock 'n' roll metaphor the defining idea for a situation or a time of one's life—that is the kind of thinking that makes sense."[6]

By 1975, Marcus had expanded that conceptualization of the "single rock 'n' roll metaphor" in his classic book *Mystery Train*, arguing that rock 'n' roll explains America—and America, rock 'n' roll. "What I bring to this book, at any rate, is no attempt at synthesis," he states in the prologue, "but a *recognition* of unities in the American imagination *that already exist*. They are *natural* unities, I think, but elusive; I learned, in the last two years, that simply because of those unities, the resonance of the best American images [with rock 'n' roll] is profoundly deep and impossibly broad."[7] Through recordings, rock musicians "delivered a new vision of America with their music, and more people than anyone can count are still trying to figure out how to live in it."[8] The best artists "dramatize a sense of what it is to be American," Marcus continues, "what it means, what it's worth, what the stakes of life in America might be."[9] Close examination of this music and their stories reveal struggles and aspirations, indeed the limitations and potentials of America itself. And it's at this point that claims about identity become assertions about a politics of freedom: "It may be that the most interesting American struggle is the struggle to set oneself free from the limits one is born to, and then to learn something of the value of those limits."[10]

For sure, Marcus is not naïve. I wonder if he's just too good a writer, too persuasive, incapable of resisting a soaring rhetorical flourish or small exaggeration in the service of his inimitable style. And certainly, not all critics have agreed with the loftier pronouncements. "Rock is *not* political theory," Langdon Winner wrote, also in *Rock and Roll Will Stand*, "and never will be."[11] So I am less interested in testing the claims that writers like Marcus make about rock music than in understanding how these claims first came to seem common-sense. That's not to say that the political labels people attach to rock music have been in any way coherent. To again use American presidential campaigns as a kind of crude barometer, every candidate since 1968 (when a young Jerry Garcia appeared fleetingly in a Nixon ad pitched to the "American Youth") has invoked the messaging power of rock in one way or another. The aim here is more modest: to catalogue some of the labels people have assigned to rock music from the 1950s and the 1980s, and to place these people within the postwar contexts that made their labeling seem not only obvious, but also essential.

Before we get to those moments, a brief note on methods. As I've suggested, the politics of popular music to many of us make sense at a gut level. We just *know* that it stands for rebellion, that it provides a means for not only challenging but also transforming the status quo. We *know* that illiberal states make policies to curtail its power, that they silence the voices of rock musicians, and we assume that this is a logical response: Rock *did* help topple the Berlin Wall, right? Its core values—self-expression, individuality, truthfulness—also undergird liberal democracy, do they not? You can actually *hear* these political values: they are woven through lyrics and productions, embedded deep within the very grain of musicians' voices and instruments.

To combat my own biases, I've set for myself a few guiding questions. How did these values and truths *become* so self-evident? Over the course of the twentieth century, why did certain values and labels stick, while others did not? And what were the broader conditions of possibility in which the politics of rock *could* emerge in postwar America? The myth is the starting point, not the destination. And instead of merely deconstructing the narrative, we must parse the conditions that made this story possible. Following the model of Jack Hamilton (who explained how Americans learned that rock was "white"), I want to "tell the story of those stories" about how rock set us free.[12] And so my object is also "to listen to [the] music against and alongside the stories we've told ourselves about it."[13] Time has worn down their rough edges, smoothing these stories into forms we recognize today. To restore their original features, the following chapters examine seven key moments when rock 'n' roll acquired its political meanings. These moments do not represent a comprehensive list; certain events, people, and ideas have necessarily been left out. Guiding my selection has been overall significance: Was a problem widely discussed in its time? Did it directly influence how future commentators talked about rock music? And could it be argued that the problem helped shape how Americans see themselves today?

Debate has often arisen when someone claimed there existed a relationship between popular music and one or another political-economic system or ideology, whether democracy or capitalism, socialism or communism, fascism or anarchism. But such political labels, as well as their broader associated constellation of values, did not simply affix themselves willy-nilly to any musical style, artist, or performance. This depended on individuals who, for diverse reasons, knotted together or articulated political ideas with rock at certain moments.[14] Nor did this process always occur smoothly or predictably, and we will encounter contradictions and counter-debates. Because there's no reason why rock had to have acquired *any* of these specific extra-musical connotations. But the music did, and this resulted in new political truths: about the power of music in general, and rock 'n' roll in particular.

* * *

And so here we are. This is a book about rock 'n' roll—some of it—and America. Or better: this is a book about rock 'n' roll and one particular story of America. It considers those musicians understood to have been endowed with an ability to express politically significant visions of American democracy, and those sounds understood to exemplify some ineffable spirit of "freedom." It is about a particular, idealized vision of the United States, especially as this vision came to be fixed within an entire constellation of values concerning autonomy, individualism, self-expression, and democracy, and primarily as these values came to be conceived as peculiarly "American."

It is not a history of the genre, but rather an allusive, at times even opportunistic, examination of the conditions that allowed these values to be attributed to rock 'n' roll. It offers scant analysis of the music itself, instead locating albums, songs, and performances within some unexpected social and political contexts. The stories recounted below hardly reveal the entire picture. Yet understanding where these stories came from, and why they once made sense to so many people, may tell us something useful about the nature of twentieth-century political power in the United States.

So, this is what this book is about: Americans imagine, or once did imagine, that rock musicians manifest powerful political truths through their live and recorded performances. What postwar conditions—cultural and demographic, technological and ideological—enabled musicians and listeners to imaginatively link rock music to certain kinds of liberal democratic values between the 1950s and the 1980s? And what have been the consequences, both at home and abroad, of telling these stories?

Put simply: How did Americans learn that rock can make you free?

1
How Rock 'n' Roll Invented the Teenager

On a cool spring evening in 1958, disk jockey Alan Freed rocked Boston. "Alan Freed Presents The Big Beat" featured Jerry Lee Lewis, Buddy Holly, Chuck Berry, and Frankie Lymon. The revue registered record ticket sales thanks in no small part to Freed's hype for what his promotional materials called this "basic American heritage."

The Boston Arena show, however, proved the beginning of the end for the showman's career. Conflicting reports emerged as to what actually happened that Saturday night. The revue seemingly proceeded as planned until the venue's manager turned on the house lights to stop teenagers "dancing in the aisles, fighting and causing disturbances." Taking the microphone in hand, Freed addressed the audience. "It looks like the police in Boston," he's alleged to have said, "don't want you to have fun."[1]

The musicians left for Maine the next morning; newspaper stories wouldn't hit Boston's front pages until Monday. "Police said the outbreak came as 6,000 Rock 'N Rollers poured out of the arena," one reported. "Packs of trouble makers formed and incidents were reported from as far away as Roxbury and the public garden." Eventually, over a dozen incidents, including two alleged muggings by groups of teenage girls and a nearly fatal stabbing, were attributed to what appeared to be another "rock 'n' roll riot." "It might be a good thing," one suburban editorialist suggested, "to give Alan Freed a bit of the bumping around that innocent Bostonians got from the kids he bedeviled into gangsterism."[2]

By Wednesday, Mayor Hynes had banned all future rock 'n' roll shows, and Freed threatened to sue the police department for libel. The next day, a grand jury deliberated only three hours before returning an indictment against the promoter. Invoking a decades-old anti-anarchism statute, the district attorney charged Freed with "inciting the unlawful destruction of property." "One thing I can state positively," Freed's attorney protested to the *Boston Globe*, "is that my client is definitely not an anarchist."[3]

The anarchy charge loomed until November 1959, when prosecutors filed the case in exchange for a no-contest plea. As we will later see, Alan Freed's career would not survive this establishment rap against rock 'n' roll. But despite the municipal bans and congressional investigations, the growing anxieties of parents, teachers, and lawmakers, to say nothing of the exponential growth of expert studies showing how the music harmed young listeners, the "big beat" that Freed had helped break nationwide did.

How did rock 'n' roll affect teenaged bodies and minds? Should authorities take measures to stanch the music's spread? And what did its frightening effects on teenagers portend for American society as a whole? In seeking to understand and regulate rock 'n' roll, authorities in the 1950s often cited its anti-democratic potentials: to stir juvenile passions, to incite violence, to "bedevil" the normal adolescent. For a broad coalition of commentators, the big beat appeared to be a means for breaking down order in a "healthy" society, a vehicle for anarchism or communism or even fascism—political labels that were assigned to this music into the 1960s.

In these debates, the figure of the teenager loomed large as society's weak link. Postwar politics gave anxieties about young people teeth, endowing claims about popular music's negative psychopolitical effects on adolescent listeners with a marked sense of urgency. And for good reason, at least according to the experts. "Ever since the bursting of the fearful bomb in Hiroshima," Dorothy W. Baruch wrote in *How To Live With Your Teen-Ager* (1953), "we have known that our children are facing an age different from any previous age."[4] How should parents in such a world raise their children? And in particular, how should they navigate teenage-hood, a liminal stage Dr. Baruch called the "neither-nor" years, neither childhood, nor adulthood?

We often hear a story about teenagers and rock 'n' roll. "In the beginning there was a great darkness upon the Earth," quoth Bruce Springsteen (or a ghostwriter) in his memoir. "There was Christmas and your birthday but beyond that all was a black endless authoritarian void. Then, in a moment of light, blinding as a universe birthing a billion new suns, there was hope, sex, rhythm, excitement, possibility, a new way of seeing, of feeling, of thinking, of looking at your body, of combing your hair, of wearing your clothes, of moving and of living."[5] In this scenario, teenagers find themselves impatiently waiting for something—anything!—that answers their hunger for release from the repressed and repressive status quo of the United States in the 1950s. This is the "demand-side explanation of the emergence of rock music," sociologist Richard Peterson writes, in which "the baby boomers demanded music that spoke to their own condition."[6] Yet as Peterson points out, the first members of the postwar baby boom cohort had just turned nine when the rock 'n' roll fad hit in the mid-1950s. Most had not yet been born.

So let's discard that story. No pre-existing condition of American teenagehood required the invention of rock. But what if we flip the formula? If the

American teenager did not invent rock 'n' roll, then we might instead ask: How did rock 'n' roll invent the American teenager?

* * *

"Nation in tizzy!" proclaimed the trailer from *Don't Knock the Rock*. "Command performance of 'rock' film in London! Rangoon riots over rock 'n' roll!"[7] In February 1957, Alan Freed was flush with optimism—and advance ticket receipts. Still fifteen months away from the anarchism charge in Boston, the disk jockey had at last cracked Manhattan. His new jukebox film, an arch apologia for the raucous new sound, was set to play six nights at the Paramount Theater in Times Square. Its financial backers hoped it would prove a global hit on the scale of the previous year's *Blackboard Jungle*.

The promoter had cut an unusual deal for these shows. The Paramount would get the first fifty thousand dollars at the door, with Freed and his associates keeping 90 percent of the gross above that. When the *New York Times* reported on "Frenzy and Furor at the Paramount," Freed was reportedly on track to earn over a hundred thousand dollars. Not bad for a former sportscaster in Akron, Ohio.

Freed had arrived in New York City after five long years "inventing" rock 'n' roll in northwest Ohio (or so he later claimed). In Akron, Freed had serendipitously filled in one afternoon for an absent disk jockey. Spinning black rhythm-and-blues records, the white deejay expected to reach local black listeners. To his surprise, white teenagers tuned in—and Freed gave up the sports beat for good. Shedding his on-air moniker, Moondog, after an experimental musician using the same name sued him, he then tried to trademark the term "rock 'n' roll" before vertically integrating his big beat empire through song copyrights, films, and live shows.

The big beat appeared to be a growth industry. Freed had booked his first New York shows at a rundown ice rink only recently converted into a gymnasium way uptown. He worked with a mobbed-up promoter from Queens, Morris Levy, who later recalled the raucous mass dancing. "The ceiling was actually dripping from the moisture," Levy reminisced. "It was raining inside the St. Nicholas Arena."[8] Buoyed by this success, Freed and Levy next booked the Paramount on Flatbush Avenue in Brooklyn. Manhattan's more upscale venues viewed the strange and sweaty rites performed at these shows with suspicion; one dance had "the atmosphere of a revival meeting," reported *Cash Box*. But the mistrust quickly dissipated as the Brooklyn shows earned nearly two hundred thousand dollars, easily besting the previous record set by Jerry Lewis and Dean Martin.[9]

The mainstream press, however, reported not on these eye-popping sums, but on scenes of rocked-and-rolled teenagers gone amok. Over a hundred policemen and twenty-five private security guards had been deployed to control the crowds that began forming the day before Manhattan's first showing of *Don't Stop the Rock*. Glass windows at a ticket booth had been shattered; two girls crushed by a surging mob were treated for minor injuries. The fire marshal threatened to shut it down. We are witnessing "mass youth hysteria," a veteran police officer told the *Daily Mirror*, which ran photos under the headline "Rock 'n' Roll Madness."[10] The skirmishes—kids "shouted, tried to crowd past policemen and burst screaming through wooden barriers," they "stood on their seats, slapped and stomped and surged"—received widespread press coverage.[11] The *Washington Post* summed up the overall mood: "Wild, dungaree-clad teen-agers by the thousands stormed the Paramount Theater. . . . They smashed glass, danced barefooted in the aisles and their ecstatic screams drowned out the savage beat of the music that held them in sway."[12]

Speaking to journalists, Freed offered to interpret this phenomenon. He had earlier sought to preempt critics by affirming the big beat's distinctively national quality. "ROCK 'N ROLL is American! It is the only basic AMERICAN MUSICAL HERITAGE we can call our own," he wrote in early programs. "And I am very proud to have helped expose the 'Big Beat' to music loving Americans—instead of suppressing it—SO LET'S 'ROCK 'n' ROLL!' "[13] But now he offered a psychological interpretation of the surging, shouting, stomping mobs: "If the kids let off steam here, they won't be doing it somewhere else."[14]

For the moment, let's look at Freed's second claim. (We'll return to the idea that the music was distinctly "American" later.) Because serendipitously, the American Psychopathological Association had been holding its annual meetings at the Park Sheraton Hotel just as the President's Day shows got underway. Founded in 1910, the APPA explored abnormal human behavior; its 1957 event was focused on "problems of addiction and habituation."[15] An intrepid reporter for the *New York Times*, Milton Bracker, trekked crosstown to tap the group's collective expertise, preserving in his article "Experts Propose Study of 'Craze' " a snapshot of the emerging consensus on the big beat's psychopolitical significance at this precise moment. One educational psychologist likened the craze to "the medieval type of spontaneous lunacy where one person goes off and lots of other persons go off with him."[16] Several men cited a 1949 study by a Dr. Reginald Lourie claiming that up to 20 percent of babies naturally "rocked and rolled" to intense musical beats, even though that work primarily discussed children rocking in non-musical contexts. "Rhythmic motor patterns are presented as quite normal," Lourie had concluded, related to the healthy child's gross motor development.[17]

The most colorful analysis came from Joost A. M. Meerloo, then a research fellow in psychiatry at Columbia University. "Dr. Meerloo," Bracker reported, "described his first view of rock 'n' roll this way: Young people were moved by a juke box to dance themselves 'more and more into a prehistoric rhythmic trance until it had gone far beyond all the accepted versions of human dancing.' Sweeping the country and even the world, the craze 'demonstrated the violent mayhem long repressed everywhere on earth,' he asserted. He also saw possible effects in political terms: 'Why are rhythmical sounds and motions so especially contagious? A rhythmical call to the crowd easily foments mass ecstasy: "*Duce! Duce! Duce!*" The call repeats itself into the infinite and liberates the mind of all reasonable inhibitions . . . as in drug addiction, a thousand years of civilization fall away in a moment.'"[18]

Here we begin to discern the shape of what, at the time, appeared to be an existential political problem faced by the United States. The problem was not quite so simple as deciding whether the big beat represented "basic American musical heritage," as Freed had suggested, or a "national menace," as a growing number of concerned adults alleged. The politics of rock 'n' roll depended instead on a cluster of longstanding concerns about adolescence as a developmental stage and the role of the teenager in fostering a "healthy" democratic society.

And so to understand how its critics and proponents alike could assign political labels to this music in the 1950s, we need first to understand the roots of these anxieties. To do that, we must revisit the decades preceding the birth of rock 'n' roll.

* * *

While American troops fought for freedom in Western Europe and Asia, their younger siblings necked in town hall basements throughout the United States. A pamphlet distributed by Royal Crown Cola, "Planning For Fun" (1944), advised these young people in the nitty-gritty details of organizing their ad hoc social clubs. The soda executives were not entirely civic-minded. ("No party would be complete without refreshments!" the instructions read. "Look up your Royal Crown Cola bottler, ask him for soft drinks wholesale, and sell 'em for a nickel apiece.") But their "teen-age clubs" (sometimes "teen canteens") did address what appeared to be an urgent problem: how to better organize American adolescents who found themselves at loose ends.

The problem appeared grave. "Our Kids Are In Trouble," explained a *Life* magazine headline. Teens' naturally high energy levels, unleashed by a conflict seemingly remaking the social order of the United States overnight, demanded administration. But were adolescents receiving oversight? To answer this question, the journalist quoted a juvenile court judge in Indiana. "We're too busy winning the war," he said. "The hell with the future—that seems to be our philosophy." During wartime, young boys had become "thrill saboteurs," thieving, vandalizing, and assaulting innocent citizens, and young girls, "patriotutes," "good-time Janes," or "Victory girls," carousing and seducing soldiers.[19]

The out-of-control teenager represented just one among several ungovernable specters that haunted the wartime United States. Certain kinds of ungovernable bodies could be brought into line through direct action. In the name of national security, the US government would intern the racially marked bodies of Japanese-born American citizens; it deported or surveilled the linguistically or culturally marked bodies of many foreign-born Europeans.

The ungovernable bodies of white suburban adolescents, however, seemed to require a softer touch. "There are three things (and only three) that your club just can't get along without," the authors of "Planning For Fun"

Figure 1 "Good Clubs Are Democratic," *Planning for Fun: How to Organize a Teen-Age Night Club* (1944). Written and published for Boys and Girls of America by Bottlers of Royal Crown Cola

instructed: "(1) a source of music, (2) plenty of chairs, and (3) adequate lavatory facilities."[20] But teen canteens did not only keep kids off the streets; they also provided a forum for them to practice appropriate civic behavior. "Good clubs are democratic," would-be organizers learned. For best results, hold regular meetings, form volunteer committees to address potential problems, and create by-laws. "Rules are fun—when you make 'em yourself."[21] As one club's charter proposed, the institution offered "clean, wholesome recreational facilities and entertainment based on the American Republican form of government."[22] Recordings of popular music provided a glue to bind young people together in this extracurricular exercise in civics, with the record player, a device essential for conditioning healthy adolescent behaviors.

The belief that social conditions could be tweaked in order to promote such behaviors depended on new ideas about "the adolescent" as a social and political problem. This modern belief emerged in part from studies on "juvenile delinquency," a technical term invented only in the late nineteenth century.[23] Policymakers had initially viewed so-called delinquents—children who stole, committed acts of violence, or engaged in precocious sexual behavior—as inherently defective.[24] Reform-minded experts, however, rejected that interpretation, locating delinquency instead as deriving from observable, and thus ameliorable, social conditions. Communities could "study and reduce their own delinquency conditions," one reformer argued.[25] A range of conditions fostered unhealthy behaviors, from poverty and malnutrition, to the delinquent's general "home conditions," as well as to what another writer termed "the industrial situation" that had caused the "disorganization of family."[26]

By 1936, two sociologists could summarize the current state of research into delinquency as follows: "[O]ne needs to regard [the delinquent] as the product of forces as well as the sum of his present constituent parts; one must study him dynamically as well as statically; genetically as well as the finished result."[27] That shift from understanding the ungovernable adolescent not as a biological problem, but as a social problem, had profound implications. For if the problem of unruly adolescents could be traced to "dynamic forces" (rather than a young person's inherent defects), then its solution depended on accurately identifying and then modifying those forces (rather than, for instance, segregating or even sterilizing individual delinquents).

This still doesn't necessarily explain why the unruly teen became such a pressing political problem by the 1940s. A second body of expert knowledge provides the key to understanding how the behavior of young people would come to be seen as a threat to the postwar order not just in the United States, but as we will soon see, worldwide. When the United States entered WWII, anthropologists had long been exploring the relationship between individuals and society. Studies of "national character" or "personality" probed the psychological basis of political structures; wartime anxieties pushed this work to newfound prominence in publications aimed at general readers. In the 1920s and 1930s, social scientists had largely focused on so-called "primitive" societies. Successors turned their diagnostic tools to Germany, Japan, and later, the Soviet Union.[28] Germans had a "split" character, a kind of national schizophrenia that made fascism possible, wrote psychologist Erik Erikson; Ruth Benedict would reach a similar conclusion in her classic armchair ethnography of Japan, *The Chrysanthemum and the Sword* (1946).[29]

But what distinguished Americans? Well, that was the question. In 1942, anthropologist Margaret Mead (named by the *Washington Post* that year one of "eight outstanding women in the world" alongside Eleanor Roosevelt and Madame Chiang Kai-Shek) turned an ethnographic lens on her own society in the bestselling *And Keep Your Powder Dry: An Anthropologist Looks at America*. Sketched in only three weeks, the character study explores how "American babies are made into Americans."[30] The American personality, at least as Mead concluded, tended toward individualism; it demonstrated an inclination for democratic forms of governance. To postwar experts, this insight suggested a focus for policy: finding and implementing the conditions that would foster the individualistic, democratic personality type—and avoiding those that would thwart it.

Capitulation by first Germany and then Japan did not lessen the urgency with which experts studied the relationship between individuals and political orders. Instead it channeled this energy, motivating them to craft generalizable theories about human nature that, they hoped, might prevent a third world war. Books such as Theodor Adorno's *The Authoritarian Personality* (1950), for instance, a thick specialist work on how anti-democratic beliefs could be instilled in people, defined the "fascist character" (the book's original title). Following the Korean War, studies on "brainwashing" theorized how agents of illiberal regimes, especially in Communist states, could actively break down the mental integrity of their subjects, engendering blind, Pavlovian obedience in otherwise normal human beings.[31]

Let's pause for a moment and begin taking these threads in hand. One concerns the nature of society itself. An individual's "personality" (or, to use the post-1945 neologism, "identity") exhibits a kind of iconicity with their nation's political status quo. Some kinds of social structures produce psychological traits that render us susceptible to authoritarian or illiberal values. Of course, the opposite could be argued, too: that some structures make us more open to democratic or liberal values. The other thread has to do with young people. Certain conditions produce delinquency, or the abnormal expression of natural adolescent tendencies. Yet his actually makes adolescence accessible to experts: if we want healthy, normal teenagers, then we merely modify social conditions until delinquency disappears.

Postwar thinkers such as psychologist Erik Erikson would knot together these threads in ways that elevated teenagers—and the music they loved—to major political significance in the Fifties.[32] Consider Erikson's bestselling *Childhood and Society* (1950), which explained how societies flourished—or degenerated. The politically healthy society, Erikson argued, comprised psychologically healthy people. Psychologically healthy people had in turn successfully navigated a series of normative developmental stages from birth to old age. The key stage? Developing an "identity," or congruence, between your internal sense of self and how others in society see you. And the period when this normally occurs? Adolescence.

How young people navigated this treacherous terrain from childhood to adulthood would determine the fate of free society. And the fact that clothing, hairstyles, films, and of course records loomed so large in their lives made teens' postwar consumption a key object for not only study, but also regulation.

* * *

As the Coney Island El train inched through Brooklyn, journalist Harrison Salisbury observed his fellow passengers. One flipped through a newspaper, reading "something about a teenage gang shooting"; another glanced at the headline, "War with Russia Inevitable." "The teenage problem and the Russian problem—there was, I suspected, a somewhat closer connection between the great issues of our times than many imagined," Salisbury wrote, using this scene to introduce *The Shook-Up Generation*, his 1958 study of adolescence. "They might, even, be regarded as two faces of one coin—the conflicts that grew in the tainted soil of neglect at home and the conflicts abroad with their deep roots in social and political neglect on a wider scale."[33]

As bureau chief in Moscow for the *New York Times*, the newspaperman had witnessed "the Russian problem" firsthand. Now back in the United States, Salisbury turned his attention to teenagers. *The Shook-Up Generation* followed three volumes on the Soviet Union; reporting had brought him not only to the blue-collar streets of Red Hook, New Jersey, but also to the manicured lawns of suburban Massapequa, Long Island. These prosperous new enclaves featured good schools and houses that were "clean, neat, stuffed with consumer goods"—but also unwanted pregnancies and street violence.[34] "Split-level delinquency in the quiet suburban communities," Salisbury would conclude, "is just as deadly a menace to the younger generation as are the festering conflicts of the housing projects and old slums."[35]

Surely something deeper must be going on. The end of World War II had resulted in economic enfranchisement for untold numbers of Americans, whether white or black, rural or urban. So why hadn't prosperity and stability produced happy and stable kids? What accounted for the problems facing the youngsters that Salisbury, borrowing the title of the song written by Otis Blackwell and recorded the previous year by Elvis Presley, called the "shook-up" generation?

Evidence of teenaged volatility could be found in its most spectacular, public forms at rock 'n' roll films and dances. "Why do teenagers rock 'n' roll?" asked Gertrude Samuels in a photo-essay for the *New York Times* in early 1958. "And should they?"[36] The adolescents she polled gave many reasons: "It's the rhythm." "It's easy to listen to." "I don't like this symphony stuff that my father puts on the radio." "It makes you feel good." "It hops us up." "We like to go crazy."

In wide-angle group shots, the photographer Samuels shoots the girls and boys as a teeming mass of conformity, of unfettered libido. Their mouths open in ecstasy. Hands tear at faces and hair. Samuels brought an eye keen to tease out the psychopolitical effects of the beat on young listeners; she had cut her teeth documenting dehumanization in Europe's refugee camps in 1946, the lens of her bulky black Leica framing for Americans the horrific end results of

Figure 2 "A Reporter Attempts to Explain What It All Means," a photo-essay by Gertrude Samuels, "Why They Rock 'n' Roll—and Should They?," in *New York Times* (12 January 1958)

fascism. Can we discern echoes of this work in her closely cropped portraits of teenybopper rock 'n' rollers? The boy with too-thick eyebrows staring dully into space? The girl in her clinging sweater gaping, glassy eyed, lips slightly parted?

Their violence is distressing. Some claim that the music provides an "outlet for impulsive behavior or sexual aggression," Samuels writes, noting "this has not been proven by any thorough studies." But most troubling is their lock-step compliance with the group's norms. "So many of the girls wear a sort of uniform—tight, revealing sweaters with colorful kerchiefs, skin-tight toreador pants, white woollen socks and loafers; so many of the boys conform to a pattern—leather or sports jackets, blue jeans, loafers and cigarettes. Physically, it would seem as though the children feared to look different from one another, or lacked confidence in individuality. Indeed, many admit to this cheerfully: 'All the kids have this jacket,' said one boy, 'and I don't want to be different.'"

The bogeyman of conformity, that threat to American productivity, to say nothing of democracy itself, loomed large in debates over rock 'n' roll as a consumer good. But let's bracket that debate for now, to instead see why the experts queried by Samuels believed these young rock 'n' rollers had spurned individualism for these insensible expressions of collectivism. "What—who— is responsible for these sorties?" the journalist asked. A mother weighs in, as does a psychiatrist; a juvenile courts judge provides the bleakest answer. "It is our fault," she tells Samuels. "We haven't stirred the children with something to live by, to worship, to put their hopes in. They haven't the inspiration because we ourselves haven't put a high value on courage and liberty and working for others."

Elsewhere, experts wondered if teens even had a choice. Research into the newly named phenomenon of "brainwashing" reveals how anxieties about the psychopolitical effects of popular culture manifested in clinical language during this period. In 1957, English physician William Sargant published *Battle for the Mind: A Physiology of Conversion and Brainwashing*. Sargant theorized that individuals could "fix" or expunge particular beliefs in the brains of unwitting dupes through physiological means. Based in part on data gathered during a residency in the United States, the book surveyed revival meetings and evangelical churches, as well as trancing practices in West Africa, Southeast Asia, and the Middle East. Its illustrative plates begin with images of seventeenth-century religious meetings—and conclude in the present-day with an image of two teenaged rock 'n' rollers in thrall to the rhythm.[37] "From the Stone Age to Hitler, from the Beatles to the modern 'pop' culture, the brain of man has been constantly swayed by the same physiological techniques," Sargant would write in the revised edition. "Reason is dethroned, the normal brain computer is temporarily put out of action, and new ideas and beliefs are uncritically accepted."[38]

The psychiatrist we met earlier speculating about the big beat dance's similarity to the fascist rally, Dr. Joost Meerloo, drew similar conclusions. Born in the Netherlands in 1903, Meerloo had emigrated to the United States in 1946. After fleeing the Nazis during WWII, he led the Dutch government-in-exile's department for psychological studies. In *Total War and the Human Mind* (1946), *Delusion and Mass Delusion* (1949), and *Patterns of Panic* (1950), Meerloo probed the psychological dimensions of "totalitarianism." Published in 1956, *Rape of the Mind: The Psychology of Thought Control, Menticide, and Brainwashing* explored technological and political practices that engendered submission to authority in quotidian contexts. Radio and television indoctrinated people: "Big Brother's voice resounds in all the little brothers."[39] The "contagious rhythm of Rock 'n' Roll,'" he wrote in a second book, "is a form of rhythmic mass hypnosis."[40]

We can see these authors engaging a broader set of intellectual problems that historian Mark Greif has termed "the discourse of the crisis of man." Do modern political orders help human beings to flourish, to realize their full potentials? Or do they enslave us? Do human beings even *want* to be free? For many, WWII had demonstrated just how tenuous a grip most people held on "freedom." Writing in 1941, Erich Fromm saw "modern man" as staring down a stark choice: "either to escape from the burden of his freedom into new dependencies and submission, or to advance to the full realization of positive freedom which is based upon the uniqueness and individuality of man."[41] Soon the concentration camp had provided an extreme proof that, in Hannah Arendt's words, we could be made "ghastly marionettes with human faces, which all behave like the dog in Pavlov's experiments."[42]

The postwar emergence of humanistic psychology represented the positive flipside to these pessimistic readings of human nature.[43] American psychologist Carl Rogers, for instance, proposed that human beings naturally behave in ways congruent with an authentic, internal self; tension and instability in the individual subsequently occur when their lived experiences contradict this inner concept.[44] Even more influentially, Abraham Maslow coined the now ubiquitous term "self-actualization," or the realization of one's true self, placing it at the pinnacle of a hierarchy of purportedly universal human needs. To feel whole, to successfully meet your psychological needs, required prerequisite conditions: "freedom to speak, freedom to do what one wishes so long as no harm is done to others, freedom to express one's self, freedom to investigate and seek for information, freedom to defend one's self, justice, fairness, honesty, orderliness."[45]

It would be another decade rock critics, listeners, and the musicians themselves flipped the script, reframing rock as a positive means for self-expression, even self-actualization. But in the 1950s, even rock 'n' roll's most strident critics doubted the more spectacular claims that heard Elvis Presley records, as Meerloo had suggested, as "a sign of the depersonalization of the individual."[46] "No music can hurt kids who haven't been already hurt by their home environment," the notoriously conservative bandleader Mitch Miller claimed. "Rock 'n' roll is simply this: A safe form of rebellion against mother, father and teacher. It's a way they can take out their feelings of independence without hurting those they love."[47] And indeed, this was quickly becoming the consensus viewpoint: Rock 'n' roll functioned as a safety release valve for wound-up adolescents. As Dr. John C. Kendel, vice president of the American Music Conference, summarized, "the beat only gives young people a chance to blow off steam and rid themselves of excess energy."[48]

For many parents that conclusion provided little comfort. "Recently a rock and roll movie was shown at a local theater," one wrote to Dorothy Ricker, the syndicated advice columnist for "Teen-Age Mail."[49] "My 15-year-old daughter and two of her girl friends went to see it the day it opened. It seems the attendance was 90% teen-agers. They caused a riot, were destructive and so noisy it was necessary to call the police." Dad hit the roof, banning the music at home (and cruelly making the girl break her records). "Perhaps he is right," mom allowed, "but I would like to know your opinion of rock and roll."

"When dance fads have come up in the past," Ricker replied, "there has not been any violence or destruction associated with them. And, if rock and roll stopped at the point of just being another fad, like the Charleston, Black Bottom, or Jitter Bug, there wouldn't be all this unfavorable publicity about it." Yet the problem, Mrs. Ricker concluded, did not have to do with "rock and roll as such," but rather with "the EFFECT it is having on certain groups of teen-agers. While these groups are only a small percentage of our teen-age population, anything which turns a group of people into a screaming, destructive, uncontrolled mob is wrong and harmful, in my opinion."

Who were those "certain groups?" That euphemistic turn of phrase suggests that maybe some anxieties about rock 'n' roll did not concern adolescents in general. "Patterns of conduct formerly exclusive to poor, working-class or lower-middle-class youngsters," one sociologist had told Salisbury in *The Shook-Up Generation*, "have spread to the middle-class as a whole and to upper-class youth." The "rock-'n'-roll fad" represented "an example of how lower-class culture and speech patterns have engulfed all American youth regardless of social status."[50] Why had this happened? And what did it portend for American society?

* * *

New York Herald columnist George Sokolsky experienced communism firsthand while in 1920s Russia, which motivated his support for the nationalist Chang Kai-shek while in 1930s China. Now back in the United States, the journalist promoted increasingly extreme conservative views in the *Herald*. (He had even denounced the *denunciations* of Joseph McCarthy, continuing to defend the senator long after even his most stridently anticommunist supporters had cut their losses.) The riots at *Don't Knock the Rock* inspired Sokolsky to devote an entire column to the big beat.[51]

For the conservative firebrand, rock 'n' roll riots stemmed not from the music's effects on adolescent bodies, but rather from social meddling by liberals. The postwar safety net was not only raising Americans' standard of living, allowing more people to attend college, purchase homes, and buy consumer goods. It was also infantilizing adolescents, keeping young people who should be out earning an honest wage in a state of arrested development. Small wonder the pent-up energies of these coddled teens often exploded in unpredictable ways. Social engineering most seriously harmed the self-image of the blue-collar youth, which in turn upset the natural order of American society itself. "[W]hile the boy wants to be a grease monkey in a garage or an electrician, he is asked to sit in a classroom in front of a kid's desk reading *Silas Marner* which can be a pain in the neck," Sokolsky wrote, "and the girl would rather be a waitress or a salesgirl or a manicurist than listen to a teacher explain that UNESCO is not a disease like polio."[52]

For sure, the rise of rock 'n' roll can be attributed in part to the increased cultural and economic clout of blue-collar consumers, the music's power, as historian Michael Roberts writes, "sustained by the increasing political power of the American working class."[53] But the structural shifts that allowed rock's spread extended far beyond high school reading lists featuring novels by George Eliot. And the nature of these shifts goes a long way toward explaining what kinds of political meaning were beginning to be assigned to this music. Technological changes included major transformations to how commercial music was produced and sold after World War II: decentralization in both radio broadcasting and record production; industrial innovations resulting in sturdier (and cheaper) 45 rpm records and newly portable (and cheaper) transistor radios. Organizational shifts in the recording industry gave rise to a new class of disk jockeys, record men, and talent scouts able to recognize, as well as tap into, previously untapped markets at the national level.

Yet material conditions, of course, do not determine political content. To take just one especially contradictory example, consider the shifting meanings assigned to playback technologies in general over the preceding decade. Though the authors of "Planning For Fun" thought record players provided a kind of social glue for binding young listeners in positive pursuits, other social reformers had linked the jukeboxes to surging juvenile delinquency, inspiring not just debate but even attempts at legislation. Jukebox operators replied sharply. "Experts in the field," one argued, "say [recorded music] is the best way to solve juvenile delinquency." Operators in San Francisco argued that one proposed ordinance was even "un-American in that it attempted to penalize an innocent occupation to give police more control over taverns."[54]

But race would by far provide the postwar condition that most significantly channeled mainstream understandings about rock 'n' roll—both its "American-ness," as we'll see in the next chapter, as well as its effects on white teenage consumers. Major wartime changes to African-American live music economies had played a key role in paving what Preston Lauterbach calls "the road to rock 'n' roll," the chitlin' circuit: remarkably dense urban networks of agents, musicians, fans, and entrepreneurs that emerged in the African-American quarters of cities in the 1930s and 1940s. Small bands fronted by charismatic singers played this circuit, proto-rock 'n' roll groups such as Louis Jordan's Tympany Five. Founded in 1938, the group comprised piano, guitar, double bass, and drum kit alongside a couple of horns, instrumentation that became standard in part due to wartime rationing (which kept larger swing orchestras off the road) and in part by changing musical tastes.[55]

The chitlin' circuit began breaking down after 1945. The Federal Housing Act of 1949, part of Truman's so-called Fair Deal, aggressively remolded black communities in the name of "urban renewal." In practice, urban renewal resulted in what novelist James Baldwin called "Negro removal." Activist Jane Jacobs, struggling against the federal fight against blight in New York City's West Village, claimed that the act destroyed urban vitality by breaking apart the commingling of habitation and commerce that motivated their vibrant, innovative economies.[56] "Racial integration, a new moral streak in city government, and a far-reaching federal program together reshaped the African American cityscape," Lauterbach writes. As a result, the creative economies that had given rise to what African-American newspapers began calling that "rockin' rhythm" started breaking apart.[57]

Dispersed beyond the formerly segregated borders of black taste and pleasure, the rockin' rhythms went to seed nation-wide, channeled toward fertile grounds by the postwar mediascape and, increasingly, without regard for racial boundaries. As the music entered the consciousness of white adolescents, race would refract reporting on its seemingly harmful effects. A dance in Chattanooga featuring African-American singer Roy Hamilton led to one of the earliest reported "rock 'n' roll riots" in February 1956. Reports differed on its cause. The fighting began either when a member of the crooner's entourage sat in the whites-only circle, or when whites began pouring drinks over the black dancers below their balcony seats. Black and white teenagers fought for nearly an hour before police restored order; in the end, a white teenager was treated at the hospital, and nine black teenagers jailed.[58] In May, a sixteen-year-old black girl in Atlanta required medical attention after a brawl described as "a riot by white teenagers during a Rock and Roll show" that ended with the arrest of "five white youths."[59]

Journalists reporting on "riots" inevitably alluded to the race of participants. That September, a "rock 'n' roll riot" at a service club in Rhode Island sent ten sailors to the hospital when people began throwing bottles.[60] "'Man, it was murder!' one sailor exclaimed. 'There must have been a thousand bottles and chairs flying around a second or two after the lights went out.'"[61] Beat reporters immediately blamed the club's integrated audience. But the commanding officer was quick to quash talk of "racial factions and friction" among the enlisted men, claiming that "the only cause of the row among white and Negro sailors and marines and their wives and women companions was the excitement accompanying the stirring 'rock 'n' roll' and the plunging of the dance floor into darkness by an unidentified person."

The headliner blamed the alcohol. "I'd say they should not have been serving that beer in all those quart bottles," Fats Domino told reporters. "That provided those fellows with too many weapons."[62] A week later, however, the Associated Press had linked the Rhode Island melee to other disturbances, reporting that this was "the second time within a month [that] a 'rock 'n' roll' dance played by singer Fats Domino has ended in a riot."[63] The singer's response? To invite journalists to a "music seminar" where he would "explain and analyze the current trend in popular music"—demonstrating (from the piano!) that it was not the beat that caused teenagers to lose control.[64]

It's worth pausing here a moment to consider the motivations at play in explaining these events. In Rhode Island, the officer soft-pedalled talk about racial tensions, explaining away what might have been reported as a "race" problem and instead attributing violence to the effects of the music.

In contrast, Fats Domino had a vested interest in assigning blame not to the music, but to external factors—in this case, the alcohol. Here we are getting into the up-close, nitty-gritty details that a birds-eye view of the more abstracted conditions in which rock 'n' roll acquired its early meanings—changing ideas about adolescence, but also heightened political anxieties about the adolescent in the postwar United States—fails to fully capture. We should bear these details in mind even as we pull back our focus to see the bigger picture. And while we are not yet finished examining how race shaped the music's political meanings, for now we need to move on to consider one final, key condition that helps explain how rock 'n' roll invented the teenager.

* * *

"The movies, the radio, the super-highway have softened us up for the bomb," novelist Mary McCarthy wrote in *Commentary* just a year after Hiroshima and Nagasaki. "We have lived with them without pleasure, feeling them as a coercion on our natures, a coercion coming seemingly from nowhere and expressing nobody's will. The new coercion finds us without the habit of protest; we are dissident but apart."[65] How well did McCarthy's thesis hold up? Because if her postwar Americans found themselves unaccustomed to protest, their younger siblings and children found nothing *but* authority figures to rebel against.

Here's one seventeen-year-old from Wyoming, moaning about his teachers: "Sure they are here to give us an education but they don't have to pry into our personal lives to do it. The things that make me mad is that they call up your folks and make it sound real bad. They say they have a few hints. You should make him stay home more. You shouldn't give him the car. He shouldn't see his girl so much. Keep your boy away from Saturday-night dances. Make him study more. They just don't leave you alone."[66]

To any Eddie Cochran fan, these complaints surely sound familiar. They could have been taken straight from "Summertime Blues," recorded in March 1958 by the twenty-year-old. Like his manager (and the song's cowriter), thirty-one-year-old Jerry Capehart, the LA-based Cochran was a California transplant; he had left high school to pursue a career in the commercial music industry just as rock 'n' roll hit. Cochran scored his first success the previous year when "Twenty Flight Rock" was included in the Jayne Mansfield vehicle *The Girl Can't Help It* (1956). (A young guitarist named Paul famously got his first gig with an English outfit in Liverpool, the Quarrymen, after successfully picking his way through this song for the group's hard-nosed leader, John, at a church picnic.)

"Summertime Blues" bested Cochran's previous hit, peaking in the United States at number 8 on the recently renamed *Billboard* Hot 100 Chart. Its lyric encapsulates a powerful distillation of particular kind of white suburban teenage drama. Cochran's singer-protagonist can't catch a break. Can't take time off from his summer job to take his girl out, can't borrow the car, can't even take a vacation. He gets no sympathy from his boss, his parents, even his congressman, none of whom seem even slightly inclined toward understanding his predicament. He's bound by a situation not of his own making, needing to exchange his precious leisure time for a few bucks, needing a few bucks to have some fun, but unable to have fun because he must work.

First World problems, for sure. But that quotation above—"They just don't leave you alone!"—comes not from the Capeheart-Cochran lyric, but from *The American Teenager* (1957), a sociological portrait of adolescence rendered in exquisite ethnographic detail from survey data and interviews with over three-thousand high school students across the United States. There's no evidence that the seventeen-year-old from Wyoming bought the Cochran single. But if he did, would he have recognized art imitating life? Or was it art imitating life, imitating art? Put simply: Did early rock 'n' roll reflect the anxieties of actual high school students? Or did it provide them a vehicle for experiencing a new kind of rebelliousness? "I liked the music," said Bob Gruen, the acclaimed photographer who successfully navigated adolescence to become one of rock's most influential chroniclers, "and it shaped me because it made me feel like an outcast."[67]

Now the first rock 'n' roll stars had traversed adolescence a decade or two before the big beat rocked America's teenagers. So forget about the geriatric Bill Haley's glass eye and dorky spit curl, not to mention Chuck Berry's age when he cut "Sweet Little Sixteen" (a not-so-teenaged thirty-two years). Instead shift your focus to the burgeoning white suburbs made possible by the postwar construction boom, to how these burbs gave rise to a new lifestyle politics, to how a new network of highways connecting them transformed the social geography of white Americans from Boston to Pittsburgh, from Texas to the 'Frisco Bay, from St. Louis to New Orleans. And we should also consider how the majority of economic growth in Southern California from the late 1940s to 1960 came via increased defense spending, with nearly 60 percent of new jobs in the greater Los Angeles area in some way related to the military-industrial complex.[68] There's Rear Admiral George Morrison, moving a growing family that includes a young Jimmy, from Melbourne, Florida, to Los Altos; there's Francis Zappa, employed at a munitions plant in Maryland, relocating to San Diego with his wife and four children, including an asthmatic Frank, Jr.

This broader context might help us understand a quirky bit of trivia about the big beat's founding charter. Recorded by Bill Haley and his Comets, "(We're Gonna) Rock Around The Clock" (1954) begins with a rimshot. And then, the revelation: "One, two, three o'clock! Four o'clock, rock!" Released by the goofy novelty act Sonny Dae and His Knights in 1953, the song initially flopped. Haley's version also sputtered until actor Glenn Ford dug into his twelve-year-old son's record collection to find a song for the opening credits to his new film, *Blackboard Jungle*. By July 1955, "Rock Around the Clock" had hit number one on the *Billboard* Pop charts, where it remained for two months, the first so-called rhythm song to do so. It reached number one in the United Kingdom in November; the following year, the film—on the back of the song—became, as we'll see, a global phenomenon. Conservative estimates suggest it sold twenty-five million copies over the next half-century, quite possibly making it the best-selling recording of all time.

So here's the trivia question. "(We're Gonna) Rock Around The Clock" was actually the single's B-side. What was the A-side? Turn the record over, and the needle lurches to an opening rockabilly riff and this lyric. "Last night I was dreaming," Haley croons, "I dreamed about the H-bomb." "Thirteen Women (And Only One Man in Town)" relates an unlikely tale of love in the age of thermonuclear warfare. Haley's narrator has survived a nuclear explosion, along with thirteen women. Somewhat improbably, the women cook and clean for him. Soon three girls are doing the mambo, with three others "ballin' the jack," a kind of prewar jitterbugging. The polygamous relationship, however unorthodox, nevertheless seems relatively anodyne. And in any event, it turns out to have been only a dream. The narrator wakes up to shuffle off, by himself, to work.

Haley's version added the part about the dream. Dickie Thompson's original, released just a few months earlier, had a jazzy Latin feel and lyrics overflowing with innuendo that the Comets' more straight-ahead cover sanitized. Dickie sits in bed, the girls rubbing his back and head. Bill's girls make "sure he's well fed," sweetening his tea and buttering his bread. Dickie's girls, he complains, were "driving me too fast"—he worries "how long I could last." Bill's girls? "Boy, they sure were a lively pack." Gee whiz. Apparently, better a lyric about nuclear holocaust than sex.[69]

The two sides of this single demonstrate in capsule form the primary challenge for understanding the long Fifties, the remarkable period spanning approximately 1946 to 1964. How do we reconcile an overweening confidence born of unprecedented prosperity with deeply felt anxieties that the world might end? The exuberance of rocking and rolling today with the threat of mushroom clouds looming tomorrow? At first blush, the two sides may appear incompatible. Yet as Americans learned, you can't have one without the other.

Major domestic reforms had grown from a groundswell of postwar support for strong government intervention. The New Deal had reinvigorated belief in a proactive state in the 1930s, with its architect, Franklin Delano Roosevelt, reclaiming the political keyword "freedom" to describe his activist vision.[70] And then came war. "World War II," H. W. Brands suggests, "confirmed a pattern of anomaly in American history. Against a background of persistent distrust of government's growth, Americans accepted the expansion—sometimes the breathtaking expansion—of federal authority during wartime."[71] With the end of hostilities, this expansion should have begun its inevitable contraction. Except the war never ended. The struggle between democracy and fascism mutated into a new form, of permanent crisis, a "cold war," to use the term coined by George Orwell and popularized by journalist Walter Lippman. Strong, interventionist policymaking flourished, a path between socialism on the one hand and unfettered capitalism on the other that historian Arthur Schlesinger Jr., American liberalism's foremost intellectual architect in the 1950s, called "the vital center." The subsequent rising economic tide lifted many, and not only in the United States. "In the span of a single generation, hundreds of millions of people were lifted from penury to unimagined riches," historian Marc Levinson writes. "The change in average people's lives was simply astounding."[72]

Commentators at the time recognized this. "Never before," *Life* summarized in 1954, "so much for so many."[73] But prosperity stayed only because peace would never come again. Orwell worried about the ideological implications of this, "the kind of world-view, the kind of beliefs, the social structure that would probably prevail in a state which was at once unconquerable and in a permanent state of 'cold war' with its neighbors."[74] Schlesinger predicted the contest would take places through cultural struggles. "Nineteen hundred looked forward to the irresistible expansion of freedom, democracy, and abundance; 1950 will look back to totalitarianism, to concentration camps, to mass starvation, to atomic war," he wrote in *The Vital Center: The Politics of Freedom* (1949). "Free society and totalitarianism today struggle for the minds and hearts of men."[75]

Abundance for all, and permanent war. As parents handed the car keys to their teenagers, they had ample reasons to be hopeful, but also to be anxious. And as those teenagers eased the family car out of their suburban driveways, they tuned the dial—past the small white triangle, mandatory from 1953, marking the CONELRAD civil defense broadcast frequencies of 640 and

1240 kHz prepared to warn Americans of imminent nuclear attack—to the sound of the big beat.

* * *

"Today's youth are war babes, just beginning to feel their oats," columnist Phyllis Battelle wrote in a four-part series on rock 'n' roll in 1956. "They live in a world of mixed emotions. Prosperity has built up financial security for them and their families, so they do not want. At the same time, they hear all the talk of world insecurity. Of psychiatry and psychology, of atomic warfare in abeyance. In the back of their minds, like an uncomfortable dream, is the inkling that living-for-today may be a wise course to follow."[76]

The big beat caused "depersonalization of the individual." It stoked rioting mobs, turning normal children to violence. It took a healthy young person and turned them toward conformity, stripped them of individuality. Or did it? Maybe the big beat allowed young people to cope with the natural pressures of adolescence, to let off steam, to relieve the stress of social conventions in a safe, controlled environment. Maybe the music even modeled the kind of rebellion that a healthy democracy required. These proposals all depended on a normative understanding of adolescence as a particularly fraught stage, one that saw a healthy child mature (hopefully) into a well-adjusted adult, a normal American whose internal sense of self successfully aligned with their role in society.

With the stakes so high, it's no wonder experts worried so much. And with the big beat so publicly, so spectacularly threatening to disrupt this process, it's no wonder the music became a key object for anxieties and expert pronouncements. But that has less to do with any property of the music itself than with new understandings of this life stage, now freighted with political significance. The health of American society, postwar experts claimed, depended on the psychological integrity of individual Americans, and the psychological integrity of individual Americans, on their having successfully navigated the teen-age years. This is how "the teenager" became not simply an object of anxiety, but also a key political category in the postwar United States.

And that's how rock 'n' roll invented the teenager. Knowledge about rock 'n' roll's psychopolitical effects helped defined the borders of this category, impelling Americans to discuss, study, and worry over their adolescents in new ways. How did normal teenagers behave? How *should* normal teenagers behave? How could their healthy development be fostered? Or more insidiously, interrupted? These questions revolved around the skeleton key of

American public discourse, "freedom," and for good reason. The history of the United States can be written by how different actors have invoked this key term, whether in using it to narrate their stories, to express their worries, or to chart their futures. This did not change after 1945. Rather, the Cold War super-charged this discourse, and Americans acquired a new pair of related concepts: free society and totalitarianism. In a free society, citizens needed to remain alert to signs of creeping totalitarianism, to signals that their capacity for autonomy had been compromised. At issue were individualized freedoms: of thought and action, and of speech and self-expression, but also of simply consuming what you like.

Extraordinary material conditions made possible "freedom from" economic obstacles, a form of freedom that philosopher Isaiah Berlin in 1958 called "negative liberty." The "consequences of taking life easy or making poor choices were not nearly as dire in the 1950s and early 1960s," historian Grace Palladino writes. Plentiful jobs, good wages, and affordable consumer goods represented "the most unique and potentially liberating feature of postwar teenage life."[77] That's hard to imagine. But not for those who lived through it. Anyone could "put a pack on his back with the collected poems of WB Yeats and a few other books and spend five months on the road with nine hundred dollars in the bank," remembered Robert Christgau, who did just that before becoming one of the first rock critics in the late Sixties. "That is freedom, and it was just *there*. If I needed to get a job I could just go get a job tomorrow. It was not an issue."[78]

As our story progresses, we'll keep an eye on these material conditions, and how they inflected the kinds of politics that could be ascribed to rock 'n' roll and, later, rock. But for now, we can give teenagers the last word.

"You asked me why we rock 'n' roll," a high school student had told Battelle. "We don't want to have repressions any more than anybody else. This gives us a change to relax, let off steam. Izzat so bad?"

"Do you think all kids like it?" Battelle asks another.

"Any kid who wants to get off the beaten track of school work and drudgery, man. It gives 'em a feeling of just wanting to let themselves go."[79]

" 'Why?' a high school girl was asked.

'It gives you a sort of feeling of freedom,' she said firmly. 'it makes you relax and want to jump. Youth's gotta have freedom today. You know?' "[80]

2
How Americans Rocked Cairo (and London, and Moscow, and Tehran, and . . .)

In May 1957, young Egyptians held a rock 'n' roll dance contest. "Rock 'n' roll," reported an American journalist, "has caught fire in the land of the sphinx."[1] Fourteen couples, the women in blue jeans and the men, sporting American-style crew-cuts, had passed through preliminary rounds in Port Said, Suez, Ismailia, Luxor, and Aswan before reaching the finals in Cairo. The band rocked as best they could. (They had only recently begun imitating American recordings.) But the dancers did not seem to care: they "stomp, they whirl, and they sing along with the musicians."

At last the emcee, a Brooklynite and recent Howard University graduate attending medical school in Cairo, addressed the crowd.

"Rock 'n' roll is one thing from America you're bound to like," Cleve Lewter Jr. said. "And when you rock 'n' roll, you'll find out there's lots more about America you're going to like. Let's rock 'n' roll 'n' everybody get together!"

Newspapers in the United States did not report the winners. But the mere existence of the big beat in Cairo, commentators suggested, helped extend American influence in this strategic region, allowing unofficial diplomats such as this African-American student to "put the American way of life over thru the medium of rock 'n' roll." Because whatever the majority of Americans might have felt about the music, no one could deny that "the 'rock' looks like the strongest link of understanding right now between the youth of Egypt and the U.S.A."

Could the big beat's popularity help the United States mend its relationship with Egypt? That relationship had been tense since the Suez Crisis six months earlier, when Israel, the United Kingdom, and France attacked the Egyptian Sinai, retreating only after heavy diplomatic pressure from both the United States and the Soviet Union. The invasion had helped recalibrate the international order, cementing Nasser's position in Cairo but straining relations among the First, Second, and Third Worlds.

The effects of rock 'n' roll diplomacy, however, could be unpredictable. As reported by Osgood Caruthers, foreign affairs specialist at the *New York Times*, the music troubled both liberal and conservative Egyptians. "To those seeking fresh ammunition for their warfare against the 'imperialist West,' this American importation had become a symbol of United States policy in the Middle East," Caruthers wrote, "part of a plot to undermine the morals of Egyptian youth and (sometimes echoing Moscow's line) a sign of Western degeneration." Those more "puritanical" parliamentarians, on the other hand,

CAIRO ROCKS: Dancers at a rock 'n' roll evening in the Abdine Palace Casino at Cairo. Rock 'n' roll records and motion pictures have become latest fad of Egyptian youth.

Figure 3 "President Eisenhower's Middle East Policies Are Being Called the Rock 'n' Roll Doctrine," by Osgood Carruthers, "Rock 'n' Roll Cuts Swath in Egypt," in *New York Times* (23 June 1957)

bristled at women contestants in pants—a necessary concession, apparently, due to the immodesty of some of the more athletic dance movements, but also "a rarity . . . frowned upon by conservative Cairenes."[2] At a Cabinet meeting in mid-June, Carruthers reported, "saner heads prevailed." "The youngsters are going to continue this fad until they are tired of it," a minister concluded, echoing the American consensus: "it is a good safety valve for pent-up energies."

And so when the big beat traveled abroad, it prompted tricky questions. What image of the United States did rock 'n' roll present to Cold War foes and would-be allies? Was rock 'n' roll, so immediately successful with young people worldwide, an appropriate means for exercising American soft power? In reporting the global spread of rock 'n' roll, many US journalists praised its success as pro-American propaganda. But others worried about the "American way of life" that it seemed to promote.

Today it seems obvious that rock 'n' roll is, in some ineffable and essential sense, "American." "There is not a bigger giant in the history of American music," President Obama said in awarding Bob Dylan the Presidential Medal of Freedom. As we saw in the prologue, certain critics have long claimed that rock 'n' roll grew naturally in the fertile cultural soils of America, the music's deep roots drawing sustenance from a natural national inclination toward rebellion and individualism. But look for rock 'n' roll not in that hoary past but in its Cold War present, and you'll find a different story. This one hinges on two major mid-century plot devices: the invention of liberal democracy and the emergence of "the Three Worlds." In a postwar order defined by the struggle between the United States and the USSR, that qualifier, "liberal," became necessary to distinguish US-flavored democracy from competing forms in Europe, both East and West. And to label the divisions of this postwar order, Americans required new terms to explain its three distinct spheres of influence: a free capitalist First World, an unfree communist Second World, and a traditional non-aligned Third World.[3]

Let's bear this new language in mind as we begin disentangling the strands of debate about the big beat's spread, debate through which the meaning of not only liberal democracy and its guarantor, the "free society," but also a new vision of America itself, began taking shape. We've seen what programs accompanying Alan Freed's first rock 'n' roll stage shows claimed: "IT'S GREAT! IT'S WONDERFUL! IT'S EXCITING! IT'S AMERICAN!"[4] But that's not a claim you need to shout out loud—unless of course you're arguing with people claiming the opposite.

So suspend for a moment the belief that rock 'n' roll simply is "American." Instead, we'll ask how it *became* American. And to answer that question, we can examine how the big beat rocked places like Cairo, and London, and Moscow, and Tehran, and...

* * *

In 1955, the Venice Film Festival screened MGM's *Interrupted Melody*. This stirring biopic about an Australian soprano's battle with polio featured works by Verdi, Puccini, and Bizet; the most musically daring inclusion was a song by Harold Arlen. It netted only a pittance at the box office, about one-hundred thousand dollars, but garnered Academy Awards for its screenplay, costuming, and singing star, Eleanor Parker. "Not since the great Caruso," the film's trailer narrated, "has any motion picture presented the world's most beautiful music, as it was meant to be heard."

Interrupted Melody had been a late addition to the festival's line-up following an unusual protest lodged by Clare Boothe Luce, the American ambassador to Italy, against the first choice, MGM's *Blackboard Jungle*. The conservative author and former congresswoman had argued that film "presented an untrue view of American life and gave a bad idea of America."[5] Arthur Loew, president of the conglomerate that owned MGM, called the ambassador's moralistic intervention "hypocritical nonsense." "We will protest against her action to the State Department as censorship," he said. But what Loew did not say was that his own executives had expressed the very same concerns just months before.

Blackboard Jungle starred Glenn Ford as a young teacher struggling to reach "juvenile delinquents" at a working-class, racially integrated high school in New York City. Even today, the teacher reads like a liberal's deepest fantasy. An ex-Navy man, he has just finished teachers' college on the GI Bill. Plans to improve his wayward charges through education purport to be colorblind, giving each student an equal opportunity to better himself. The film culminates with Artie West, a tough white delinquent, pulling out a switchblade. "Step right up and taste a little of this, daddy-o," he mocks, flipping it open. The other students in the interracial classroom, won over at last to the teacher's side, pin West against the wall using a flagpole flying the stars-and-stripes. The message is none too subtle: the problems of postwar delinquency and race will be solved by well-meaning individuals (and a healthy measure of patriotic gumption).

Based on the bestselling novel by Evan Hunter and directed by Richard Brooks, the film presents itself as semi-fictionalized docudrama. Hunter said his short stint as a substitute teacher inspired the story; Brooks kept a large file of newspaper clippings about the "adolescent problem" for reference during production. "Today we are concerned with juvenile delinquency," instructs an opening cue card scrolling over a martial snare rhythm. "The scenes and incidents depicted here are fictional. However, we believe that public awareness is a first step toward a remedy for any problem." The snare's rhythm gradually becomes jazzier, then comes the snare shot, and then: "One, two, three o'clock, four o'clock, rock!"

Bill Haley's "Rock Around the Clock" for a moment crackles with static, the credits fade to the opening scene, and the problem appears in black-and-white. Crude young men hanging outside the school, wearing the delinquent uniform of cuffed pants, short jackets, and greased-back ducktail haircuts, tap along to rock 'n' roll played through the tinny speakers of a transistor radio. The ever-present threat of teenage delinquency lingers in the air, as one throng crouches, bopping to the beat, while another catcalls a young female teacher, peering through the bars of a wrought-iron fence like caged animals.

"Music and sound," the director Brooks said, "are major characters."[6] Indeed, the soundtrack of *Blackboard Jungle* catapulted the film to notoriety in the United States and then worldwide. "Rock Around the Clock" rose quickly to the top of the Billboard pop charts, though its inclusion in the film had been a fluke, the fortuitous suggestion of thirteen-year-old Peter Ford, son of lead actor Glenn Ford. This success not only touched off a rush of imitators, but also planted new associations in the ears of listeners. "Suddenly," Greil Marcus writes, "the festering connections between rock and roll, teenage rebellion, juvenile delinquency, and other assorted horrors were made explicit."[7]

But did *Blackboard Jungle* represent an *authentic* picture of the "assorted horrors" found in mid-century America? The film's depictions generated anxious responses. New York's assistant superintendent staged tours at the school where Evan Hunter had taught in order to show off its bland normalcy; the *New York Times* described journalists watching a high school teacher play Tchaikovsky records to his students.[8] An executive at Loews International suggested MGM include disclaimers. Might the film note that delinquency "has always been an aftermath of war and the present wave of unruly children is found in all countries?" And might, perhaps, the film reference the *global* character of delinquency by also discussing Soviet problems with unruly youth? MGM's producer sought to assuage the theater chain's fears. "You need have no concern over its foreign distribution," he reassured. The film would not provide grist to the Soviet propaganda mill. In fact, by demonstrating the triumph of the teacher, the producer claimed, *Blackboard Jungle* painted a "portrait of democracy at work."[9]

Concern about the film's reception abroad persisted. Another executive "thought it an outrage that America was exposing our own weaknesses on the screen."[10] The agency that enforced Hollywood's voluntary ban on sex and violence, then directed by Geoffrey Shurlock, received regular briefings on perceptions about American films in foreign countries. While *Blackboard Jungle* was in production, Shurlock had received a report on Marlon Brando's *The Wild One* (1954), another rebellious-teen-flouts-social-conventions film. "A savage society like the American capitalist society, where the only law is that of the jungle, produces a terrible deformation in the minds of the young," an editorial in a communist newspaper in Santiago had argued. "Here we have in the flesh the 'American way of life' that they wish to import to Chile."[11]

Sure, that kind of criticism was propaganda. But at a moment when the export of "the American way of life" constituted a major plank in US policy, policymakers took it seriously. Because these cold war elites also took seriously the symbolic, cultural struggle to win the hearts and minds of people worldwide. A far-reaching infrastructure created to export US-produced films, music, and print media has ensured at least the possibility of American cultural hegemony since World War II when, as Jeremy Tunstall argued in his provocative classic, *The Media Are American*, "the United States reached its pinnacle of political, military and media supremacy." The United States dominated by controlling raw materials in a period of strict rationing, vastly outproducing its competitors (in 1948, Hollywood produced 432 films to Italy's fifty-four and the Soviet Union's twenty), and through sheer manufacturing capacity. From 1953, American influence became more indirect, as global shortages eased and media capacities worldwide began to be rebuilt. At this point, it was too late. The United States had ensured "the foundations were laid of a new post-war doctrine and system of free trade in the media."[12]

This structural shift coincided with the US government's discovery (and deployment) of soft power. Founded the 1954, the State Department's Cultural Presentations program funded performances abroad in order to foster mutual understanding between the United States and the rest of the world. The program depended on an understanding of the postwar world in which American interests were, in no small part, determined by the struggle to conquer the world through a new art of government, cultural diplomacy. (Or more cynically, the struggle to fashion consent for American political-economic goals?) "Cultural diplomacy," as Danielle Fosler-Lussier writes, "was always an uncomfortable mix of information propaganda (intending to shape the thoughts and opinions of the world's citizens . . .) and a gentler, high-minded vision of mutuality and respect, regarded as separate from politics."[13]

While state-funded programs to export American culture were subjected to close technocratic deliberation, by contrast, the market forces that shaped the informal export of American popular culture seemed chaotic both to postwar liberals and to conservatives alike. Should these kinds of mass culture be policed? And who should police them? In 1954, Senator Alexander Wiley, a member of the Foreign Relations Committee, had stumped for hearings about how to restrict depictions of "an America of sex, sin and sadism, of gangsterism, corruption, filth and degradation." Concerned that same year that violent films were "hurting American prestige abroad," *Variety* suggested a board of volunteers that could suggest banning certain films from foreign distribution.[14]

Yet until a voluntary commission composed itself to regulate films such as *Blackboard Jungle*, individuals such as Clare Boothe Luce would need to step up. A staunch Catholic and even stauncher anti-communist, Boothe Luce campaigned for Dwight Eisenhower, who named her ambassador to Italy, where she lobbied tirelessly for US funding to fight local communists. Boothe Luce previously shaped America's image through her articles in *Life* magazine, an imprint published by her media mogul husband, Henry. Along with *Time*, *Fortune*, and *Sports Illustrated*, *Life* taught Americans to recognize what was special about their nation. Henry Luce himself had offered an especially compelling vision in a rousing call against wartime isolationism in 1942. "We have some things in this country which are infinitely precious and especially American—a love of freedom, a feeling for the equality of opportunity, a tradition of self-reliance and independence and also of co-operation," he had written. Separated by oceans from the dark storm clouds gathering over both Europe and Asia, America had hitherto served faithfully as sanctuary to these ideals and to "all the great principles of Western civilization." But the time for isolationism had ended: "It now becomes our time to be the powerhouse from which the ideals spread throughout the world and do their mysterious work in lifting the life of mankind from the level of beasts to what the Psalmist called a little lower than the angels."[15]

Were Bill Haley and His Comets appropriate emissaries for the American values and ideals Henry Luce had in mind when he heralded this new "American century?" Surely not. Even one of the more ardent pro-US journalists, a reporter from Santiago who also appeared in the report about *The Wild One* discussed above had voiced doubts: "When he leaves the theatre, the spectator asks himself, overwhelmed, 'is *this* American civilization?'"[16]

When Clare Boothe Luce successfully lobbied to keep *Blackboard Jungle* from appearing in the Venice Film Festival, she no doubt thought she had scored a victory for civilization. Her success against rock 'n' roll films, however, was short-lived. She soon resigned her post in Italy, laid low by a mysterious illness. Rumors ran rampant in Rome: Had the Soviets poisoned one of liberal democracy's most formidable spokespersons? (The culprit turned out to be dust from the lead paint in her seventeenth-century villa.)[17]

And her victory ultimately proved pyrrhic. The Venice Film Festival scandal helped promote *Blackboard Jungle* worldwide, priming international audiences for sex, violence and, of course, rock 'n' roll. Over the next year, the film would earn another two million dollars on release in Western Europe and help launch the big beat globally. And as Boothe Luce had predicted, the music shaped how American allies and foes alike viewed the United States, though not always in predictable ways.

* * *

On a hot and humid afternoon in July 1957, several hundred European exchange students waited to depart from Pier 88 on the Hudson River. The atmosphere was jubilant. Singing rock 'n' roll songs and wearing cowboy hats and blue jeans, reported the *New York Times*, the teenagers left with a favorable impression of the United States. "I think there is on the average much more comfort here," eighteen-year-old Armelle told a reporter. "Americans are often misunderstood because it's hard for Europeans to understand a people who are both idealistic and materialistic."[18]

By 1957, the United States had rocked Western Europe. But two years earlier, before most these teenagers had even heard a rock 'n' roll record, their parents were reading spectacular stories about the phenomenon in Europe's mainstream press.[19] At Elvis Presley concerts, reported *Der Spiegel*, American teenagers danced "like haunted medicine men of a jungle tribe governed only by music—rock 'n' roll."[20] "It is nothing more than an exhibition of primitive tom-tom thumping," sniffed Sir Malcolm Sargent, conductor of the BBC Symphony Orchestra, echoing criticisms found in the United States.[21] And newspapers in Denmark compared rock 'n' roll to "the ritual feasts of faraway natives" and "African orgies of dance and drums."[22]

Exotic, primitive, dangerous: did newspapers in Europe prime local listeners for sex and violence? Following riots in Copenhagen, one Danish sociologist claimed that "newspaper reports of a sensational nature may have exerted a certain influence, if not otherwise, then at least by contributing to induce such a great number of individuals to set out for [public spaces] on the days concerned."[23] But for our purposes here, we are less concerned with what *Europeans* thought about the big beat than with the kinds of meanings that American journalists assigned to its global spread. The first stories about the effect of rock 'n' roll on Western Europe's adolescents examined riots in Oslo prompted by a September 1956 screening of *Blackboard Jungle*.[24] "Police charged with horses and swung clubs, but it was several hours before they could restore order. No casualties were reported."[25] As the US reporting on rock's European travels expanded, newspaper accounts of specific incidents were replaced by more general—and generalizable—stories on how American popular culture affected European youth.

The *Boston Globe* reported that London police increasingly encountered music-fueled violence: insults against passers-by, smashed bottles, and the destruction of private property all by "gangs of boys and girls who have been turned into unmanageable mobs by the throbbing of drums and the strum of guitars."[26] As in the United States, many British experts urged calm. "It is one of the few permitted forms of basically sexual expression," a welfare officer told reporters. "And that is a good thing in a society which allows young people so little self-expression, anyway." Writing from the *New York Times* London bureau, Thomas P. Ronan provided more context.[27] Brits were "puzzled by [the] un-British actions of crowds of teen-agers," he reported. They seemed to be asking the same questions as Americans: "Does the music madden them? Does it appeal to some latent jungle strain? Is it an outlet for the frustrations and insecurities that seem to afflict teenagers?" Everyone—"psychiatrists, churchmen, social workers, editors and the plain man-in-the-street"—offered different answers.

Yet it was another fad from across the Atlantic, unreported in the American press, that first muted, and then amplified, rock 'n' roll's effects on British youth. A homegrown folk-blues mash-up played on acoustic guitars, tea-chest bass, and washtubs, skiffle exploded via Lonnie Donegan's smash recording, "Rock Island Line," a strange, DIY cover of a Leadbelly song that coincidentally entered the charts just as Haley's "Rock Around The Clock" climbed to number one. "Lonnie Donegan broke the fourth wall of Britain's popular culture," Billy Bragg writes, "except rather than making the audience feel that the performer was talking to them personally, his suburban background made it possible for working-class British teens to suddenly imagine themselves stepping out of the audience and into the pop pantheon."[28] Young would-be musicians across Britain, from a schoolboy Jimmy Page in London, to a pre-Bowie (and -Ziggy and -Aladdin Sane and . . .) David Jones at summer camp on the Isle of Wight, and of course, to a John, a Paul, and a George in Liverpool, all commandeered washtubs and tea-chests, begging or borrowing cheap acoustic guitars. In just a few short years, these young Brits (who received scant attention from American journalists) would reintroduce rock to the United States.

Across the English Channel in France, the rock 'n' roll situation looked very different. "Paris moviegoers have seen the rock 'n' roll epic 'Rock Around the

Clock,'" Reuters reported, "and given it a polite, amused, but never for one moment a frenzied reaction."[29] Quelle surprise, right? "What's with French youth?" asked the quirky columnist Art Buchwald. "Would they dance in the aisle and jump over the balconies, would there be gang fights? Would the French world of jazz survive the new bomb?"[30] Reactions at three theaters ranged from the blasé to the ho-hum. On the Avenue des Champs-Élysées, a mostly middle-aged crowd remained so docile "we might as well have been sitting at a screening of 'The Swan.'" Same scene at the Moulin Rouge in Montmartre. And at the Rex, there was no chance for any mischief, as a policeman (purportedly) took Buchwald's bag of rotten vegetables. The lack of violence reflected, the journalist winked, "a sorry commentary on French youth."

If the postwar French public remained wary of Anglo-Americanization, the creeping ubiquity of American popular culture soon became unavoidable.[31] Young working-class, leather-clad adolescents called *blousons noirs* consumed American films and records, taking their cues from James Dean and Elvis Presley. Almost overnight, French record producers began creating homegrown rock 'n' roll to meet this demand and, perhaps, to help assimilate this potentially destabilizing social group into French society as consumers.[32] The team of Boris Via and Henri Salvador first capitalized on the rock 'n' roll craze with "Rock and Roll Mops," an unlikely novelty song released under an even more unlikely name, Henry Cording and His Original Rock and Roll Boys. ("We hugged and kissed all evening long," the lyrics go, "And listened to some Pelvis song!") A singer named Richard Anthony (née Btesch, an Egypt-born crooner) released French-language covers in nearly pitch-perfect imitation of Elvis, Buddy Holly, and Paul Anka, as did breakout star Johnny Hallyday, a Franco-Belgian singer with an American uncle. An Americanized nom-de-rock became a requirement: Johnny had been christened Jean-Phillipe, while elsewhere an "Eddy" replaced a Claude and a "Rocky," a Jean Joseph.[33]

In contrast to the light-hearted, often tongue-in-cheek coverage about France and the United Kingdom, reporting on West Germany emphasized the music's dangerously destabilizing effects in the postwar context. In one typical overview, "Rock 'n' Roll Adds to Woes in Germany," a Reuters journalist reviewed the violence wrought by fans in 1956 and 1957. *Blackboard Jungle* inspired only one riot, but it had been a big one, with nearly a thousand fans vandalizing storefronts and cars before police dispersed them.[34] The scale of the problem, journalists suggested, raised troubling questions about the psychological makeup of young Germans. Police reported "smashing-up-parties," preplanned riots among high school students or young tradesmen, these "adventure-starved youths" rearing for "a battle" with authority figures.

Just like in France, rock 'n' roll in Germany soon found itself domesticated. The "German Elvis," Peter Kraus, cut his first attempts at the big beat in early 1957. The "17-year-old son of a cabaret artiste," Reuters reported, Kraus "rocks and rolls in the manner of Presley's stance and technique."[35] Kraus's first single was a prissy Presley cover, though "Hafenrock" (meaning "Harbor Rock") had shifted the location of the American's original jailhouse, taking a sophisticated view of rock and putting it in the harbor. With his female sidekick, Conny Froboess, Peter quickly became a teen idol, the clean-cut face of rock 'n' roll for West Germans. And as in France, these covers helped smooth the music's sharp edges; Peter and Conny's bland chirping—"*Teen! Teen! Teenager melody!*" in one song—so completely desexualized, so wholly deracinated the original style as to make it nearly unrecognizable. Good, clean fun, and a way to let off some steam.

The reserved Brit, the blasé Frenchman, the overly intense German: American journalists explaining how "the virus of the rhythm has jumped the Atlantic" often offered more in stereotypes than nuanced analysis.[36] By early 1957, Leonard Ingalls summarized the situation in a special to the *New York Times* with characteristic understatement. "Europe," he wrote, "has had its share of rock 'n' roll riots."[37] But the American craze had not conquered the continent: "Old countries which have seen many fads come and go are not disturbed," and "everyone seems to be taking the phenomenon in stride." So much so that not only had a British physician called the music a positive force allowing young people "self-expression and release," but a hospital in North Kent reportedly planned to incorporate rock dances into physiotherapy sessions.

Ultimately, American journalists may have underestimated the influence of rock 'n' roll on Western Europe. In their reporting on Eastern Europe, however, they almost certainly overestimated it.

* * *

In May 1958, a Senate sub-committee discussed a proposal put forward by a group of patriotic radio men. Murray Kaufman, better known as "Murray the K," wanted to "give the Soviets a sampling of rock 'n' roll music."[38] Disk jockeys such as Kaufman represented a powerful, albeit paradoxical, force. A team of researchers at Columbia University's Bureau of Applied Social Research had recently concluded that these men simultaneously "were the key gurus in making the hits of the day," while also tending "to follow rather than lead popular taste."[39] As we will soon see, debates about that paradox helped transform the political valence of rock 'n' roll in the Sixties. But for now, back to the US

Senate. Should the United States recruit disk jockeys in the struggle against international Communism? No, as it turned out. Live rock 'n' roll shows, one anti-communist disk jockey from New Hampshire testified, represented "powder kegs" that a "few Communist plants" could use to initiate riots. Murray the K's plan died in discussion, and the chastened disk jockey agreed to tour American army bases under the strict supervision of the USO—and without the big beat.[40]

But *could* rock 'n' roll have been weaponized against the Second World? Some ideologues in the communist bloc did worry that the music represented an American plot. The East Germans called it *Unkultur*, or non-culture. It expressed the "anarchism of capitalist society," First Secretary Ulbricht said. "Rock 'n' roll," claimed his Defense Minister Willi Stoph, "was a means of seduction to make the youth ripe for atomic war."[41] (Recall how, as we learned in the last chapter, Americans had precisely the same worry.) And Ulbricht told comrades in 1957 that "it is not sufficient to condemn capitalist decadence in words and speak against 'hot music' and the ecstatic 'songs' of a Presley; we must offer something better."[42]

This statement hints at a major change in cultural policy. As the big beat arrived in the eastern bloc, state-socialist policymaking on "the Youth" had coincidentally entered a radical new phase. As in Western Europe and the United States, leaders in Eastern Europe assigned special significance to young people. Nearly half the Soviet Union's population was under eighteen, and on these young people authorities pinned their hopes for postwar reconstruction (and anxieties about social change), just as they had in Western Europe.[43] But unlike in capitalist countries, youth in the Second World also served a specific ideological function: the "building of socialism," and its subsequent transformation into Communism.

At the 20th Communist Party Congress in 1953, the famous "secret meeting" where Krushchev denounced Stalin, the first secretary of the youth organization Komsomol, A.N. Shelepin, had also announced a bold change of direction. No longer would top-down policies be directed at young people. Soon "youth initiative clubs" opened throughout the Soviet Union in order to foster participation from below.[44] This policy shift resulted in an increased emphasis on the creation of locally produced programming, and the proliferation of new committees for producing socialist popular culture that might compete with commercially produced Western music.[45] Many domestic creations failed. The Lipsi, a new couple's dance that East Germany heavily promoted as an alternative to Western-style dancing, received a lukewarm reception in 1956; local bandleaders like Alo Koll fared a bit better, but still had trouble (not unlike in West Germany) competing with American imports. A year later in Leipzig, rock 'n' roll first figured in a series of demonstrations: "We want no Lipsi and we want no Alo Koll," young people chanted, "we want Elvis Presley and his rock 'n' roll!"[46]

As John Fell Stevenson toured the Soviet Union in 1958, he did not seem to know about these changes. The son of Adlai Stevenson, the former vice president, John had just graduated from Harvard. His dad was busy reinventing himself as a voice of reason in an unreasonable world, then (as now) a popular post-office career path for liberal politicians. While accompanying his dad, John noted his impressions of the USSR for an essay, "The Russians' Big Obsession: You!" (His previous effort, "My College Roommate Rules 10 Million Moslems," had profiled the Aga Khan, a university buddy.)[47]

To help readers understand the Soviet Empire, Stevenson invoked both rock 'n' roll and recording technology throughout the essay. When the Stevensons arrive at the Kremlin for dad's audience with Krushchev, they take "a slow, old-fashioned elevator" up to an eerily silent set of offices lacking the hustle and bustle found at even, say, a regular American company. John leafed through pamphlets while his father met with officials. There is a phonograph in the room, and an American recording of works by Ralph Vaughan Williams, but the machine will not function; an embarrassed aide tries to explain that this model is not yet in production. The Stevensons then leave the Kremlin and meet some Russian teenagers. (Definitely not intelligence plants, right?) Adlai asks the boys, clad in cheap imitations of American jeans, why they wear their hair so long. (In Russian? In English?) "That's the way they wear it in America," the boys reply. John invites one boy up to his hotel room for a gift. "Since I had been advised previously that Elvis Presley was popular in Russia, I had a few Presley records with me," he writes. "As I handed him the recording, he grinned, examined the colourful record jacket approvingly, and slipped the recording out and passed his fingers lovingly over the grooves. Then he handed it carefully back to me. He thought I had brought him up there merely to *show* him this treasure!"

The misunderstanding is sorted, and the young Russian jumps for joy; he returns the next morning to gift John a Russian record. "Russians are *fascinated by everything American*," John Fell Stevenson concluded. To him, this fascination is a bit silly, unseemly; it proves that the Soviet Union lags far behind the United States. This trope can be found throughout reporting on the eastern bloc, with rock 'n' roll a ready device used by journalists to lampoon the humorless Reds. "Bulgarian Communists," Reuters snarked in 1958, "are trying to chase pony-tail hairdos, blue jeans, and rock 'n' roll back across the Iron Curtain as manifestations of 'hooliganism.'"[48] In stories about popular culture in the Soviet Union, it became compulsory to reproduce in stilted English translation a goofy pronouncement by Dmitri Shepilov: "All this nervous and insane boogie woogie and rock 'n' roll," the former foreign minister had told a congress of Soviet composers, "are the wild orgies of cavemen."[49] And in his contribution to the *New York Times* series, "Global Report on Rock 'n' Roll," special correspondent Max Frankel used this lede: "The only Soviet composer ever to publish a note of rock 'n' roll did it for a theatrical scene depicting hell."[50] Nubile young girls, dressed as devils, had apparently shimmied in a revival of a Mayakovsky satire. "No one in [Moscow] can recall an authentic performance this side of hell," Frankel concludes. "Mother Russia is safe!"

Perhaps understandably, humorous depictions in the American press lacked much context. But how were the political statements of eastern bloc officials that American journalists sometimes reproduced actually received in Eastern Europe? The rock 'n' roll devil dance, to take just one example, on closer inspection poses a puzzle. The use of Western dances to illustrate negative characters or themes in Soviet productions seems to have been widespread: a foxtrot, for instance, might represent a student who cheated on university exams. Yet these depictions could mean several things at once to savvy locals. For some, they challenged gender roles; for others, maybe they simply titillated. But their very existence, historian Gleb Tsipursky argues, allowed young people in the Soviet Union "to exhibit officially condemned dances and thus to negotiate and expand the limits of tolerance for non-Soviet styles."[51]

Needless to say, that level of nuance did not reach readers in the United States. Depictions of rock 'n' roll's popularity in the Second World instead dramatized what US commentators saw as the yawning gap between the tenets of "official" policy and the worldviews of ordinary citizens. "Wherever I went in Russia," as John Fell Stevenson wrote, "I saw evidences of disbelief in official Soviet propaganda." So too did journalist Harrison Salisbury, taking break from his juvenile delinquency beat, in a three-part special on Bulgaria. The second essay explores young people's tastes in popular culture. The *Times* reporter first encounters two gormless representatives from the local youth organization in Sofia. "I saw rock 'n' roll in Russia at the Youth Festival," one young woman sniffs, "but it made no impression on me. It is only beat and no melody." Just two weeks later, however, Salisbury learns the truth. He attends a dance where a visiting swing band from Czechoslovakia plays fusty Glenn Miller charts. Soon the bored teenagers cannot stand it any longer. "Clamorous youngsters at the Sofia Summer Theatre took up a chant: 'Rock 'n' roll! Rock 'n' roll!' Finally the orchestra leader yielded," Salisbury reported, "and swung into a rendition of 'Rock Around The Clock.'"[52]

These depictions characterize the Second World as defined by the decoupling of politics from truth. To understand socialist societies, such accounts suggested, readers cannot simply take the statements of their leaders at face value; intrepid reporters like Salisbury need to interpret these statements, peeling back the hollow words to reveal how deeply (or not) "propaganda" has infiltrated the inner lives of regular citizens. Sometimes this formulation is explicit. An article on Czechoslovakia, for instance, estimates that upwards of 90% of people oppose Communism. In this context, "an American sticks out like a sore thumb": "Not because of his clothes or speech but because he talks, laughs and acts *spontaneously*." Socialist citizens repeat the same rote answers, ask the same rote questions. "It takes a while before the significance of this sinks in: the people are 'acting,' playing a part."[53] In young people's unvarnished reactions to rock 'n' roll, the accounts above suggest, could be discerned the truth of their beliefs. Because when people are unfree, experts need to read between the lines.

We might be getting a bit too abstract. The key point here is that Cold War contests between the First and Second Worlds were, in large part, struggles over knowledge. And for good reason. The stakes of armed struggle had become too high, given that each side had thermonuclear weapons as the big beat hit the eastern bloc. In the United States, the impulse to acquire knowledge about the world quickly became institutionalized after 1945. Senator William Fulbright influentially pushed for the creation of exchange programs to bring foreign students to American universities, and Americans to foreign ones. The notion that the United States must cultivate "cultural understanding" with other countries, an idea fundamental to liberal conceptions about how the world works, soon dominated postwar thinking. In this context, knowledge about the Soviet Union and its satellites especially became a key priority, with centers for the study of Soviet politics and culture founded at major universities such as Columbia University in New York City, and programs to learn languages like Russian, Polish, Serbo-Croatian, Tatar, even Albanian, receiving state funding.

For sure, the average American did not participate directly in this Cold War knowledge economy. But its assumptions trickled down into mainstream thinking through the kinds of journalistic accounts we have just examined. "One comes away from Russia wondering," John Fell Stevenson ended his travel diary, "whether the Russian people's genuine friendliness toward, and interest in, Americans will eventually triumph over their fierce competitive spirit and the aggressiveness of their leaders."

But of course the problem was not quite that simple. American ideology shared a key assumption with Soviet thinking, and this assumption would ultimately make it impossible for either side to budge an inch. Each side not only viewed itself as a torch-bearer for progress, but also as charged with spreading its political values globally.[54] This universalism, this secular messianism, played out most visibly in their struggle to win over people in the non-aligned countries of the Middle East, South America, Southeast Asia, and Africa. And in this contest, Americans believed, rock 'n' roll provided a powerful secret weapon.

* * *

In February 1958, the *New York Times* published a short human interest piece headlined "Kuwait Student Digs Rock 'n' Roll." The Columbia PhD student "speaks three languages, plays the violin and is 'hip' to rock 'n' roll."[55] He'd even seen Alan Freed's show at the Paramount Theater—twice. The headline notwithstanding, much of the interview focuses not on the student's record collection, but on his political views. The reporter asked about Nasser (a "sincere man trying to do good for his country") as well as the recently deposed King Farouk ("a corrupted monarch"). But the hook, and shorthand for this Kuwaiti exchange student's pro-American feelings, remained the music.

"The craze of America's teen-agers has met a mixed reception abroad," Harry Gilboy wrote in a "Global Report on Rock 'n' Roll" illustrated with photographs of young people dancing not only in London and Rome, but also in Buenos Aires, Tokyo, Cairo, and Warsaw.[56] So too claimed "Rock 'n' Roll Exported to 4 Corners of Globe," published just after Manhattan's *Don't Knock the Rock* riots. "The rock 'n' roll mania that gripped Times Square yesterday," the lede stated, "has manifested itself in just about every corner of the world."[57] Teens had torn up theatres in London, danced in the streets of Sydney, bootlegged Elvis in Leningrad, rioted in Japan, even swarmed a

Figure 4 "Rock 'n' Roll is a Controversial Subject in the World," photo collage from a "Global Report on Rock 'n' Roll," in *New York Times* (20 April 1958)

Vancouver singer (who required a police rescue). "As at the Paramount in New York," the author claimed, "the balcony of a local theatre in Jakarta, Indonesia once swayed precariously to the stamping feet of youths in the grip of the rocking rhythm."

Coined in 1952, the term "Third World" referred to those countries aligned neither with the capitalist North Atlantic Trade Organization countries nor the socialist Warsaw Pact countries. One reason this term caught on so quickly, historian Carl Pletsch suggests, is that it was part of "a general Western tendency to clean up the language of government, journalism, and social science in reference to the rest of the world."[58] The former subjects of European colonies became citizens of "developing nations"; "primitive" groups became "traditional." This euphemistic term obscured (without erasing) two key assumptions in Western thought: that individuals in the Third World were inherently backward, and also in need of modernization. In that deeper ideological context, rock 'n' roll represented a sign of progress, evidence for the penetration of American consumerist modernity into "traditional" or "developing" societies.

But not everyone in the so-called Third World, American journalists reported, swayed to the big beat. Newspapers also reported on "rock 'n' roll bans" in places like Singapore, Havana, and Tehran. In 1959, Jakarta had prohibited rock 'n' roll, at least temporarily, leading several of its neighbors to follow suit. "Indonesia has banned rock 'n' roll and hula hoop dances and films," the *Washington Post* relayed from an editorial in Singapore's *Malay Messenger*. "As the dances are very obscene, we must do the same here."[59] In pre-revolutionary Havana, a Cuban official tried to prohibit rock 'n' roll from being shown on television in February 1957. Televised almost daily, the dancing (according to local killjoys quoted in the *New York Times* reporting) is "immoral and profane and is offensive to public morals and good customs."[60] The ban lasted just two days before the official in charge of culture and the arts "yielded to nation-wide protests from teenagers." (Though broadcasters promised to "delete three steps from a dance the Minister considers 'degrading to public morals.'")[61]

In Iran, Reuters reported, officials "banned rock 'n' roll dancing as 'harmful to health.'"[62] "This new canker can very easily destroy the roots of our 6000 years' civilization," a police spokesman told the press. Authorities reported rock 'n' roll dancing had caused grievous bodily harm to several persons: a fractured knee, a broken back, and two tongues bitten clean off. The problem first came to light after a photographer secretly photographed the dancers for a national magazine, providing proof of the "decadent, degrading and lascivious" dancing. An upscale hotel imported an Italian band named

"The Rock 'n' Rollers," which inspired Radio Tehran to spin a few rockin' records. While the dancers were at first upper-class boys, girls soon caught the rock 'n' roll fever: removing their veils, wearing "I Like Elvis!" buttons, even enrolling in dance lessons from instructors claiming to hold "certificates of competency" signed by Presley himself.[63]

A year later, the *New York Times* confirmed the popularity of the big beat in a profile of two Iranian exchange students headlined "Youths Studying in U.S. Like Rock 'n' Roll Music." The young woman, Behjat, and her cousin, Jeemie, had come to the United States to study (respectively) interior design and engineering. In response to the interviewer's questions, each explained that at home they enjoyed picnicking—and American popular culture. "We love to dance," says Behjat, "folk dancing, waltz, mambo, rock 'n' roll we like best." They come from a privileged background. While life in Iran may be difficult if you are poor, they say, for the rich it can be quite "jolly." They not only relate their tastes in popular culture, but also explain other cultural similarities. "We wear clothes like Americans," Behjat tells the interviewer. "I buy most of my clothes in the big store (there is one department store in Tehran)."[64] The suggestion here seemed to be that (at least some) Iranians were not so different from Americans. They dress like us, they consume like us, and they listen to rock 'n' roll like we do, too. Had they been, or could they be, in some sense Americanized through their consumption? Was the big beat actually conquering non-American hearts and minds?

We shouldn't forget that rock 'n' roll imperialism worked alongside the more direct exercise of American power abroad. In 1953, Tehran had been the site of the first successful postwar attempt at regime change by the United States government (a previous plan to dislodge the communist government in Albania failed). Operation Ajax deposed Mohammad Mosaddegh, a democratically elected leader who had sought to nationalize the Iranian oil industry—and exert more oversight on American and British corporations operating in Iran. As rock 'n' roll went global, so too did covert American interventions. Were the rock 'n' roll bans so diligently reported on by American newspapers reactions to these interventions a form of cultural resistance? In some cases, certainly. But we might also better understand such reactions more broadly part of the collateral damage resulting from the politically—and socially—destabilizing machinations of the US government abroad.

This context helps explain why American journalists reported on the big beat's global spread to certain areas of the world (and not others). If the success of rock 'n' roll in places such as Cairo, Tehran, Havana, or Singapore evidenced openness to the United States, then protests against American popular culture potentially signaled resistance to American hegemony. Yet resistance, journalists reported, seemed futile. As Henry Luce had predicted, this would be the American century. "From Cuba to Trinidad," a journalist suggested approvingly, "rock 'n' roll is in strong competition with calypso, the rhumba and the cha-cha-cha." Floor shows in Havana even featured rock 'n' roll singers, whose "performance is generally a complete carbon copy, down to the slightest action, of some stateside rock 'n' roll artist."[65]

In Dar es-Salaam, Reuters reported, the local police band had performed "Rock Around the Clock" on the occasion of Princess Margaret's tour of the British colonial territory Tanganyika in October 1956. The bandmaster somehow procured a score, which bandmembers dutifully learned. Squint and you might discern a shift that's just beginning. Five years later, this territory would declare its independence from Great Britain; today it is part of the sovereign state of Tanzania. Would cultural imperialism directed by the United States simply replace an older, more direct colonialism? We'll need to address this question much later. Now back to Dar es-Salaam.

"The order from Gov. Edward Twining caught the band napping," Reuters reported, "because no one had heard of rock 'n' roll, even tho its beat is said to be African jungle rhythm."[66] So perhaps the music was not so strange to local listeners in sub-Saharan Africa, even though, in following the big beat as it traveled worldwide, journalists had assumed that it would inevitably be heard as some exotic American confection. Back in the United States, however, a vocal and racist minority was emphasizing the music's "Africanness." And they were doing this to argue that rock 'n' roll was fundamentally un-American.

* * *

"It has been three years now since American youth began to writhe with the shake and pound its feet like a Ubangi at the tom-toms," Phyllis Battelle had introduced her four-part series on rock 'n' roll.[67] "I suppose the natives must have been worked into a frenzy by tom-toms," Boston disk jockey Fred Cole told her. "[Rock 'n' roll] works the same way on kids."[68]

Today these kinds of quotes are often used to show that early reactions to rock 'n' roll were inherently racist. An archbishop damns "Rock 'n' Roll tribal rhythms"; a psychologist, quoted in an article suggestively headlined "Rock and Roll Riots Sweep Thru Anglo-Saxon World," calls the music "cannibalistic and tribalistic."[69] But this primitivist language seeks to denigrate the music as not simply non-white, but also premodern—as non-American twice over. And if rock 'n' roll functioned, as Glenn Altschuler has argued, as a powerful "metaphor for integration," then we need to remember that criticism of the music's blackness also functioned analogously to criticisms of integration itself at the precise moment when civil rights reforms demanded a reckoning with who should (and shouldn't) receive full membership in the American body politic.[70] For these reasons, the music—"a poor white trash version of a music formerly called 'Rhythm and Blues,'" as Battelle called it—represented a flashpoint for political debates among both black and white commentators.[71]

"Would you describe rock and roll," the white celebrity gossip columnist Joe Hyams asked Dizzy Gillespie, "as a revolutionary kind of music?" "Now look here, man, I didn't say anything is revolutionary," Gillespie replied. "I've just come back from a State Department tour, and I watch my words. I'm a conformist."[72] When African-Americans criticized rock 'n' roll, they often did so on aesthetic rather than political grounds.[73] "It's musically trite," another musician told the jazz magazine, *Down Beat*. "It's obviously gimmicked up with old boogie-woogie phrases, pseudo-Spanish rhythms, recurring triplets *ad nauseum*.... Harmonically, a lot of it is incorrectly written, and worse than that, incorrectly played."[74] Jazz had long been subject to similar racist criticisms. We might read these criticisms by jazz musicians, I think, as a strategy, a way they distinguished their music from the new style. This coincided with a broader process of aesthetic legitimation through which artists such as Charles Mingus and Nina Simone claimed jazz should be heard as high culture, through which musicians such as Gillespie exported jazz abroad as a quintessentially *American* form of art music under the auspices of cultural diplomacy programs.[75]

In contrast, the criticisms of white racists arose from avowedly supremacist political grounds. Much of their invective blended white supremacy with anti-Communism. As early as March 1956, segregationists in the South called to ban rock 'n' roll—and not simply because it was "primitive." The leader of the pro-segregation Northern Alabama's White Citizens Council, Asa Carter, had called it "jungle music," decrying its "Congo rhythms"; he demanded jukebox operators stop playing "immoral" rock 'n' roll records. But he went even further. The music, Carter claimed, represented an attempt by Northerners to "infiltrate" the white South.[76] "[A] plot to mongrelize America," "be-bop, 'Rock and Roll,' and all Negro Music" had been engineered by the NAACP and its sympathizers to impose "Negro culture" on the South. The notion that rock 'n' roll was an African-American plot elicited incredulous reactions. "Some people in the South are blaming us for everything from measles to atomic fall-outs," said Roy Wilkins, the NAACP's executive secretary.[77]

This idea proved powerful within the warped and muddled logic of 1950s racism, a logic that knit together "blackness" with "redness" in often convoluted ways. For sure, integration had earlier fueled far-reaching conspiracy theories in the South that predated these criticisms of rock 'n' roll. The arrival of federal troops in Little Rock, Southern newspapers reported, represented the "military occupation which always accompanies a Communist coup"; praise for Eisenhower's directive by the *Communist Daily Worker* evidenced Soviet machinations.[78] Conservative thinker Zygmund Dobbs called "race turmoil" a communist tactic pitting American against American, suggesting that the NAACP was a front organization with deep ties to the Kremlin.[79] The relationship between the federal government and Arkansas, other white journalists wrote, was no different than that between the Soviet Union and Hungary.[80]

When the big beat hit, these conspiracy theories could be mapped directly onto the music in part because white Southern racists had long viewed the mass media with suspicion. As we will soon see, a broader debate over the media and its effects on Americans shaped postwar ideas about individual autonomy and freedom. But a particular, fringe conspiracy theory generated by white supremacist activists claimed loudly that communists had wrested control of the postwar media. A 1957 editorial cartoon, for instance, juxtaposed two television sets under the caption, "A Fair Exchange?" The set labelled USA-TV featured a great big Russian bear growling, its teeth bared; a tiny Uncle Sam peered out from the one labelled USSR-TV to say, "Peep peep!"[81] Sinister suggestions even reached the floor of the House of Representatives during this period. Introducing legislation that would prohibit media outlets from censoring racist song lyrics, one Southern congressman portrayed antiracist media policies as fascist or anti-democratic: "Hitler got his start doing things this way—now Russia does it in a 1957 version because the Kremlin controls all media of communication."[82]

Political anxieties about integration just barely masked more visceral fears of what white historian Charles Dew, in his 2016 memoir *The Making of a Racist*, called "the sexual violation of the color line."[83] "[N]othing, absolutely nothing, was more important to white Southerners, and particularly white Southern men, than defending the purity of white Southern womanhood," Dew writes.[84] He cites a congressman who claimed that American communists and their misguided liberal allies were scheming "to bring about a forced amalgamation of the white and black races." As Governor Wallace would claim explicitly, Northern liberals "were betraying the South through their commitment to the false doctrine of communistic amalgamation." "If left unchecked," Dew interpolates, "this pernicious doctrine would result in the creation of a 'mongrel unit of one' in the South, 'under a single all-powerful government.'"[85]

Red, white, and black: their intermingling, potential or real, prompted frantic efforts to ensure racial and political purity in the postwar United States. It inspired Asa Carter's group to stir unrest outside a Nat King Cole concert in 1956 by calling his anodyne crooning akin to the "openly animalistic obscenity of the horde of Negro rock 'n' rollers." The following day a local newspaper, *The Southerner*, published photographs of Cole singing alongside young white fans, stoking racist reactions with the captions, "Cole and his White Women" and "Cole and Your Daughter." The singer was badly beaten.[86] A white supremacist group in California used a similar tactic, distributing pamphlets with images of African-American boys dancing with white girls.[87] A chapter of the White Citizens Council in Alabama subsequently picketed another concert featuring Billy Haley, Bo Diddley, and the Platters, holding signs that read, "NAACP Says Integration, Rock & Roll."[88]

For white American liberals, race had seemed peripheral to more pressing economic concerns into the 1940s. The aftermath of World War II made "the race problem" central to their agenda.[89] In the age of Three Worlds, the position of African-Americans in US society loomed ever larger on the global stage. "At the United Nations General Assembly," Henry Cabot Lodge said, "you see the world as a place in which a large majority of the human race is non-white. The non-white majority is growing every year, as more African states gain their independence. . . . I can see clearly the harm that the riots in Little Rock are doing to our foreign relations."[90] (For its part, the Soviet Union pointed out the hypocrisy of the American government's position at every opportunity.)

At the same time, anti-communist campaigns also helped marginalize the class-based politics that had formerly dominated liberal agendas.[91] Anti-Communism pushed civil rights groups toward problems (such as segregation) with technocratic solutions (such as court cases); it also weakened coalitions among labor, civil rights activists, and leftist thinkers both black and white, leeching the significance of economic struggle from contemporary debates.[92] This followed closely a shift in understandings of the roots of intolerance. Racism, Gunnar Myrdal argued in his massive study, *An American Dilemma: The Negro Problem and Modern Democracy* (1944), represented "a problem in the heart of the American."[93] If the "race problem" resided in the hearts of white people, could its solution be found in transforming their personal relationship to, if not African-Americans themselves, then perhaps their music and culture?

Isn't that the (white) liberal dream? A dream that emerged just as blackness itself was being radically reconfigured for white consumers, though mainstream white record buyers rarely articulated this shift as eloquently as explicitly as their counterparts at the countercultural margins of postwar society. Following the "psychic havoc" wreaked by the atomic bomb, wrote Norman Mailer in his celebrated essay in *Dissent*, "The White Negro" (1957), individuals faced two options. Submit, and melt passively into the "the totalitarian tissues of American society."[94] Or rebel.

A few caveats. At this moment, the dissenters walking at lilac evening, desiring—like Sal, the protagonist of Beat author Jack Kerouac's *On The Road* (1957)—to be Mexican, Japanese, black, anything but white, were listening to be-bop, not teeny-bopper rock 'n' roll.[95] Moreover, the notion that black expressive culture provided white consumers an imaginative resource for self-making was definitely not new.[96] But as we will see in the next two chapters, the claims that white consumers of rock 'n' roll would begin making about non-white musical practices transformed rock music's political potentials by the end of the 1960s. Blackness came to represent the model and the vehicle for evading conformity—for eluding the tranquillizing grasp of the quotidian in American society.

* * *

When Elvis "wiggled and wriggled with such abdominal gyrations," critics charged, he seemed to be doing "an aboriginal mating dance."[97] This is why, as Presley performed on the Ed Sullivan Show for the third and final time in January 1957, Sullivan infamously instructed he be filmed from the waist up.

"Elvis the Pelvis" performed "Hound Dog," "Love Me Tender," "Heartbreak Hotel," "Don't Be Cruel," and "Too Much," songs exemplifying the threatening racial ambiguity of the singer, and rock 'n' roll itself. ("If I could find a white boy who could sing like a black man," Sam Phillips at Sun Records supposedly told anyone who would listen, "I'd make a million dollars.")[98] But the final song that Presley performed was not a rock 'n' roll record at all. Introducing the song, Sullivan told viewers that Elvis would soon hold a concert to benefit the Hungarian Relief Fund, with proceeds going to support anti-communist Hungarians fleeing after their failed uprising. Backed by the Jordanaires, Elvis then solemnly sang "Peace in the Valley," a gospel tune.

Two days later, Presley turned twenty-one and received A-1 status from his local draft board. His manager, Colonel Parker, saw the draft as a public relations coup, a means to remake the singer into an all-American idol as he transitioned from teenybopper music to more lucrative films. Some American officials did, too, even floating plans to create a special unit for him. Wary of the US government making money off his cash cow, Parker instructed Elvis to accept a regular commission. Sideburns shorn and now stationed in West

Germany, Private Elvis Aaron Presley embodied the new form of American soft power in almost too-literal terms.

Would rock 'n' roll itself survive the absence of its biggest star? Many hoped not. Trade papers even began reporting on the new fad set to eclipse the big beat: Caribbean dance music. "Don't blame it on Elvis for shakin' his pelvis," sang the Fabulous McClevertys, a five-piece calypso outfit from the US Virgin Islands, "shakin' the pelvis been in style ever since the River Nile."[99]

Back at the actual River Nile, the uneasy consensus about rock 'n' roll that Osgood Carruthers had reported on in Cairo at the beginning of this chapter broke down after just two days. According to the *New York Times*, Nasser's cabinet had banned rock 'n' roll—its films, its public performance, even its mere mention in local newspapers—"as sinuous imperialism." (That report ended with a knowing wink: "the ban means a not too sad return to the more frankly sensuous oriental dances that are Egypt's own home-grown product.") His fifteen minutes of fame as a rock 'n' roll dance emcee over, the African-American medical student Cleve Lewter completed his degree and returned home the United States.

Presley eschewed the big beat when he raised money for Hungarian dissenters, while Lewter—barred from medical school in the Jim Crow South—became a mini-celebrity in Egypt after accepting a scholarship from Nasser. Peeking around the corners of stories about rock 'n' roll's early protagonists, we find some complicated questions about how Americans rocked the First, Second, and Third Worlds. Did rock 'n' roll represent a form of American imperialism? Should the big beat represent the so-called Free World? And just how "free" was that world?

The self-anointed position of the postwar United States as "the leader of the free world," historian Susan Carruthers reminds us, remained "relational, forged in opposition to an Other imagined as its absolute antithesis: the 'slave world' of Communism."[100] A new, postwar sense of exceptionalism inflected this relational identity. For the United States, as Hans Kohn wrote in *American Nationalism* (1957), "was not founded on the common attributes of nationhood—language, cultural tradition, historical territory or common descent—but on an idea which singled out the new nation among the nations of the earth."[101] The spread of that idea, "liberty," became the centerpiece of a new manifest destiny, what historian John Fousek calls "American nationalist globalism." "This ideology combined traditional nationalist ideologies of American chosenness, mission, and destiny with the emerging notion that the entire world was now the proper sphere of concern for U.S. foreign policy," Fousek writes. "In a global age, America was called upon to exercise its now extraordinary power globally in the name of traditional American values—values that had always been deemed universal."[102]

And this is how the United States rocked Cairo, and London, and Moscow, and Tehran. For sure, the seeds of these ideas about the universality of that US-led project of liberal democracy would only later be knitted fully into mainstream narratives about the music. Before that could happen, rock first had to become American, and it began to be seen as American in part through stories about the United States and its relationship to the rest of the world. Few would explicitly label it "native American music," as one supporter claimed in the African-American newspaper *Chicago Defender*.[103] But these seeds had been sown. Now another obstacle remained, blocking rock 'n' roll from becoming rock music and acquiring its contemporary democratic bona fides: its commodity status.

Yet as Americans came to define themselves by their standard of living, capitalism itself, as well as its mass-produced consumer goods, assumed positive, extra-economic political meanings. The relationship between free markets and a free citizenry, commentators pointed out, still had some kinks to work out. "Slowly, sometimes painfully, most of us have come to realize that mass production implies mass consumption, and that mass consumption in a free economy requires mass purchasing power," Adlai Stevenson had stated in a lecture titled "America, the Economic Colossus" (1955). "It is bad economics for too high a proportion of our total income to go into too few hands ... in our society social justice and economic well-being go hand in hand and there can be no fruitful coexistence between prosperity and selfishness."[104]

"Give me money!" screamed a twenty-one-year-old Liverpudlian, covering the Motown hit by Barrett Strong, "Money (That's What I Want)," at his beat group's failed audition for Decca in 1962. "Whole lotta money! I wanna be free!"

That rock-crazed white teenagers drove consumption, and that their consumption enmeshed itself with new forms of leisure that adults often found frightening or repugnant—this would, as we will soon find out, exponentially complicate matters. So before John Lennon's Beatles could launch their invasion of the United States, helping to transform rock 'n' roll into rock, American commentators first needed to more fully grasp the political implications of this music as a form of mass culture.

3
How Trash Became Art

In December 1964, the Primitives released "The Ostrich" on Pickwick City Records. Put on the record now so you can hear their singer scream and cluck, begging you to do an impossible dance. "Come *on*!" the speakers shriek. "Stand on your *head*! Now do the Ostrich! Do the Ostrich!"

The singer had just finished an English degree at Syracuse University in upstate New York. Now back home, Lou Reed took the train each day from his parents' house in suburban Freeport to industrial Long Island City, Queens, where he sat cranking out "songs on command, like a songwriter machine."[1] Many of the singles written at Pickwick were lazy rip-offs, imitations of chart toppers recorded quickly and rushed to market. But the best of Reed's dreck—like "The Ostrich"—hinted at an outré sensibility that would propel him to underground stardom.

Reed got the Pickwick gig after Terry Philips, the label's talent scout, heard him perform a Beach Boys–esque pastiche about a street-racing girl from Pasadena named "Cycle Annie." To promote "The Ostrich," Philips then cobbled together the Primitives, fronted by Reed. The band played a few radio stations, a high school dance, even the opening of a new supermarket.[2] The single flopped. But the promotional gigs for this crass cash-in played a key role in rock history, connecting Reed to Welshman John Cale, a member of New York City's experimental music scene. Backed by Pop Art impresario Andy Warhol, Reed and Cale were soon making records that, once and for all, destroyed the distinction between rock music and art.

But for now let's return to "The Ostrich." Reed's little bit of meta-dance-craze fluff encapsulates the inherent silliness of rock 'n' roll in its commodity form. The exaggerated send-up parodies *du jour* teenybopper fads of the early Sixties, the ephemeral 7-inch singles demanding listeners frug and shimmy, shake and stomp and twist, "do" the Monkey, the Pony, the Mashed Potato, the Watusi. It's not difficult to see how these dance crazes generated widespread anxieties about the effects of so-called mass culture on young consumers. "You gotta *swing* your hips now!" Little Eva begged in 1962. "Jump up! Jump back! *Do* the Loco-Motion with me!" An entire industry mass-produced these commodities: songwriters and lyricists, not to mention newly powerful A&R men ("artists and repertoire" specialists) charged with developing and managing marketable talent. "Every day we squeezed into our respective cubby holes," recalled Carole King, co-writer of "The Loco-Motion" and a songwriter employed at the famous Brill Building (across the East River from Reed's dingier Pickwick digs). "You'd sit there and write and you could hear someone in the next cubby hole composing a song exactly like yours."[3]

Mass production of rock 'n' roll motivated serious critiques about the anti-democratic nature of popular music. Otherwise serious people believed three-minute-long banalities such as "Boney Maroney," "Wooly Bully," "Louie Louie," even "Rama Lama Ding Dong," raised existentially troubling questions. Were listeners passive or active? Did industry men dictate or respond to public taste? Does a listener's taste for rock 'n' roll records express their individuality or conformism? In short, does the marketplace of sounds foster—or suppress—democracy?

Well-worn tropes juxtaposing the repressed Fifties with the liberated Sixties often foreground sex, drugs, and (of course) rock 'n' roll. But after the hot white heat of rock 'n' roll's opening salvo, popular histories often claim, the real music (nearly) died. Jerry Lee Lewis married his thirteen-year-old cousin, while Chuck Berry went to prison for taking a fourteen-year-old girl across state lines; Elvis Presley served in Germany, and Buddy Holly died in a plane crash in Iowa. Even Little Richard retired after rediscovering religion while on tour in Australia. (The fireball in the Sydney sky, which the rock 'n' roll screamer had taken to be a sign from heaven, in fact turned out to be Sputnik I, launched by the Soviets a few weeks before.)[4] Into that vacuum pranced cheap commercial pop idols, teenybopper trash pushed by crass businessmen, frauds, and con artists.

And so before rock 'n' roll became rock, and schlock could be displaced by something more meaningful, four plucky Brits had to invade America and a teenaged-Little-Richard-cover-artist-turned-Woody-Guthrie-impersonator had to go electric. And *this* is how rock became capable of real political and social change. At least, that's the story. For sure, we find within this narrative grains of truth. But the broad strokes obscure more than they reveal. How did mass culture, long seen as frivolous at best (and a threat to individuality at worst), come to be lauded as a serious expressive means for exploring the human condition between 1958 and 1966? How could a mere commodity, rock 'n' roll, morph into a vehicle for critique, rock music?

Put simply, how did mass-produced trash become politically meaningful art?

* * *

In early 1959, George Avakian sat in his New York City apartment watching *77 Sunset Strip*. He didn't like what he was seeing. Kookie, the teenage lead played by Edward Byrnes, wore greased back hair and a surly grin. "I was offended," Avakian later recalled.[5]

The veteran A&R man had left Columbia Records one year earlier. Over twelve years there, the Russia-born producer had championed early jazz giants and collaborated with leading classical musicians; he greenlit major recordings of figures such as Krenek, Carter, Khatchaturian, and Cage; and he curated a groundbreaking concert series, *Music for Moderns*, which featured leading improvisers alongside contemporary composers at Manhattan's Town Hall. Now charged with building a commercial label for Warner Brothers, Avakian showed his pragmatic side. In one early coup, he poached Bill Haley and His Comets from Decca. In Kookie, Avakian now mused, he might have found his very own rock 'n' roll star. Teenagers loved him, and parents hated him. Could he sing? Did it matter?

In a feature about the phenomenon of the "no-talent singer," journalist John Wilson asked Avakian this very question. A square-jawed, pouty-lipped head, perched atop a magnetic tape recorder, croons into a Rube Goldberg-esque contraption in the illustration accompanying the essay; someone has plugged the singer-cyborg into a wall socket. The "synthetic" or "no-talent" singer can now be created in the studio, the article explained, because "'sounds' have often taken precedence over music." (Think Elvis's voice awash in echo; or Fabian, the doo-wop idol from Philadelphia who had vanquished a handful of voice teachers, only the last of whom had "managed to open up [his] voice slightly, although he was not able to inculcate any sense of pitch.")[6] Aided by the modern recording studio, handsome young men like Edward Byrnes realized "their limitations as singers have been no handicap." Avakian found this to be true, at least to a certain extent. In April 1959, "Kookie, Kookie (Lend Me Your Comb)," Byrnes's (mostly spoken-word) duet with actress Connie Stevens, reached #4 on the Billboard Pop Charts, though his subsequent single, "Like I Love You" (b/w "Kookie's Mad Pad"), edged only briefly into the Top Fifty.

Kookie was not an isolated case. That same year, RCA Victor began transforming one Roger Strunk, a James Dean look-a-like from suburban California, into teen idol Rod Lauren. The constructed nature of "Rod's" celebrity was no secret; insiders called him "the recording industry's new guinea pig." Roger is a nice boy, one journalist reported, "but still generates enough sloe-eyed sullenness to stimulate girls, aged 13 to 19, into buying the two recordings he's made to date: 'If I Had A Girl' and 'No Wonder.'"[7] A&R man Dick Pierce had discovered him a year before. His interest piqued by the boy's naturally moody demeanor, Pierce hoped he could carry a tune. "It turned out that he *could* sing," Pierce said, "so we signed him to a contract, changed his name, and decided to build him up as the nation's no. 1 ballad boy." A press agent then began the delicate balancing act "to present Rod Lauren to the parents of the nation as a fine, decent, talented boy-from-next-door, while simultaneously convincing teen-age girls that Rod is a romantic, individualistic, strong-willed, ballad-singing rebel."[8]

This crass commercialism inspired some resistance. "I refuse to make that trash," bandleader Mitch Miller told anyone who would listen. Others hopefully predicted the music's imminent demise. "Teenagers get tired of seeing the same thing over and over again," producer Albert Zugsmith said. "Their tastes are improving and rock 'n' roll is on the way out."[9] Indeed, there were signs, songwriters Jack Fulton and Lois Steele claimed, that "the popular music pendulum is beginning to swing away from the sexy beat of rock 'n' roll and is moving again in the direction of sentiment, love, and romance."[10] But these arbiters of good taste agreed the big beat—"this raucous distillation of the ugliness of our times," as Pablo Casals put it—had no redeeming qualities. "The French have a word, *abrutissant*, for anything that brutalizes man and tends to turn him into a beast," the renowned cellist continued. "That's the word for this terrible, convulsive sound. It is against art, against life."[11]

Against art, against life. So how had this trash gained a stranglehold on America's airwaves? Did the American public actually want to hear these new balladeers, or were these young men being foisted on young consumers? As we have seen, the idea that postwar media fostered social control, that "he who is master of the press and radio," as psychologist Joost Meerloo wrote, "is master of the mind," became popular just as rock 'n' roll exploded in the United States.[12] Deejays did not necessarily disagree. Alan Freed, for instance, proudly branded himself the "Pied Piper of Rock 'n' Roll." Yet in ascribing nearly limitless powers of consumer persuasion to these men, critics begged the question: if industry insiders had made the big beat fad, then surely they could also break it? "If all the A&R men got together and agreed," Don Costa at Paramount Records claimed, "there'd be no more rock 'n' roll. But they aren't going to do it, and there's no question but that rock is what the kids want."[13]

Rock 'n' roll's fiercest critics soon realized that if industry men would not solve the problem, then the state would need to step in. The US government had first addressed the rock 'n' roll problem, albeit indirectly, three years earlier. In September 1956, Rep. Emanuel Celler (D-NY) chaired an inquiry by the Antitrust Subcommittee of the Committee on the Judiciary in the House of Representatives into monopoly practices in the television industry. At the hearing, a long-simmering struggle between ASCAP, the performing-rights organization founded in 1914 and representing old-guard performers and songwriters, and the upstart BMI, founded in 1940 and representing the newer country, rhythm, and rock 'n' roll set, erupted. Following testimony by BMI's president, Carl Haverlin, lyricist Billy Rose spoke.

"An ASCAP standard like 'Love Me' and 'The World is Mine' has been replaced by 'I Beeped When I Shoulda Bopped,'" the ASCAP board member told the committee. "A lovely song like Irving Berlin's 'Always' has been shunted aside for 'Bebopalula, I Love You.' It is the current climate on radio and TV which makes Elvis and his animal posturing possible."[14] And in a perverse twist, Rose reported, he had been able to escape the "untalented twitchers and twisters" ubiquitous on American airwaves only in the Second World. On a tour of five Communist countries, the lyricist heard works by George Gershwin, Cole Porter, and Rodgers and Hammerstein. "In other words, our best musical talent seemed to be having an easier time crashing through the Iron Curtain," Rose summarized, "than through the electronic curtain which the broadcasting companies have set up through their three-way control of the airwaves, the outfits which publish and the companies which make phonograph records."[15]

The consummate showman's image of an "electronic curtain" proved attractive to both the subcommittee and the press. This so-called electronic curtain allowed pro-rock 'n' roll industry insiders to not only exercise "domination of the public taste," but also to actively degrade this taste in order to push more product. Its continued existence, then, had potentially far-reaching consequences for a purportedly free society.

"It would mean that musicians and songwriters would have to conform to the old pattern, and that if they off the beaten path they might be yanked back," Rep. Celler prompted Rose. "That certainly does not spell creative genius as far as American music is concerned."

"I couldn't agree with you more," Rose replied.

"America has a great deal to contribute, as far as music is concerned," Celler continued.

"In the popular field certainly more than any five other nations," Rose dutifully agreed.

This initial hearing spurred little change in the short term. The "synthetic singer" continued to be pushed by media companies such as Warner Bros and RCA Victor; the spat between ASCAP and BMI smoldered without resolution. In 1957, Frank Sinatra reignited the debate with a statement that, according to *Time*, had been "transparently timed to pump a little publicity pizazz into the weary, long-running argument between [the two organizations]."[16] But that same year, the Senate Commerce Committee declined to hold hearings, with chair Sen. John Pastore (D-RI) telling *Billboard* that he cared only "whether the listening public can call up its stations and ask for a tune and get it played—regardless of who wrote it, or what licensing outfit cleared it." In his estimation, they could.[17]

Yet officials continued to worry about the problem of rock 'n' roll on the airwaves. A Massachusetts congressman decried the federal government for subsidizing "musical illiterates" like Little Richard and Elvis Presley by designating all phonograph records as "educational material," and thus able to be mailed through the US Postal Service at a reduced media rate. "Putting 'Itchy Twitchy Feeling,' 'Honeycomb,' 'Stagger Lee' and 'Splash Splash' in the same category as the three B's of Bach, Brahms and Beethoven is a horrible perversion of the intent of Congress, who tried to further the purchasing of educational records," said Rep. Torbert "Torby" MacDonald. "If any changes should be made, it seems to me we should make it more difficult for the phonographs of our teen-agers to blare from coast to coast daily and nightly with this trash."[18]

* * *

Two years later, concern over "trash" records finally culminated in a series of government hearings. In New York City, the district attorney launched an investigation. So did the Special Subcommittee on Legislative Oversight in the House of Representatives, which had recently concluded a spectacular investigation into rigged television quiz shows. Each targeted the widespread phenomenon of surreptitiously paying disk jockeys to play a record on the radio, a devious practice that, Americans learned, had a name: payola.

Payola manipulated citizens, stripping them of their full rights as consumers. "The public owns the airwaves," said the subcommittee's chair, Oren Harris (D-AR). "It is entitled to hear what it wants to hear—not what somebody secretly is buying."[19] The payola hearings provided a platform for the music's sharpest critics. "Do you think without payola that a lot of this so-called junk music, rock and roll stuff, would not be played?" one congressman asked a witness. "Never get on the air," he responded.[20] The coverage took on moralistic overtones. "Wages of Spin," according to *Time*, represented a form of dishonest "hanky panky" that "prospered in the shade offered by official indifference."[21] Endemic corruption had seemingly allowed rock 'n' roll to flourish, and in doing so, to conquer the nation's teenagers. Fallout from the payola scandal disproportionately affected those who had first championed rock 'n' roll: small-fry radio men at regional stations, as well as promoters at the independent labels that produced most rock 'n' roll recordings.

The larger record companies largely escaped censure.[22] And this despite widespread reporting on how record companies plied disk jockeys with drink, drugs, even prostitutes, or how industry men took royalties on songs and owned shares of the labels whose singles they promoted. Dick Clark held song-writing credits on over a hundred songs, for instance, and stakes in nearly three dozen labels—and got off scot-free. Alan Freed was not so lucky. "Payola may stink but it's here and I didn't start it," a defiant Freed initially told reporters. "What they call payola in the disk-jockey business, they call lobbying in Washington."[23] But for once Freed's bluster failed him. Just months later, New York's WABC fired the deejay after he refused to sign a pledge stating he had never taken payola; charged with bribery, Freed pled guilty in December 1962 to taking a $2,700 payment. He received a small fine and a suspended sentence, which effectively ended his career.[24]

By 1960, two congressmen had introduced legislation to ban "deceptive practices" in the media. "Payola in the selection of musical work and records for broadcast," one said, "is a kind of corruption that should have been dealt with years ago."[25] Some stations stopped playing the big beat. In Boston, WEZE replaced its rock 'n' roll program with "The Wonderful World of Music," replacing Frankie Lymon with Frank Sinatra, and Buddy Holly with the Boston Pops.[26] "The caliber of the performers on upcoming disks will be of pro-caliber," predicted *Variety*, "in contrast to the anything-goes amateurish quality of so many platter hits over the past few years."[27]

But could nefarious disk jockeys actually force young listeners to buy that trash? After all, that's the claim behind the payola scandal. Four disk jockeys at WCMS in Norfolk, Virginia, tried to find out. The team played "Pachalafaka (Pronounced Pachalafaka)" three hundred times over the course of one day. A novelty song by Irving Taylor, "Pachalafaka" appeared on the 1958 compilation *Terribly Sophisticated Songs (A Collection Of Unpopular Songs For Popular People)*, one of the first albums released by George Avakian on his new Warners Brothers label. The disk jockeys never found out if they could break "Pachalafaka." As day two began, WCMS executives brought the experiment to an abrupt end by firing all four.[28]

For sure, the payola scandal would not have occurred without Americans' pre-existing, deep-seated anxieties about race and its influence on young white listeners. "If they were paying people to put Glenn Miller on the radio, [the government] would never have stepped in," a white disk jockey in Minneapolis later claimed. "The payola scandal let people get off their chests their resentment of youth and their music, and blacks."[29] But these debates also unfolded against concerns about the effects of commercially produced music on individual consumer-citizens. We've previously seen traces of these debates—the handwringing about adolescents, or the Second World critiques of profit over uplift in capitalist societies. Now journalists began weaving these threads together, ensnaring longstanding worries about democracy, autonomy, and consumption.

Otto Zausmer, foreign affairs correspondent for the *Boston Globe*, pondered the relationship among all three in a 1959 think-piece titled "Mechanical Slaves Bake A Bigger National Pie." "Mechanical slaves" (the automobile, for instance, or the all-electric kitchen) had made life almost unthinkably more efficient over the course of the twentieth century. "There is a great hope," Zausmer wrote, "in using these mechanical slaves properly: this generation can perhaps say it is the first in all human history which has a choice of all three freedoms: the political, economic and intellectual freedom which always has been the dream of man."[30] This is "freedom for the asking": a single Shakespeare telecast brings the bard to more viewers than he'd encountered his entire life; radio broadcasts of opera stars and classical performers democratize the musical arts in ways a Caruso might just barely have imagined; inexpensive paperbacks of literary classics allow anyone to accumulate a library that would've been inconceivable even a generation before. But in practice, the consumer's "freedom of choice" tempered the promise of cultural democratization. "It depends on what we read and what we skip; on whether we fill the newly won spare-time with Westerns and rock 'n' roll or with Shakespeare and Beethoven," Zausmer concluded. "There is no shirking the duty of choosing. In the life of the individual and in the life of the nation, opportunity rarely knocks twice."[31]

Here in the broadest of strokes we encounter the key problem with mass culture. Is the consumer's freedom to choose among products compatible with other forms of freedom? Since World War II, thinkers across the political spectrum had said no. Conservative culture warriors tended to advocate on simple moral grounds, entwining their political-economic agenda with a religious-social one. Thinkers on the left, however, set the terms for debate by elaborating a philosophical basis for opposing mass culture. For them, political democracy stood at odds with cultural democracy. These postwar intellectuals romanticized the past as a period of creative autonomy and self-expression, with the postwar present, as historian Neil Jumonville writes, "characterized by the destruction of the individual's critical and expressive capacities."[32] And after 1945, our modern world seemed suspended between the tyrannies of capitalism and communism. "[W]e may establish totalitarianism in the United States without concentration camps through the use of mass media," intellectual Bernard Rosenberg worried. Though resistance seems futile, "would any man who cherishes his sanity withdraw from the battle against kitsch and Khrushchev for that reason?"[33]

These ideas became mainstream through popular sociological studies that confirmed the United States had become a nation of followers. Its prosperity had broken the bonds of tradition, David Riesman and his co-authors argued in *The Lonely Crowd* (1950), bringing a new danger: conformity. Meanwhile, increasingly sophisticated forces shaped our lives. In *The Hidden Persuaders* (1957), Vance Packard explained how "mass psychoanalysis" and the lessons learned from "psychiatry and the social sciences" resulted in a situation where "professional persuaders" could sell us nearly anything: from household products, to political candidates, to ideas and values. The continued existence of the American as a free agent appeared fraught. "Freedom is placed before him and snatched away," Rosenberg would write in the essay introducing the monumental essay collection, *Mass Culture: The Popular Arts In America* (1957). "And even if the incubus of hydrogen war could be lifted, these specters would still hover over us."[34]

But the blurring of those lines separating potentially distinct "freedoms"—political, economic, cultural—also presented an opportunity. "As the engines of postwar industry thrummed," historian Fred Turner writes, "politics, economics, and the making of American selves became so entwined that to many theorists, choices in one realm often seemed to be choices in the others as well."[35] Could democratic citizenship be exercised through the freedom to consume mass-produced goods? In articulating the difference between the First and Second Worlds, Richard Nixon had suggested as much in his so-called Kitchen Debate with Krushchev, proposing that access to high quality consumer goods indicated a person's high quality of life, and privileging consumption as a quasi-official expression of belonging to the American nation-state.

Not all mass-produced commodities, however, had been created equal. Kitchen appliances and automobiles obviously, it seemed, represented American progress. But trashy dance singles? These still represented a threat to the psychopolitical integrity of the normal citizen, albeit a threat that, for mainstream commentators, would increasingly seem quirky rather than dire. (My favorite example is the scene in Billy Wilder's 1961 comedy *One Two Three* where East German secret police torture a suspect by playing on repeat the novelty song "Itsy Bitsy Teenie Weenie Yellow Polka Dot Bikini".)

And we shouldn't simply dismiss out of hand all observations about the mass production of rock 'n' roll. Many songs did, for instance, sound remarkably similar. Songwriter entrepreneurs churned out big beat product just as they had the Tin Pan Alley tunes now viewed as passé by rock's supporters.[36] Composer-lyricist teams (Gerry Goffin and Carole King, or Jerry Lieber and Mike Stoller) competed to create hits in the new youth style, while session musicians (the Funk Brothers at Motown, the Wrecking Crew in Los Angeles) pumped out recordings. Would-be hitmakers tried to strike the one-hit-wonder lottery, men such as Murry Wilson in Hawthorne, California, remembered today not for his minor dance single "Two-Step Side-Step" (1952), but for purchasing a reel-to-reel tape recorder for his son in June 1958.

Young Brian quickly taught himself to overdub, recording multi-part vocals with his brother, Carl, and cousin, Mike. They quickly found a lyrical schtick: cars, surf, girls, and more cars. The music was derivative, too. The boys' first top-ten hit, "Surfin' USA" (1963), so obviously followed Chuck Berry's "Sweet Little Sixteen" (1958) that dad Murry uncharacteristically ceded the copyright to him without a fight. Young would-be pop stars didn't worry too much over the line between homage and imitation; at about the same time, another teenager, James Taylor, christened his first group the Fabulous Corsairs after another local group, the Corsairs, who had named their doo-wop group after the car model. Not as bad as naming your group the New Regulars after finding out the Regulars already exist, but still not great—originality doesn't seem to have been anyone's strong suit.

Yet originality had potentially important political implications. Does true freedom exist in a consumer society? Could commodities—even recordings of rock 'n' roll—possibly promote freedom? We're not there yet, but this idea now appears on the horizon. "Take out the papers and the trash!" orders the authoritarian father in Jerry Leiber and Mike Stoller's 1958 smash hit, "Yakety Yak." "Or you don't get no spending cash!" "This is essentially a song of protest," Stoller had claimed. The journalist interviewing the songwriter did not exactly disagree, but instead told readers that "these kinds of songs represent something of a rock 'n' roll Rorschach."[37]

"Yakety yak! Yakety yak!"

What do you see? Conformity—or individualism?

* * *

"Young and old in England, Germany, France and behind the iron curtain and elsewhere," Otto Zausmer had written, "are anxious to have their car or motorcycle at least, a refrigerator, electric stove or TV set."[38] The spirit of American consumerism—not only the *desire* for things, but also the urge to *identify oneself* with those things—seemed universal. What did that suggest about the preeminent American consumer product (besides blue jeans) to conquer the world, the rock 'n' roll record? We'll need to return to that question. But back in 1959, as Zausmer sat pondering the nature of liberal democracy in Boston, a young bandleader in Liverpool, just about to christen his new guitar group the Silver Beetles (in homage to four Crickets from Texas), was rehearsing an invasion.

That invasion came four years later, coinciding with an assassination that stunned the United States. ("Each of us has some share in the crime," Harrison Salisbury later wrote introducing the Warren Commission's report, "because we had a role in a society which made it possible.")[39] The youngest person ever elected to the American presidency, John F. Kennedy helped usher national politics into the television era.[40] He had star power: Marian Anderson sang at his inauguration, and the night before, Frank Sinatra had hosted a sparkling reception. His administration represented itself as a new beginning, with "the best and the brightest" (as David Halberstam would later ironize) promising major reforms at home.[41] Kennedy and his technocrats survived their first major international challenge, the Cuban Missile Crisis, in October 1962. ("Heard the roar of a wave," a Minnesota folk singer had warned listeners at Carnegie Hall a month before, "that could drown the whole world.")[42] But the president wouldn't live to face the next one.

At the recently renamed Kennedy International Airport in New York City, thousands of teenagers roared in February 1964. The object of their mania, four British musicians who "make non-music and wear non-haircuts," had first appeared on American television two months earlier (coincidentally, the very morning Kennedy had arrived in Dallas).[43] Visiting the United States to perform on Ed Sullivan's variety show, the marauding mop-tops relayed their demands at a press conference. "We have a message," one told the two-hundred-odd journalists. "Our message is: Buy more Beatle records!"[44]

Early coverage invoked the language of military conquest with a knowing wink. Beatlemania's arrival represented "B-Day": "the incomparable Beatles came and conquered."[45] "In '76 England lost her American colonies," another journalist wrote. "Last week the Beatles took them back. Washington surrendered, and New York's Carnegie Hall was all but obliterated."[46] "After surviving two World Wars this country is about to be invaded by a group who call themselves the Beatles," a parent wrote to *Life* magazine. "It makes one wonder if it was worth it all."[47] *Life* depicted the hysteria in full color, its photo-essay depicting girls pressed against barricades. In one disturbing photo reminiscent of wartime photography, police officers carry distressed, sobbing young women past a chain-link fence. "A disaster?" the caption asks. "Well, not exactly. . . ."[48]

Before the Beatles arrived, gossip columnist Jack Gould thought it unlikely that Beatlemania would succeed. "Hysterical squeals emanating from developing felinity," he wrote, "really went out coincidental with the payola scandal and Presley's military service."[49] Other commentators thought the phenomenon a significant political shift. "Their departure on a 10-day American tour will mark for British fans a form of sweet revenge," the correspondent at the *Times* London bureau wrote, "a satisfying reversal of the postwar transAtlantic traffic in popular singers."[50]

But no serious observer doubted that Beatlemania was a media invention: a craze, a fad, mere hype. One journalist reported a "genial conspiracy" making the rounds that record men had paid high school girls to scream at Kennedy Airport.[51] Police officers in Miami, the Beatles' second stop in the United States, alleged press agents had bussed in screaming girls (a claim later retracted).[52] The hysterical scenes prompted a renewal of psychological interpretations about the effects of popular music on mobs of adolescents: their need for revolt against authority, their quest to acquire status, and most especially their "frenetically felt urgency for having a good time and living life fast in an uncertain world plagued with mortal dangers."[53] A young fan from New Jersey confirmed as much in a letter to the *New York Times*: "All I know is, when I see the Beatles on television, they make me feel happy, enthused, just plain good. With all the stress and strain there is in our complicated society, I'm glad the Beatles arrived to take our minds off these problems."[54]

Was that a good thing? In 1962, psychologist Harold Mendelsohn had confirmed this phenomenon in his study of teenagers' listening habits for WMCA in New York City. Buffeted by constant stimuli, Mendelsohn concluded, teenaged listeners enveloped themselves in "a blanket of sound that keeps them apart from the world they walk through."[55] A mother on Long Island, responding to the Beatles fan in New Jersey, agreed. "Seeing and hearing these very ordinary, untalented young people from England," she acidly noted, "gave [the average listener] pleasure and a sense of gratitude at having her mind taken off the problems of our 'complicated society.'" The group's success, she concluded, depended on "the cooperation of naive, unsophisticated audiences who lacked the shrewdness and the wit to see that they were being skillfully used."[56]

Here we're stuck again at that perennial problem: Were industry men manipulating the Beatles' fans? Had the Beatles been "brought to their preeminence in latter-day vaudeville by artful contrivance," as McCandlish Phillips suggested in an article examining the phenomenon?[57] Advance newspaper accounts of Beatlemania in Great Britain, Phillips argued, created the expectation of hysteria, which American teenagers docilely provided. This represented almost a mirror-image of the hype preceding rock 'n' roll's spread to Western Europe nine years before.

Yet almost overnight that kind of handwringing would become passé. Wearing the right clothes, owning the right things, listening to the right records, playing the right guitar: hip consumption would soon mark not mass conformity, but free individualism. But first the key terms of debate over popular music would need to shift. How could this shift happen? "Teen-agers display considerable conformity on other issues besides the Beatles," a commentator was still writing in March 1964. "Guitar-playing, for example, is a favorite indoor sport, and numerous teen-agers confide that the most coveted graduation present today would be their own spanking-new guitar."[58]

"What counts is what you wear, drive or play," another journalist explained. "This may be why the guitar is the all-purpose symbol from coast to coast. If you own one, you are immediately identified as a person of arts, one who is conversant with Bob Dylan and Joan Baez."[59]

* * *

"I've been lecturing my classes about middle-class conformity for a whole semester," a sociology professor told *Time* magazine, discussing Malvina Reynolds's recent folk hit, "Little Boxes." "Here's a song that says it all in 1½ minutes."[60] A sixty-year-old with a PhD in literature, Reynolds penned the satire on suburban life in 1962. The "little boxes," tract housing thrown up Levittown-style throughout the United States, may come in different colors, but still "they all look just the same." The people buying these ticky-tacky houses? White-collar professionals, the business "ek-ZECK-you-teeves": "And they all get put in boxes / little boxes all the same."

In contrast to singles by groups like the Beatles, commentators viewed much of the commercial music released by white folk singers like Reynolds as artistically and politically significant. And no white folk singer would be more prominently ascribed political significance in the early Sixties than Bob Dylan, né Robert Zimmerman. Raised in Hibbing, Minnesota, Dylan—like John, Paul, George, and Ringo—requires only a brief introduction. As a teen-aged rocker, he played piano and whooped like Little Richard in a high school band, the Golden Chords, before enrolling at the University of Minnesota. In 1959, the high school senior who loved Elvis inevitably matriculated as a sweater-clad freshman who listened to the Kingsmen. And in the small business district just north of the university, Dinkytown, that's what happened to Zimmerman. He discovered the folk revival.

What was the folk revival? "It was the sound of another country," Greil Marcus writes in *Invisible Republic*, "a country that, once glimpsed from afar, could be felt within oneself." Singing and listening to folk songs, he continues, allowed access to "both peace and home in the purity, the essential goodness, of each listener's heart. It was this purity, this glimpse of a democratic oasis unsullied by commerce or greed, that in the late 1950s and the early 1960s so many young people began to hear in the blues and ballads first recorded in the 1920s and 1930s."[61]

In more prosaic terms, the folk revival had multiple, contradictory sources, from vaudeville and blackface minstrelsy, to song collecting and folklore studies, to the music of the Popular Front and union choruses.[62] For young enthusiasts, the specifically socialist, leftwing political connotations that folk-singing acquired over the previous two decades were not always obvious.[63] More salient for them was the revival's recent split into commercial and "authentic" wings. A major singer in the latter category, Tom Rush, remembered learning about this division when he arrived in the "green pastures" of Cambridge, Massachusetts, in 1960. "And I had to be totally reeducated," he recalled with a healthy dose of irony. "It was like being sent to a camp by the Communist Party, to cleanse your aberrant belief. I was told that Josh White was commercial and that was bad. What they wanted was ethnic.... So I was reeducated and I did my best to be ethnic, although it was difficult for all of us because we were a bunch of Harvard students singing about how tough it was in the coal mines and on the chain gang."[64]

The unresolved tension of that division suffused the tenth anniversary issue of *Sing Out!*, which hit newsstands in January 1961, the same month Bob Dylan arrived in Greenwich Village. Editor Irwin Silber included a broad range of voices in the pages of this expanded issue, which even included greetings from Soviet composers Dmitri Shostakovich and Aram Khachaturian. Malvina Reynolds idealized an earlier period before industry men "discovered" folk music. "It was an easier time," she wrote. "No one was cutting throats, or stepping on hands to climb the ladder of life with a guitar and a couple of Library of Congress albums strapped to his back."[65] George Avakian (now with RCA-Victor after leaving Warners) reminded the "purists" that commercial labels couldn't release music that "remained the province of rarefied and very 'inside' listeners." To survive, the companies (and lest we forget, the musicians themselves) needed to turn a profit.[66] Silber himself praised those who "added their own stamp of individuality to the songs and the stories, created something new when nothing in the old could speak for them."[67] Pete Seeger implored younger musicians to more deeply master "the finest folk traditions of the past."[68]

From within these messy, convoluted debates emerges the possibility of political significance for a voice like Dylan's. The first ingredient was the creation of an origin myth, repeated verbatim by obliging journalists and critics: the authentic heir to Woody Guthrie, the songwriter had travelled across country hopping trains like a hobo with a guitar strung across his back. Yet a rebel brand, no matter how compelling, could not by itself move product. Dylan had been signed to Columbia in late 1961 by John Hammond, part of what *New York Times* music critic Robert Shelton reported as a "scramble among several labels to increase their stable of city folk singers." Savvy hitmakers marketed them as "real" folkies; an A&R man reassured Shelton they recorded with "a minimum of splicing" to ensure performances "as free as possible."[69] This didn't keep *Bob Dylan* (1962) from selling so poorly that the singer became known briefly (and famously) as "Hammond's Folly."

The second ingredient arrived a year later with *The Freewheeling' Bob Dylan* (1963). On his sophomore album, Dylan embraced topical "finger-pointing songs" (a term he'd soon use to denigrate these political songs). A new girlfriend had shifted Dylan's politics. Suze Rotolo's parents had been Communist Party members; she had volunteered with civil rights groups in the South. The songs addressed nuclear annihilation (in "Talkin' World War III Blues"), race relations (in "Oxford Town"), the military-industrial complex (in "Masters of War"), and the Cold War's apocalyptic geopolitics (in "A Hard Rain's a-Gonna Fall"). But it was the opening anthem—especially as covered by Peter, Paul, and Mary, the poppy folk trio his manager Albert Grossman had created a few years before—that broke Dylan as a political voice nationwide. "Blowin' In the Wind" first appeared in Pete Seeger's *Broadside*, and it quickly became a civil rights anthem, famously inspiring Sam Cooke to write "A Change Is Gonna Come" (1964). "Someone was always putting his album on the turntable," one African-American organizer later recalled. "It was very compatible with what we were doing at the time."[70]

Might we be ascribing too much importance to a mere singer? Well here we come to the third ingredient: Dylan's reception. It began with glowing reports from *Times* critic Robert Shelton, who first encountered the singer at Gerde's Folk City in September 1961. He had gone to review the Greenbriar Boys, a bluegrass outfit (who performed a whimsical cover of a cold-war country gospel tune, "We Need A Whole Lot More of Jesus and a Lot Less Rock 'n' Roll"). But the opening act stole the show, and Shelton's mythologizing leapt immediately into high gear. To the critic's ears, Dylan was "one of the most distinctive stylists to play in a Manhattan cabaret in months." He "composes new songs faster than he can remember them, [and] there is no doubt that he is bursting at the seams with talent."[71] Over the next three years, Shelton's reviews shaped an enduring image of the individualistic artist-rebel: Dylan is simultaneously "comedian and tragedian"; he "resembles a Holden Caulfield who got lost in the Dust Bowl"; not merely an entertainer, he is "a latter-day James Dean who knows what he is rebelling against, perhaps an American Yevtushenko."[72]

America's version of the dissident conscience of the Soviet Union? Maybe that was taking things too far? Others suggested the praise didn't go far enough. Since the death of William Faulkner, author Thomas Meehan suggested in a late 1965 thinkpiece, the United States lacked a "Public Writer No. 1." Had Dylan assumed this mantle? "We're concerned with things like the threat of nuclear war, the civil-rights movement and the spreading blight of dishonesty, conformism and hypocrisy in the United States, especially in Washington, and Bob Dylan is the only American writer dealing with these subjects in a way that makes any sense to us," a university student told Meehan. "As far as we're concerned, in fact, any one of his songs, like 'A Hard Rain's Gonna Fall,' is more interesting to us, both in a literary and a social sense, than an entire volume of Pulitzer Prize verse by someone like Robert Lowell."[73] (Others were not yet convinced. "I am afraid I don't know his work at all," W. H. Auden said. "But that doesn't mean much—one has so frightfully much to read anyway.")[74]

An archetypical dissident, a real individual, even an artist: Dylan had become, in Shelton's words, "the brilliant singing poet laureate of young America." He represented individuality as "a personality who makes his own rules." And in songs like "It's Alright Ma," he proposed "a coruscating inquiry into the nature of personal freedom, the dread of tyrannical authority, the horrors of war, the demonic visits of a sensitive modern musical poet."[75] But that political voice, of course, had been accompanied by an acoustic guitar.

* * *

"Facing a rude and immature audience," Robert Shelton wrote in August 1965, "Bob Dylan gave a program Saturday night at the Forest Hills Music Festival in Queens in which he was a model of patient composure."[76] As he had throughout the tour, Dylan played the first set alone, accompanied only by his acoustic guitar and harmonica. He then welcomed an electric guitarist, organist, bassist, and drummer on stage for the second set. But the jeering had been directed not at his American-made Fender Stratocaster, but at the emcee who introduced the acoustic set: teenybopper disk jockey Murray the K, the Fifth Beatle.[77]

A year before, the Beatles had met Dylan after their gig in Forest Hills. Paul had introduced *The Freewheelin' Bob Dylan* to the group a few months earlier; Bobby would introduce the four to marijuana that night (or so the story goes). The politics of each side's music had seemed pretty clear-cut at the time: the one's "coruscating inquiry into the nature of personal freedom" versus the others' "strangely hypnotic effect on the female species of humanity in the teen-age bracket."[78] After Dylan's electric set at the Newport Folk Festival in July and the release of Lennon's Dylanesque "You've Got To Hide Your Love Away" in August 1965, however, that distinction began to seem less meaningful.

This shift occurred just as the Beatles, thanks to mass media, became truly global. "Naked Indians, who have never seen an electric light, sit mesmerized along river banks in the Amazon basin as missionaries' hymns or the Beatles' latest records flow from the village's transistor radio," a foreign correspondent in Bolivia reported. "The 'little talking box' holds the promise of the wheel and the terror of the atomic bomb ... It tells of child care and home economics—and how to conduct guerrilla warfare against established governments."[79] At various points, authorities in Israel, South Africa, and Spain banned the group's music, which received a mixed reception behind the Iron Curtain. One communist official described the Fab Four as "folk-singers" appropriate for young East Germans. ("But the Rolling Stones are out," he said. "Too animalistic.")[80] In July 1965, the Soviet Union's minister of culture told British reporters she'd be open to discussing a tour. (Though an American commentator snarked that "it was not entirely clear whether she knew who the Beatles were.")[81] In 1966, Japan had to hold a lottery to distribute 30,000 tickets to nearly 200,000 would-be Beatlemaniacs; the Philippines jeered them following rumors they'd snubbed the Marcos family.[82] (Communist China, the American press reported, remained mired in "an offensive against 'Western bourgeois music'—a phrase that is applied to almost anything from Beethoven to the Beatles.")[83]

Back in the United States, commentators tried to make sense of the new hybrid style, "folk rock," that Dylan had seemingly created out of thin air, and that the Beatles (alongside a score of others) quickly adopted. We've seen how folkies worried about commercialism. The explosion of "the Dylan sound" or songs written "in the Dylan mode," as Shelton described John Lennon's contributions to *Help!* (1965), now seemed to portend a potentially more insidious threat.[84] The critic saw the new vogue as "a lot of hopping on the bandwagon image-shifting and confusion," whether from singer-songwriters like P. F. Sloan or Barry McGuire, who scored a major hit with "Eve of Destruction" (1965), or groups like the Byrds or the Lovin' Spoonful. Yet overall, Shelton considered folk rock a "healthy movement," and robustly defended this "whole new area of rhythmic, up-beat music that couples the meaningfulness of folk lyrics with the vitality of rock 'n' roll."[85]

And folk rock needed defending. "When culture is treated as a commodity, its salesmen and producers must constantly feed the monster new ideas and new talent at a prodigious rate," Irwin Silber wrote in one polemic against the new hybrid style. "It is a result of this voracious process that the new commercial phenomenon of Folk Rock has emerged."[86] More perniciously, this new phenomenon came out of a "'white only' bag—it represented integration once again on the white man's terms." Had folk rock simply whitewashed rock 'n' roll? Silber's respondents didn't really engage that question. Instead, Shelton argued that Dylan had been made a "convenient symbol" for reactionaries. "Like a young Picasso racing through developmental stages, the controversial songwriter will not be hemmed in by the simplistic rules of the ethnic or political determinists," he wrote. "Curiously, Mr. Silber thought Dylan was to be lionized until the singer stopped repeating the social-protest catechism. Now he scorns Dylan for his 'psychotic vision' and his 'Tin Pan Alley gimmickry.'"[87]

At last the editor of the *Little Sandy Review*, Paul Nelson, challenged the very terms of debate. Calling Silber "a grand master of the nineteen-thirties' and forties' cliché," he mocked his "jargon": "such ancient doughboys as 'commodity,' 'money-changers' door,' 'mass culture' and 'Tin Pan Alley.'" "Where other men dream of gods and devils," Nelson smirked, "Mr. Silber's nightmares are always in capital letters: Cash Registers, Success Syndromes, Machines, and Systems haunt him and keep his mind from contemplating Mankind and its Problems."[88]

Here we have jostling together a number of competing ideas about commercialism, about creativity, about originality. Armed by the folkies' ideology of authenticity, Simon Frith writes, rock 'n' roll could begin to "claim a distinctive political and artistic edge."[89] But in order for critics like Nelson to draw these threads together in commentaries on popular music, that old jargon about mass culture first had to lose its explanatory power. Tragically unhip, Silber's "ancient doughboys" remained only as embarrassing relics of a now unfashionable politics of the past. While we'll soon encounter a few of the old folkie's nightmares as they persisted during the Sixties, albeit in new guises, we'll also meet a new medium for addressing Mankind and its Problems: rock, shorn of both its prefix (folk) and suffix ('n' roll). Because now, it seemed, certain kinds of popular musicians had something to say.

* * *

"The Beatles are about to enter," the press agent said, preparing the room at New York City's Warwick Hotel in. "I'd like to ask you people in front to kneel."[90] The assembled journalists tittered; the agent hurriedly explained that photographers standing at the back needed a clear shot. The Beatles entered looking haggard, exhausted from a tour that featured not only screaming fans but also death threats inspired by Lennon's ill-conceived comparison of the group to Jesus Christ. There were no more questions about their haircuts (shaggier) or George's favorite candy (Jelly Babies). Instead they fielded requests for statements on the escalating war in Vietnam ("we don't like war, war is wrong") and whether they'd like to tour the eastern bloc ("I don't fancy it," George said).

The mainstream press now wanted to hear what pop singers thought about the pressing problems of the day. In October 1966, *Time* magazine praised these "new troubadours"—the Mamas and the Papas, Donovan, Paul Simon and Art Garfunkel, and the Lovin' Spoonful—as groups with messages that mattered, and for having left rock 'n' roll's immature roots behind:

> "Zeeks!" gasped one teenybopper. "You can't even dance to it!" She was referring to the Beatle's latest release, "Eleanor Rigby," in which the shaggy four sing to the accompaniment of a double string quartet. "Rigby" is typical of the newest and in many ways most welcome upheaval to rock 'n' roll in years. To begin with, the familiar big beat of rock 'n' roll is receding—not in sales, but in decibels. The reason is simply that there is a big message in lyrics nowadays, and the kids want to hear it.[91]

Time attributed the change to an influx of ex-folkies: older, better educated, more musically sophisticated. Gone now were pop idols "wailing away in tongues that sounded like a cross between banshee and Bantu."[92] In their place were literate, poetic young men (and given the racially charged language of this framing, it's hard to disagree with Silber's charge that this represented "integration once again on the white man's terms").

Rock's connection to the folk movement provided one source for its newfound political heft. Its reframing as a form of high art solidified the big beat's final transition from crass commodity. In late 1966, a headline in *Music Maker* heralded Lennon for "pushing the pop song to the limit"; *Village Voice* critic Richard Goldstein called the Beatles' latest album, *Revolver*, "a revolutionary record."[93] It featured poetic lyrics about modern alienation and experimental tape loops, an entire song constructed over a single drone-like chord, and a radically expanded sonic palette that included sitar, electronic sounds, and orchestral instruments. Goldstein whiffed on their next record, infamously panning *Sgt Pepper's Lonely Hearts Club Band* in the *New York Times*. Other critics, however, rushed to the album's defense. Tom Phillips called *Sgt Pepper's* "the most significant artistic event of 1967"; *Time* lauded the group for "leading an evolution in which the best of current post-rock sounds are becoming something that pop music has never been before: an art form"; Robert Christgau praised them for refusing to "prostitute themselves for their fans."[94]

As art, the critics claimed, the album could not be evaluated according to its sales numbers (though it did sell a staggering 2.5 million copies in its first three months).[95] "[Listeners] are unprepared," a disk jockey told the *New Yorker*. "Just as people were unprepared for Picasso. That's because this album is not a teen-age album. It's a terribly intellectual album."[96] In 1963, *Please Please Me* had taken just over twelve hours to record, costing about £400.[97] *Sgt. Pepper* had no deadline; its sessions had extended over four months.[98] "Now we are working with pure sound," producer George Martin said, sounding more like the avant-garde composer Pierre Schaeffer than a pop producer who once crafted novelty songs by Spike Milligan and Peter Sellers. "We are building sound pictures."[99]

Journalists recognized this shift in status. "The funny thing about teenage idols," one wrote in reviewing the Beatles full recorded output up to this point, "is that some of them turn out to be artists."[100] The musicians themselves also loudly proclaimed their intentions for rock as a form of art. "We are just creating doubts," Paul Simon told *Time*, "and raising questions." "Pop music is the most vibrant force in music today," Art Garfunkel agreed. "It's like dope—so heady, so alive."[101] And as artists, pop musicians could grow. "We weren't as open and as truthful when we didn't have the power to be," Lennon told teenybopper magazine *Look* in 1966. Now done with "Beatling," he wanted to explore new roles: "painter, writer, actor, singer, player, musician. I want to try them all, and I'm lucky enough to be able to. I want to see which one turns me on."[102] This same sentiment had emerged in the infamous "bigger than Jesus" interview a year earlier. "You see, there's something else I'm going to do, something I must do, only I don't know what it is," Beatle John had told Maureen Cleave. "That's why I go 'round painting and taping and drawing and writing and that, because it may be one of them. All I know is, this isn't it for me."[103]

Rock's link to high art was not completely new. Underground filmmaker Kenneth Anger, for instance, had already set experimental films to pop songs, including a three-minute short funded by a Ford Foundation grant in 1964. (In *Kustom Kar Kommandos*, the camera lovingly following a blonde-haired, blue-eyed hunk erotically buffing a hot-rod to "Dream Lover" by the Paris Sisters. The more conspiracy-minded reader might be forgiven for wondering why the Ford Foundation, with its close ties to the CIA, funded an experimental short about the erotics of consumption set to that quintessential intangible American commodity, a Phil Spector-produced girl group.) Just a year later, Pop Art entrepreneur Andy Warhol placed a curious advertisement in the back pages of the *Village Voice*. "I'll endorse with my name any of the following: clothing[,] AC-DC, cigarettes small, tapes, sound equipment, ROCK N' ROLL RECORDS, anything, film, and film equipment, Food, Helium, Whips, MONEY!!"[104]

Warhol's intermedia happening, The Exploding Plastic Inevitable, featured the Velvet Underground, the group that finally allowed Lou Reed to quit his day job at Pickwick. We'll very soon return to these kinds of artworld "happenings." For now let's attend a meeting of music educators at the venerable Tanglewood Music Festival to mark just how mainstream rock's new image as a meaningful form of artistic expression had become. "If you want to know what youths are thinking and feeling," one symposium participant said, "you cannot find anyone who speaks for them or to them more clearly than the Beatles."[105] (Compare that statement with the criticisms made by teachers only a few years earlier.)

And rather than promoting conformity, the music portended nothing short of revolution for young listeners. "We urge them to be creative and original," ethnomusicology professor David McAllester said, "and suddenly they are—with hair styles, clothing, art, dance and music that we cannot stand the sight or sound of."[106] The new voices in popular music, these self-taught "composer-performer-heroes," are mounting a challenge to the "dominant culture." And that, MacAllester thought, is not a bad thing.

"Pete Seeger, Paul McCartney, Bob Dylan and many others are the leaders of a social revolution," the professor concluded. "They are the voices of dissent of our youth."[107]

* * *

In April 1967, CBS aired *Inside Pop: The Rock Revolution*. Produced by David Oppenheim, long-time director of the classical music division at Columbia Records, the hour-long documentary featured host Leonard Bernstein, who discussed the artistic—and political—significance of folk rock and pop. "I think this music has something to tell us," Bernstein told the audience, sitting at a piano and demonstrating technical aspects of recent releases by the Beatles, the Left Banke, and the Monkees.

What did young people want to say? "Next to universal love," Bernstein intoned, "freedom is their main concern." As we'll soon see, debate over the precise meaning of "freedom" had by this point begun shifting into its contemporary form, with American commentators—both liberal and conservative—well on their way toward a final split that reshaped the political landscape of the United States. Counterculturalcalls to "drop out" created sharp new divisions, with New Left critiques about how society deforms us replacing the agonistic handwringing of postwar liberals about human beings' theoretical capacity for autonomy after Auschwitz.

Meanwhile on the right, a new conservative fringe's approach to rock exemplified what Richard Hofstadter had deemed "the paranoid style" in American politics: "Bob Dylan was an obscure songwriter until he signed a contract with Columbia Records," a man's voice darkly suggests in "The Hippies," a 1967 educational filmstrip. "The man responsible for Dylan's contract at Columbia was John Hammond. It isn't surprising that Hammond would be interested in Dylan's brand of culture, for Mr. Hammond—according to official United States government records—has made himself a party to at least seven Communist fronts."[108] The John Birch Society funded this filmstrip; they also published pamphlets warning parents about Dylan, the Beatles, and the emerging "rock culture." For the moment, however, these views were not to be taken too seriously.[109]

As Leonard Bernstein told CBS viewers, we *should* take rock music seriously, and not as a threat but as an expressive form bearing important messages. Many young Americans agreed. In 1965, a philosophy major at SUNY-Stony Brook began writing his undergraduate thesis on rock 'n' roll. Richard Meltzer soon realized he was part of a network of deep young white men "helplessly dumping quotes from Plato on Beatle hits and Dylan albums," as Greil Marcus later described, "attempting to make sense of the emotions the music was provoking, trying to talk about the world the music seemed to be changing."[110] Their early methods were idiosyncratic. "I huffed, I puffed, read Nietzsche's *Birth of Tragedy*, saw the Beatles at Shea Stadium, revisited the sides of every scratchy 45 (and 78) I still possessed," recalled Meltzer, who also lovingly transcribed the inanely repetitive lyrics of songs like "Surfin' Bird" by the Trashmen ("buh-buh-buh-bird bird bird . . . ").[111] And their claims veered into overwrought rock-criticism-cliché even before rock criticism had been invented. "Rock is the brute actualization where all earlier art is potential," Meltzer wrote in the thesis that became *The Aesthetics of Rock*. "Rock is the only possible future for philosophy and art."

But one thing was sure: the revolution was coming. And that's how this mass-produced schlock became so significant, so fast. "A lot of the kids that you see from time to time, and that you retch over," the Mothers' Frank Zappa told Bernstein's *Inside Pop*, "are going to be running your government some day." "There's some sort of guerrilla warfare, psychological warfare, going on, and I feel like a guerrilla," said the Byrds' Roger McGuinn. "I feel good."

Bernstein proved sympathetic to these aims, translating the musicians' words into language presumably more palatable for the average CBS viewer. "They are hoping for a return to the human-centered life they feel modern life has moved away from," the conductor explained in one voice-over. "And they think that they, together with other young people like them, are forming a model upon which that society can be constructed."

And here the CBS documentary segued to Brian Wilson, leader of the Beach Boys. Seated at his piano, Wilson performs "Surf's Up," a track from then-in-progress album titled *SMiLE*—an infamous concept album, later abandoned due to Wilson's mental health problems, that was then generating enormous press. Wilson had hired the Beatles' former publicist to help re-brand his band's fun-in-the-sun image. A parade of mainstream and underground journalists visited to hear demos and meet "the seeming leader of a potentially revolutionary movement in pop music" at work.[112]

Not five years earlier, this musical genius had markedly less lofty aims. Back then, Wilson was teaming up with songwriter Gary Usher to record a Little Eva soundalike who wanted to cash in on the success of "The Loco-Motion." "If you haven't tried it you don't know what you missed / It beats the Mashed Potato, the Loco-Motion, the Twist," sang Betty Jean Willis, soon rechristened Rachel. "Re-e-e-e-volution!" "The Revo-Lution" (1962) fizzled on the charts, and Betty Jean/Rachel remained unknown.

"What does all this mean?" Bernstein asked in 1967, after rock 'n' roll had become rock, and that mass-culture trash had become politically meaningful art. "I think it is all part of a historic revolution, one that has been going on for fifty years. Only now, these young people have gotten control of a mass medium: the phonograph record. And the music on the records, with its noise and its cool messages, may make us uneasy."

"But we must take it seriously—as both a symptom, and a generator, of this revolution. We must listen to it, and to its makers."

4
How the Counterculture Dug Deeper

"Freedom, freedom, freedom," the hoarse mantra rings out across the fields of a dairy farm in upstate New York, its bearer urging on a ragged voice on the verge of giving out: "Freedom, freedom, freedom . . ."

Next a New York City–based guru draped in pink robes addresses the assembled masses. "I am overwhelmed with joy to see the entire youth of America gathered here in the name of the fine art of music," he begins. "In fact, through the music, we can work wonders. Music is a celestial sound and it is the sound that controls the whole universe, not atomic vibrations."

"The entire world is going to watch this," the yogi then concluded. "The entire world is going to know that what the American youth can do to the humanity." And with that he leads concertgoers, close to three-hundred thousand by this point, in a series of chants on the syllable Om.[1]

For attendees, the revolution had arrived. "We heard that there wouldn't be any reserved seats, that we'd be free to wander, and that the townspeople weren't calling out the militia in advance," one later recalled. "We were exhilarated. We were in a mass of us. People became aware of the land around us. Somebody said, 'It's like being part of an encamped army that has won.' We felt as though it were liberated territory."[2]

It's August of 1969, and we have reached an inflection point in our narrative, with this chapter a fulcrum connecting the book's first half to its second. There's really no good way to write about 1966 to 1970, perhaps the most over-mythologized five-year period in the history of American popular music. We'll need to examine well-trodden topics such as the Haight and the Sunset Strip, the Beatles and Dylan, psychedelia and the New Left. But I'll try to shift our focus just off-center, squinting to make out lesser-known figures peeking from around the corners of twice- and thrice-told stories. But for now, back to Richie Havens, Sri Satchidananda, and that teeming mass of youth, the Woodstock Nation, assembled at a dairy farm owned by the conservative Republican son of Jewish Russian immigrants in upstate New York.

Liberated territory, a mass of humanity chanting to transform the world, that clamorous, impatient demand, "Freedom! Freedom! Freedom!": in the late Sixties, listeners and musicians alike increasingly claimed that rock music provided a vehicle for the emancipation of humankind. But if the problem of liberation became central to what commentators began calling the "rock counterculture," that's not because there's something special about the music itself. This problem troubled jazz and classical musicians, visual artists, dramaturgs, and media theorists, not to mention activists in movements advocating for the rights of women, racial minorities, and homosexuals. And of course, not everyone thought that rock could make you free. As we'll see, criticisms of the rock counterculture came not only from the usual suspects on the conservative end of the political spectrum, but also increasingly from the most progressive members of the New Left.

For sure, the so-called rock revolution was not a monolithic movement. The contradictory, messy proliferation of claims about rock's political significance in the Sixties would be tidied up only later by the mythmaking of the Seventies and Eighties. But its protagonists did share in common a number of key questions. Did society make you unfree? Could its social institutions be tweaked, finetuned by experts to allow people to live better, more free lives— or did they need to be smashed, replaced by new ones? And what responsibility did individuals have to liberate themselves? In retrospect, the story goes, rock music helped remove the scales from the eyes of Americans, allowing them to more clearly apprehend the true nature of society, and to register their dissent from the status quo. This was "a big period of freedom," Brother Paul told interviewers for *The Beatles Anthology*, "which I always liken to God opening up the waves for Moses and then closing them down again."[3]

A period of freedom, a moment of clarity in which the stakes of social life were at last revealed fully to rock's true believers: How *did* rock music become a way for some people to diagnose the true limitations of American society, and then to transcend them? How did rock help young Americans dig deeper?

* * *

In 1967, the pop critic from the *Village Voice* found himself face-to-face with a dour communist bureaucrat in Prague. "In an office that looked like a set from *The Third Man*, he grilled me about all things Top 40," Richard Goldstein later recalled. " 'Tell me,' he said in the earnest, faintly melancholy tone I came to love in the Czechs. 'What is Surfing Bird? What means, *bird is the word*?' "

Goldstein called this visit behind the Iron Curtain as "the most important political experience of my life."[4] A year earlier, the twenty-one-year-old would-be journalist had talked his way into a full-time job reviewing rock and popular music. The job title "rock critic" did not yet exist (though Paul Williams's rock 'n' roll fanzine *Crawdaddy* did predate by a few months Goldstein's *Voice* column "Pop Eye"). He would help invent this role by taking seriously songs like "Surfin' Bird" (1963) by bands like The Trashmen, a land-locked surf rock group founded just a few hours' drive south of Hibbing, Minnesota. ("Buh-buh-buh-bird, bird, bird, bird is the word"—and so on.) And he did this by subjecting the 45s piled high in his family's Bronx walk-up to the conceptual frameworks of thinkers such as Susan Sontag or Herbert Marcuse, social theorists he had only just encountered as a first-generation college student.

"How do we tell what is noise and what is good, even artistic, rock 'n' roll?" Goldstein famously wrote in an early column. "A pop critic needs his eyes, his ears, a typewriter, and an impressive German vocabulary."[5] Words matter. They shape how we understand the world. The postwar period proliferated diverse frameworks for explaining how society worked, generating an explosion of expert terminology aiming to describe or diagnose social phenomena, and in so describing or diagnosing these phenomena, hoping to solve problems or chart new pathways into the future. And words beget more words. Marcuse's work explaining how capitalist democracies fostered "unfreedom," of course, provoked not just Goldstein's approach to pop records, but more significantly, a sustained critical response by young activists of the New Left. These middle-class, university-educated activists in turn helped popularize new language for describing social structures (the System, the Establishment, the Plastic Society) and human actors (the Youth, the Man, the Counterculture) after 1964.

Schismatic, such language forced into sharp relief long-standing social cleavages. "One assumption of the mid-century era was that a society normally should have an overall cohesion," historian George Marsden writes. "It would be shaped by a prevailing 'climate of opinion' that ideally would be shared to some degree at all levels of society."[6] Yet by the mid-Sixties, society appeared to many Americans increasingly fragmented, if not irrevocably broken.

To many the rot seemed pathological, the system itself irrational in its infliction of violence on the bodies of Americans and non-Americans alike. Violence in American cities, especially during "race riots" (to use the newly coined term), pointed to an untenable situation at home. In 1967, over 150 cities experienced rioting; in the bloodiest example, fighting and looting in Detroit left at least forty-three people dead and over two thousand injured. Meanwhile, the persistent psychological violence predicted by early theorists of the early Cold War such as Mailer and Orwell seemed to have mutated, spiraling into unchecked military aggression abroad. Captain George Morrison oversaw one precipitating event among many at the Gulf of Tonkin in 1964. He had said good-bye to his family at a naval base in

California seven months earlier (after insisting that his son Jim receive a crewcut from the navy barber).[7] An aircraft carrier, the USS *Maddox*, had reported an attack by North Vietnamese boats, which Morrison dutifully reported back to Washington in late August. In a nationally televised broadcast two days later, President Johnson made the case for military escalation; Congress then authorized support for any ally in the region "requesting assistance in defense of its freedom."[8] (Documents later revealed that the so-called Gulf of Tonkin incident never happened, at least not as described in official public accounts.)

Direct indictments of the irrational sadism of the American state came from college activists. "There's a time when the operation of the machine becomes so odious, makes you so sick at heart, that you can't take part!" Marco Savio of Students for a Democratic Society (SDS) declaimed in 1963. "You can't even passively take part! And you've got to put your bodies upon the gears and upon the wheels . . . upon the levers, upon all the apparatus, and you've got to make it stop! And you've got to indicate to the people who run it, to the people who own it, that unless you're free, the machine will be prevented from working at all!"[9] The Columbia University students Savio addressed had spent their summer in the South volunteering on civil rights campaigns; Joan Baez would lead them in song after his famous speech. This issue was not simply academic. Over the next decade, the American state drafted nearly two million eighteen- and nineteen-year-olds, with most sent abroad to defend "freedom" in Southeast Asia.

Early campus activists tended to come from elite universities in the Northeast.[10] New Englanders in suit jackets and ties, their cultural tastes favored folksingers such as Joan Baez over the Beatles, Peter, Paul, and Mary over Peter and Gordon. Some remained folk partisans, launching fierce criticisms against the growing political pretensions of the rock counterculture; others broke rank and helped knot together rock and new ideas about the political potentials of popular culture. But in some important ways, this knitting together of musical sounds with political values did not necessarily represent a rupture with the past. Writing in 1966, the revisionist historian Christopher Lasch located the roots of these burgeoning political movements in a decades-old "new radicalism." "The originality of the new radicalism as a form of politics," he suggested, "rested on a two-fold discovery: the discovery of the dispossessed by men who themselves had never known poverty or prejudice, and the mutual self-discovery of the intellectuals."[11]

Indeed, the political consciousness of white campus radicals crystallized through their imagined affinity with marginalized communities in the United States and abroad. This proved an important inflection point in the history of American liberalism, albeit one encompassing deep internal contradictions and even outright misidentifications. "At present, in the United States," sociologist Paul Goodman wrote in 1967, "students—middle-class youth—are the major exploited class."[12] Really? The white Jewish activist Jerry Farber took this idea to its most extreme conclusion in *The Student as Nigger* (1969), arguing that "students are society's slaves," whom educational institutions had stripped of their "human birthright": "freedom to learn, to change, to transcend yourself, to create your life."[13]

This shift helped pave the way for black-invented rock 'n' roll to become white-dominated rock, and for the guitar groups that surged in the wake of the British Invasion to become emblems of a new social consciousness in the United States.[14] For many of its proponents the music's political meaning went unarticulated, at least at first. It worked as a kind of social glue, binding together small scenes across the United States. The Coffee Gallery, a beatnik haunt in San Francisco's North Beach, began booking guitar groups like Bay Area amateurs the Great!! Society!! (fronted by Grace Slick) in 1965; Whisky A Go Go, a nightclub on Los Angeles's Sunset Strip, shifted to guitar groups at the same time, booking groups such as the Byrds, Buffalo Springfield, and Love, as well as a band fronted by Captain Morrison's son, the Doors. (At least until Jim got the group fired in August 1966 following an explicit rendition of their Oedipal song-nightmare, "The End." "Father: I want to kill you. Mother: I want to. . . . ")

But rock would also begin to function as a privileged form of social commentary. The notion that the bonds of "the System" needed slipping, or that the primary problem Americans faced resulted from a deficit of "freedom," was not new. We've encountered the Beats walking at lilac evening, their emancipation arriving through experimentation with black and non-white lifeworlds; we've examined critiques of consumerism (with a new "hip capitalism," as Thomas Frank calls it, now appearing just ahead). But what has intensified is the pace and reach of these new forms of knowledge identifying the structure of American society as the problem, and "freedom" from this structure as the solution.

Some of the most potent attempts to put into action a politics of freedom came from the liberation movements spearheaded by women, African-Americans, Spanish-speaking immigrants, and LGBT-identifying persons. The first point of the Black Panther Party's "What We Want Now!" Ten-Point program (1967) demanded in stark terms: "We want freedom." But the idea that American society was "sick" or broken also appeared in forms more easily digested by white middle-class consumers. The best-selling *One Flew Over the Cuckoo's Nest* (1962) by author Ken Kesey, for instance, presented a fictionalized account of a mental institution where the inmates, not the staff, were most rational. Similarly, in a series of wildly popular mass-market paperbacks, Scottish psychiatrist R. D. Laing popularized the claim that what we call mental illness often represented a rational response to irrational social conditions—or to put it simply, that society makes you sick.[15]

The notion that society needed to be fixed featured no less prominently in mainstream liberal political thought. As an agenda for reform, the Great Society—not the band, but the term coined by President Lyndon Johnson in 1964—aimed to tweak social institutions in order to somehow "improve" society. It targeted consumer protections, public housing, welfare entitlements, arts' funding, and of course civil rights. But it ultimately rested on a radical faith in technocratic solutions. Liberals acknowledged that America had problems: racism, poverty, inequality, war. If only the causes of these problems could be identified, then experts might find solutions, tweaking the capitalist-democratic formula just so in order to fashion a more just, equitable, and free society.

And that's where, for many people, a reliance on tropes of liberation in political discourse began to lay bare the hypocrisy of the American state. Because bipartisan appeals to "freedom" justified the expansion of the military-industrial complex at home—and its violence abroad—in difficult-to-rationalize ways. "Victory for the Vietcong," Richard Nixon wrote in a letter to the *New York Times* in 1965, "would mean ultimately the destruction of freedom of speech for all men for all time, not only in Asia, but in the United States as well."[16] If we failed to face this "incorrigible aggressor, fanatically committed to the destruction of the free world," Senator Thomas Dodd (D-CT) claimed, "we may find ourselves compelled to draw a defense line as far back as Seattle."[17] Such claims revealed a new chauvinism, a "will to power," as Charles de Gaulle spotted twenty years before, that "cloaked itself in idealism."[18] An idealism that many Americans no longer bought. "If it is necessary to approach genocide in Vietnam to achieve [our] objective," Noam Chomsky wrote bluntly in *American Power and the New Mandarins* (1969), excoriating the state's perverse logic, "then this is the price we must pay in defense of freedom and the rights of man."[19]

But what was to be done? A non-capitalist system did not seem to be a viable solution. After Prague, Richard Goldstein had discarded his rosier ideas about actually existing Communism. Meeting so many young Czech rock fans, however, suggested something important about the music. "We were all facing the military power of irrational governments convinced that they were rational," he realized. "Something bigger than systems and borders tied young people across the West together, and rock had a lot to do with it."[20]

Would rock prove a vehicle for escapism—or for dissent? For eluding "the System?" Challenging the state? Or even fomenting revolution? Singing in a nasally faux-folk twang, another California transplant offered a Dylaneseque pastiche (replete with harmonica) following the 1965 Watts riots. "If a million more agree there ain't no Great Society," Frank Zappa sings in "Trouble Every Day" (1966): "As it applies to you and me, our country isn't free."

* * *

Black R&B records blare as a group of young white friends stroll into a nightclub on the Sunset Strip. The men wear beards and longish, unkempt hair, while the women turn heads in modified thrift shop dresses. The strange group mills around for a song or two before one begins moving, apparently in thrall to the beat. Head lolling back, he whips both arms and legs, brightly patterned tights clinging pornographically to a slight frame. The white dancer, Carl Franzoni, considered himself a freak with a capital F—though the large letter embroidered on his satin cape actually referred to his nickname, Captain Fuck.

The term "freak" preceded "hippy," a derogatory diminution of "hip." It appears in the title of the album, *Freak Out!* (1966), by Frank Zappa and the Mothers of Invention, with whom Franzoni danced until early 1967. The label's adoption signaled a self-conscious rejection of mainstream, plastic society; it came to Franzoni and Zappa via a fifty-one-year-old sculptor named Vito Paulekas. In early 1965, Paulekas began collecting the runaways and dropouts who formed his loose dance troupe a few years earlier. For a time, the troupe shared a Hollywood studio space with Jerome Robbins, where the Byrds (who also took a few of the dancers on tour) sometimes rehearsed. Paulekas and his group staged "freak-outs," taking over dance floors on the Sunset Strip; they held love-ins, essentially orgies with dozens of people. They cultivated a bizarre image defined by the secondhand clothing the women, inspired by Pauleka's wife Szou, modified as a "freak subversion of middle-class values."[21]

Like the growing number of Americans seeking to maximize their experience of "freedom," the freaks placed music and dance at the center of their communal experimentation. "We dance the joydance, we listen to the eternal rhythm, our feet move to unity," another freedom-seeking commune leader put it, "live-love-joy energy are one."[22] Free-form dance, jarring electric sounds, strobe lights, projections: the multimedia spectacle of the "freak-out" or the "happening" represented for a brief window in the mid-Sixties a kind of utopian political space. In New York, Andy Warhol's Exploding Plastic Inevitable featured an impossibly chaotic tangle of movement, color, and light, with his coterie of dancers such as Gerard Malanga accompanied by feedback and noise produced by Lou Reed and John Cale's Velvet Underground. For media theorist Marshal McLuhan, the total envelopment of an audience simulated the ideal pre-modern tribal state that "everyone knows about, and therefore participates in, everything that is happening the moment it happens": a theoretical form of radical democracy.[23]

In practice, the constant bombardment—Cale's screeching, overdriven viola, the multiple projectors, the black bullwhip-wielding Malanga's sinister sadomasochistic pantomimes—induced sensory overload. "The Velvets played so loud and crazy I couldn't even guess the decibels," Warhol remembered. "I'd usually watch from the balcony or take my turn at the projectors, slipping different colored gelatin slides over the lenses."[24] "To experience it is to be brutalized," one reviewer wrote, "helpless."[25] This multimedia spectacle bombed in California, where the group's harsh brand of experimentalism jolted the emerging West Coast scene. (The feeling was mutual: "We didn't like that peace and love shit," drummer Moe Tucker confirmed. "We didn't like hippies."[26])

The multimedia spectacles developed by West Coast groups such as the Mothers and Jefferson Airplane (née The Great!! Society!!) would find their home at Bill Graham's Fillmore Auditorium. Born Wulf Wolodia Grajonca, Graham had fled Germany for the Bronx as an eight-year-old in 1939, making the hardnosed businessman a decade or two older than the acts he booked. Graham took over the Fillmore in 1965, upgrading its lighting and sound systems. While the venue had anchored for decades San Francisco's black entertainment district, "the Harlem of the West," it now became the epicenter of the white rock counterculture.[27] Its first show, a benefit for the radical political-theater collective, the San Francisco Mime Troupe, featured the Great Society, Jefferson Airplane, and the Warlocks (soon rechristened the Grateful Dead). Light-show artists collaborated with the musicians, with performance-art groups such as the Light Sound Dimension (LSD, who also worked with Graham's counterpart, Chet Helms, at the Avalon Ballroom) or the Brotherhood of Light (formed in 1968) drawing increasingly large crowds.

What did these new multimedia events mean? In *Bomb Culture* (1968), British author Jeff Nuttall saw a revolutionary process at work. "Young people are not correcting society," he wrote. "They are regurgitating it." These events functioned as an emetic for purging yourself of the irrationality of everyday life: "The battery of curdling colours projected round the room, the brutal stroboscopes, the aggressive gobbling of the lead guitars, the belligerent animal wails of the singers ... the stunned trance of the crowd and the total bleak despair of the registered junkies always hovering around the door like predatory crows, all contribute to a ritual that can be nothing if not profoundly disruptive of most things that life has been about till now."[28] If you think society needs disrupting, this is a good thing. But the idea that the electronic mass media could provide a means for subverting social norms, rather than facilitating consent to the status quo, also represented a remarkable about-face from earlier anxieties about media technologies. Media seemingly now fostered not atomization, but unity.

Historian Fred Turner calls this "ecstatic multimedia utopianism," a belief that such spaces allowed people to explore "a new way of being: personal, authentic, collective, egalitarian."[29] If the radio had the potential to turn us into fascists, unfree automatons, these new forms of media might produce free, democratic, socially conscious citizens. Their "profoundest political implications," wrote Richard Schechner, editor of *The Drama Review*, resided in disrupting media's usual function "by forcing on the receiver the job of doing the work usually done by the artist/educator/propagandist."[30] The end result would be a more equitable, unified society. "Our new environment compels commitment and participation," McLuhan influentially argued. "We have become irrevocably involved with, and responsible for, each other."[31]

Multimedia experiments in democracy had developed parallel to, but separate from, some of the debates we've traced to this point. These experiments seemed to exist outside commercial relationships, theorists claimed, because you could not sell an experience. Rock's sacralization as a form of meaningful artistic self-expression, rather than a lowbrow commercial product, provided one precondition for its use in these kinds of events. Rock's inclusion allowed these democratic, egalitarian values to be knotted with the music. But at the same time, the music itself also helped popularize multimedia shows, democratizing these utopian spaces in practical terms by helping them spread beyond the bohemian fringes of larger cities.

We'll see how conservatives railed against these events for spreading antisocial behaviors and promoting drugs. But so, too, did some members of the counterculture criticize multimedia shows. As early as 1969, one underground journalist was reporting that the "dancehall form has been dying of old age." Too expensive, the dance-light-rock experiment in democracy had lost its revolutionary appeal, and the Fillmore and other venues "had become nightclubs for the middle class pseudo-hip."[32] These utopian spaces also displaced African-Americans, in both a symbolic and literal sense. "There were black bands and only black bands—Motown and that stuff was just hummin,'" Franzoni later recalled, discussing the early Sunset Strip in Los Angeles. "There were no Byrds, no Buffalo Springfield, there was nothing. They were in incubation in the garage, all of them. Back in Hollywood we were dancing to records or R&B black bands. They got pushed out of Hollywood because of the white music."[33]

And experiences that had seemed so resistant to commodification became quickly integrated into the new hip economy.[34] By 1966, tourists already came to ogle Pauleka's freaks. In response, the Mothers included an ironic map of "FREAK OUT Hot Spots!" in early pressings *Freak Out!* Farce became reality in San Francisco a year later with the "Love Guide," an informational pamphlet for hippie-watching. A local merchant group, HIP (for the Haight Independent Proprietors) soon formed to meet the growing market demand for countercultural fashion; one savvy bar owner even rebranded his normal pub grub, selling "loveburgers" and "love dogs."[35]

But the meaning of "hip" proved a fast-moving target. "A lot of the places marked on this map were, at one time or another, relatively groovy in terms of atmosphere, clientele and vibrations," Zappa's map had explained, "and are included just so you can cruise by and observe what's left after the AMERICANS get through with them."[36]

The unhip versus the hip, the non-freak versus the freak. The tourist versus the local, and the American versus the ... what? The non-American?

* * *

In Bearsville, the frigid winter air in December chills you to the bone. That concerned the wife of Bob Dylan's manager, Sally Grossman, as she rousted her houseguests from India for an impromptu photoshoot for the cover of Dylan's new album, *John Wesley Harding* (1967). "I don't know if they've ever worn shoes," she worried about Purna and Lakshman.[37]

So that Dylan could see the images for his new album's cover at once, the photographer used Polaroid film, holding the prints tightly under his arm as the group rushed back and forth from the yard to the house to protect them from curling in the cold.[38] Dylan's earlier message-songs were now history. The first single on his last album, the sprawling *Blonde on Blonde* (1966), had featured a dumbly repetitive Beatles-ish refrain ("I want you! I want you! I want you! *Sooooo* bad!") poking out from among a concatenation of impressionistic imagery tailormade for stoned college students with nice hi-fis and too much time on their hands. The music on *John Wesley Harding* (1967) now signaled another turn: this time, toward roots, and the powerfully generative sounds of what Greil Marcus would call "the old, weird America."[39]

With gory rumors circulating about a motorcycle accident in Woodstock, Dylan had vanished from public life and missed the Summer of Love. But his manager's houseguests—brothers Purna and Lakshman Das, along with fellow musicians Hare Krishna, Sudhananda, and Jiban—arrived just in time to for its conclusion. Albert Grossman had "discovered" these Baul musicians following a tip from Allen Ginsberg (who after short stints in

Cuba and Czechoslovakia had spent a two-year period in India that, as Raj Chandarlapaty writes, "catalyzed his rebirth as prophet, icon, and countercultural messenger").[40] The poet had hipped the Grossmans and Dylan to the existence of the Bauls, an ethnic minority who seemed to put into practice a countercultural ethos of liberation. "He learned some philosophies, ideas," Purna recalled, "and when he came back he said [to Grossman] 'Bring [the Bauls] here, I think it is a joyful philosophy and a joyful music.'"[41] Dylan now referred to himself as "an American Baul"—and Grossman began corresponding with someone who claimed to manage the group.

Based in Calcutta, Asoke Fakir had worked as Ginsberg's local guide.[42] He soon rebranded himself as the founder-director of "a Socio-Spiritual research institute for Neo-Spiritual movement." He later claimed to be an American who had been reincarnated in India, a "SPY, who did a great lot of spiritual espionage work," and was now bringing that knowledge "home" (that is, back to the United States).[43] Yet despite claiming to manage the musicians, Fakir had remarkably little knowledge of them. At one point he even wrote to an American academic in Chicago to learn more. The scholar enclosed a 1959 scholarly essay analyzing the Bauls' literary representation in exoticist poems by Rabrindranath Tagore. "Many things are left unsaid by the Bauls, things which are reflected in their attitudes but not in their thought," the linguist had

Figure 5 "If Ravi Shankar is *the* classical music guy of India, then the Bauls are the Muddy Waters," Bob Dylans's manager, Albert Grossman. Album cover, *The Bengali Bauls... at Big Pink* (1969) Buddha Records BDS 5050

written mysteriously. The Baul has "only the wind as his home," he quoted a West Bengal man saying; their name means "madcap."[44]

But in more prosaic terms? The group's leader, Purna Das, came from a well-known family of performers. With his celebrated father, Naboni Das Khepa, he had traveled throughout India, earning praise in the pages of the mid-twentieth-century urban cognoscenti's leading literary and cultural journals; in 1962, he had even represented India at the Moscow-sponsored World Youth Congress in Finland.[45] Purna Das's acclamation by the learned class was the culmination of a nearly century-long process rehabilitating the Bauls, a minority long vilified as sexual deviants, hashish users, and religious heretics. The intellectual Tagore had played a key role in reframing the group as emancipated from social constraints and, as ethnomusicologist Charles Capwell summarized, imbued with "an emotional sensitivity that cannot be fully expressed in speech and therefore must have recourse to song."[46]

After signing the musicians to Buddah Records, a subsidiary of Elektra, Grossman wired them money for airfare. They missed their first gig, opening for the Byrds at the Fillmore on September 9; Fakir had taken them on an unplanned holiday in Japan. Five days later, they played with Mother Earth and Electric Flag, billed as the LDM Spiritual Band (after Fakir's spiritual institute-*cum*-tourist agency, Lok Dharma Mahashram). Hair newly shorn, the would-be guru had hectored the audience with a lengthy pseudo-mystic rap before Sally Grossman ran him off. (He'd stolen most of the musicians' advance, vanishing only to later reemerge as an advisor to Timothy Leary.)[47] The Bauls next played Provo Park. Jim Schreiber at the *Berkeley Barb* interviewed them, with a Berkeley grad student translating. "They are a gentle people with long hair, beads, and bare feet, who dress unconventionally, go begging, turn on, create songs with messages of love, and live communally apart from the rush of commerce," Schreiber wrote, "but they're not hippies." Their philosophy "transcends national barriers," he quoted Purna as saying. And it seemed to provide a kind of spiritual shortcut: "Anyone can join their community and train under a guru to master their music and learn their direct, simple point of view which cuts through the subtle complexities of Indian philosophy."[48]

Hashish-smoking mad musician-philosophers at society's margins: the Bauls fit almost too snugly into the countercultural stereotype of music, drugs, and personal liberation. Rock musicians' taste for "Eastern" sounds had exploded with the Beatles' film *Help!* (1965) and its exoticist plot about a murderous cult. A prop sitar on set had intrigued George Harrison, who began lessons with virtuoso musician Ravi Shankar, and the Beatles began adding Hindustani classical elements to their ever-expanding sonic palette. Imitators as well as sincere fellow-travelers quickly followed suit across 1966, from the

Byrds cutting "Eight Miles High" to the Rolling Stones releasing "Paint It Black."

How did so-called raga rock so quickly gain such traction with musicians and listeners? "Simply stated," Sandy Pearlman would write in *Crawdaddy!*, "with these patterns rock has learned to speak without words . . . in ways that words never could."[49] The idea that "the East" provided a means for more authentic forms of self-expression was at this moment gaining wider purchase not only among rock musicians, but also among young people in general. Members of the Doors, for instance, met at one of the newly fashionable meditation centers that began cropping up in cities such as Los Angeles. Millions of young Americans and Brits even traveled the so-called hippy trail.[50] These seekers considered their physical journeys through places like Nepal and India to be spiritual treks toward personal emancipation. "Wow, wow, wow, I've been ignorant all of my life!" an ex-Vietnam vet later described his epiphany on one such trip. "All I could do was lay down and continue to feel the liberating effects of that experience . . . I wrote down in my blue notebook . . . 'Today I am reborn.'"[51]

Recordings of so-called Eastern music could also facilitate self-discovery, allowing listeners to strip away the stultifying layers of American socialization to reveal their fresh, spiritual core. "it seems that in some places there are some people who still know they are thinking when they are," one such person wrote in *The Rag*, reviewing an album by Ravi Shankar, "because nobody as yet tells them every few minutes buy left tackle because mickey mantle shaves in it and mrs. miller bathes in it." If consumerism destroys our minds, this recording provides a means for repair, for self-care. "the idea is to get the record and shut yourself up with it, leaving your mind behind: these are songs of spirit and the public-school-system-developed type occidental mind means shut down to spirit everytime."[52] Intuitive and closer to "reality," non-Western musicians could be shoehorned into American racial categories for white consumers. Liner notes to the album released by the Bauls, for instance, called them "India's soul music." And Albert Grossman had used another racialized analogy in introducing the group to Dylan and the Band. "If Ravi Shankar is *the* classical music guy of India," Grossman told them, "then the Bauls are the Muddy Waters."[53]

Rock could absorb the sounds of the non-Western world, and could do so promiscuously, both for the talismanic qualities of these sounds and for their seeming ability to intuitively reveal the contradictions between a false surface reality of bondage and the true inner reality of liberation. This resonated with how African-American and non-white music functioned more generally in the new white rock counterculture. Robert Johnson revealed to

Dylan "a deep reality," and yet the collage-like photograph on the cover of *Bringing It All Back Home* (1965) featured a pile of LPs that included not only Robert Johnson's *King of the Delta Blues* (as well as a fallout shelter sign, a book of Beat poetry, and glossy American magazines), but also Ravi Shankar's *India's Master Musician*.[54] Richard Goldstein would call Mick Jagger "Shango Mick," comparing him to the Yoruba god of thunder, sex, and rhythm. The Stones would render "Sympathy for the Devil" (1968)—a musical history of human violence—by layering the drumming of Ghana-born sideman Rocky Dzidzornu, accompaniment Jagger much later remembered as "a primitive African, South American, Afro-whatever-you-call-that rhythm," over the pouty singer's own animal shrieks.[55] Jim Morrison called himself a "shaman," and the Doors scored the Lizard King's most extended deep dive into the darkness of the human psyche, "The End," using Robby Krieger's sitar-like open guitar tuning (he had sat in on a few classes with Ravi Shankar in Los Angeles).[56]

At the same time, the fad for "raga rock" was just that—a fad. The sudden popularity of "the Eastern sound," one critic wrote, "shows the constant pressure for trends in the struggle for a hit."[57] Consider the twanging sitar in the middle eight of "San Francisco (Be Sure To Wear Flowers In Your Hair)" (1967), a savvy branding exercise from Monterey Pop Festival organizers Lou Adler and John Philips. Or consider how the hip marketers who now began mining the counterculture to sell "a never-ending rebellion against whatever it is that everyone else is doing" in the service of a "forced and exaggerated individualism," as Thomas Frank writes, coveted these sounds. Here's how one agency pitched their admen's countercultural bona fides in the industry journal, *Madison Magazine*: "He sat on his inflatable plastic sofa, his beard curling over his turtleneck sweater, beads and Nehru jacket. Sitar music played over the loudspeaker. He and the copywriter in the transparent blouse had just told the client what to do."[58]

Ravi Shankar pushed back against the commercialization and the stereotyping. "I see a sincerity in these young people," he explained to the *New York Times*. "But I don't like the music's association with glassy eyes and the haze of drugs."[59] And he criticized the "go-man-go" attitude of hippies "looking for instant karma," noting that he had spent two years just learning how to hold a sitar, never mind understand its music.[60] Yet it was the promise of a shortcut to consciousness, as Richard Goldstein sharply observed in the *Village Voice*, that so attracted many listeners. "His following wants something so new and miraculous even Marshal McLuhan can't understand it," Goldstein wrote. "They don't want Eastern exposure. They want Buddhahood on a long-play record, Tao on a tap, a bath in the Ganges without getting wet. And they want

Ravi Shankar (who studied 14 hours a day for seven years to learn the basics of raga) to sock it to them."[61]

Back in upstate New York, the Bauls soon made a pilgrimage to Big Pink, the unassuming clapboard house (so named for its garish paintjob) that famously housed Dylan's backing group, the Band. The Band rehearsed in its fabled basement, and the material they worked out here resulted in *Music from Big Pink* (1968) as well as Dylan's heavily bootlegged Basement Tapes. But right now, as the liner notes to *Bengali Bauls . . . at Big Pink* (1968) put it, we arrive at "December of 1967, and the Bengali Bauls want to get it on."[62] After getting stoned with the Band in their upstairs lounge, everyone headed down to the basement to make some music. "'Wait a minute,' we said, 'let's record this,'" Robbie Robertson remembered thinking. He and his bandmates tune up, thinking "maybe we could have an interesting world-music, East-meets-West connection any moment now."

That moment never materialized. "It became clear," Robertson remembered, "this was not a jam band; you might as well do yourself a favor and stay out of the way."[63] So what does it mean that this rehearsal space generated not only *Bengali Bauls . . . at Big Pink*, but also the Band's *Music from Big Pink* and Dylan's *Basement Tapes*? Greil Marcus has called this room a "laboratory where, for a few months, certain bedrock strains of American cultural language were retrieved and reinvented."[64] Illustrated by one of Dylan's naïve paintings (and featuring bassist Rick Danko in Native American headdress), *Music from Big Pink* did herald a back-to-roots sound—an inset photo even featured the musicians looking like hairy nineteenth-century homesteaders. But where do visitors Purna, Lakshman, Hare Kirshna, Sudhananda, and Jiban fit into this laboratory?

You might look to the past, the Band and *Big Pink* seem to suggest, in order to find a viable way of living—though you might also look outside the borders of the United States. As historian Philip Deloria suggests, we should focus on *the search itself*: the pressing need that young white Americans felt "to find reassuring identities in a world seemingly out of control." The irony, he continues, is that these individuals found themselves "bent on destroying an orthodoxy tightly intertwined with the notion of truth and *yet desperate for truth itself*."[65]

The search for truth occupied so many people in so many different ways. But what if you didn't need to travel to the past? Or outside the United States? Maybe true freedom had resided within you all along. And all you had to do was look inside yourself to find it.

* * *

Their countercultural garb embellished with faux military "shoulder patches, arm patches, hashmarks, bars, stars, epaulets," Ken Kesey and his Merry Pranksters set out for Berkeley in their newly repainted rust-red school bus. They had daubed "military symbols on the dried blood, swastikas, American eagles, Iron Crosses, Viking crosses, Red Crosses, hammers & sickles, skulls & bones, anything as long as it looked rank." Records blared from powerful speakers mounted on the roof: the Beatles, Joan Baez, Mississippi John Hurt, Bob Dylan.[66] (The American Baul had bailed on this Teach-In, organized by the Vietnam Day Committee for October 1965, though he too had shared their absurdist, inscrutable vision for protest, planning to bring a bunch of "picket signs—some of the signs will be bland and some will have the word Orange or Automobile or the words Venetian Blind."[67])

Royalties from Kesey's *One Flew Over the Cuckoo's Nest* (1963) funded the group's home base, a rustic retreat in La Honda, just an hour north of San Francisco where he and his collaborators had begun staging free-form experiments in acid-fueled community-making. The author had participated in CIA-funded LSD trials in the late 1950s; his Acid Tests were intended to facilitate an exploration of consciousness. These multimedia events, Walter Hinckle wrote in a *Ramparts* essay on "The Hippies," consisted of "rapidly changing the audience's sensory environment what seemed like approximately ten million times during an evening by manipulating bright colored lights, tape recorders, slide projectors, weird sound machines, and whatever else may be found in the electronic sink, while the participants danced under stroboscopic lights to a wild rock band or just played around on the floor."[68]

The spirit of Kesey's events resonated with those organized by political organizations such as the Vietnam Day Committee—at least to a point. Formed in May 1965 by Jerry Rubin, the VDC linked radical student groups with left-wing political organizations to sponsor protests and "teach-ins." An innovation of the New Left, teach-ins raised public consciousness about specific political issues and, more ambitiously, sought to "increase the number of people who are opposed to the structure and value system of American society."[69] VDC organizers also incorporated entertainment—such as puppet shows, comedians, and musical acts—into speaker line-ups featuring academics, labor organizers, and other radical thinkers.

Not all activists, however, supported the mixing of these two registers. And as Kesey reached the stage and approached the microphone, many began to shift nervously. "You know, you're not gonna stop this war with this rally," Kesey said, producing a harmonica to honk out "Home on the Range." Boos enveloped the stage. He pushed on. "I went to see the Beatles last month, and I heard 20,000 girls screaming together at the Beatles," he said. "They're screaming, 'Me! Me! Me! Me! I'm me!' That's the cry of the ego, and that's the cry of this rally. Yep, you're playing their game."

As related by Tom Wolfe, the crowd looked deflated: "It's the only thing the martial spirit can't stand—a put-on, a prank, a shuck, a goose in the anus."[70] But could self-discovery be political? Could digging down into your own consciousness represent a form of activism? "The first revolution," Beat-poet-turned-folk-rock-Fug Tuli Kupferberg claimed, "is in yer own head."[71] Or as Kesey's East Coast counterpart put it, emancipation began with your own self. "If all the Negroes and left-wing college students in the world had Cadillacs and full control of society," Timothy Leary told a *Playboy* interviewer in 1967, "they would still be involved in an anthill social system unless they opened themselves up first."[72]

As a clinical psychologist at Harvard University, Leary had traveled to Mexico to ingest the naturally occurring hallucinatory compound found in psilocybin mushroom. So-called magic mushrooms first gained prominence among white North Americans in 1957, when a CIA-funded researcher and his Russian-born wife published a photo-essay in *Life* magazine. That story helped popularize the use of hallucinogens with posh would-be bohemians in the United States and the United Kingdom. (Clare Boothe Luce and her husband, *Life* magazine publisher Henry, took acid in the early 1960s; the Beatles were turned on by a particularly hip Harley Street dentist.) Previously, psychiatrists had used LSD for its psychomimetic properties, or the ability to induce a simulation of psychosis. But for Leary, psychedelics positively answered a more pressing problem: how best to help human beings attain their full potential within the bounds of a stifling society. "Madness need not be all breakdown," he later wrote in *The Politics of Experience* (1967). "It may also be break-through. It is potential liberation and renewal as well as enslavement and existential death."

To explore how hallucinogens facilitated liberation, Leary and his collaborators at Harvard devised an experimental protocol. Positive effects, they claimed, seemed to require "the congenial surroundings of a tastefully furnished room containing a tape-and-record player console and carefully chosen works of art."[73] As another collaborator wrote: "Music, of course, is most useful, and attention should be paid to the subject's favorite selections and composers. The music of Wagner, Sibelius, Saint-Saens, Richard Strauss, Liszt, Chopin, Mozart, Tchaikovsky, Mahler and Grieg is suggested."[74] The Harvard experiments resulted in the dismissal of collaborator Richard Alpert (later Ram Dass), and then Leary's resignation. Freed from his academic duties, Leary and Alpert decamped to Millbrook, a massive estate in upstate

New York where with Ralph Metzner they completed their classic manual of self-discovery and spiritual liberation, *The Psychedelic Experience* (1964)—a "psychedelic Baedaker to the Other World."[75] The group lived rent-free at the invitation of the estate's owners, a branch of the wealthy Mellon family, and organized weekend retreats and group therapy sessions.

Kesey and his Pranksters made a pilgrimage to Millbrook in 1966; Dr. Leary did not deign to meet them, instead remaining upstairs in bed. By this point, Leary had begun preaching the acid gospel to larger and larger audiences. But these events organized by his new organization, the League for Spiritual Development (get it?—"LSD"), usually incorporated not rock, but non-Western music. Staged at a small theater on Second Street, "The Re-Incarnation of Christ," featured incense, chocolate bars, psychedelic screen prints, and copies of Leary's journal *Psychedelic Review*, as well as "Hindu bells," raga music, and drums. Leary played the role of celebrant to the shaggy audience, with lysergic acid diethylamide, their sacrament. A world music fusion recording (a Latin Mass "in pure Congolese style," according to the liner notes) enveloped attendees from speakers placed around the space.[76] This multimedia surround fostered a dream-like, utopian sensorium: "Words become things, thoughts are music, music smelled, sounds are touched, complete interchangeability of the senses."[77] To achieve its full effects, this sensorium required a curator, a guru, a "guide." "He is literally a liberator," Leary explained, "one who provides illumination, one who frees men from their life-long internal bondage."[78]

The psychedelic populist Kesey disdained the hierarchical emphasis of Leary's bag—and its squareness. "You should take it in some serene and attractive setting," Tom Wolfe wrote, channeling the West Coast scene's mocking condescension, "a house or apartment decorated with objects of the honest sort, Turkoman tapestries, Greek goatskin rugs, Cost Plus blue jugs, soft light—not Japanese paper globe light, however, but un-tasselated Chinese textile shades—in short, an Uptown Bohemian country retreat of the $60,000-a-year sort, ideally, with Mozart's Requiem issuing with liturgical solemnity from the hi-fi."[79] In contrast, rock music soundtracked Kesey's chaotic, free-form events in late 1965 and 1966. The handbill for the first Acid Test listed "happeners" that included the poet Allen Ginsberg, but also bands. New York City's the Fugs were advertised, as was a group of Palo Alto folkies who had just gone electric.

Née the Warlocks, the Grateful Dead began life as a jug band. Their manager, Rock Scully (ex-Family Dog, a psychedelic San Francisco band), first encountered the Dead during an Acid Test at the Big Beat Club in Palo Alto. Acid entrepreneur Stanley Owsley had made the introductions, freaking Scully out by telling him Kesey had "got the place wired."

"Wired? As in, wired into a sound system?" Scully had asked.

"No, no! Wired into *him*, into his brain, Rock," Stanley replied. "He's *in* the wires—and when you walk into the Big Beat you are going to get wired, too. He's figured out how to control people, through electricity. That's how he does it. I've seen it."[80]

The Big Beat Club had a stage for the band at one end, with screens, white fabric, and a Native American-style tipi against which were projected images and colored lights. At the other end of the hall a lower stage had a microphone. The microphone represented an experiment in democratic participation: anyone could clamber up to amplify their "gourd shaking, Stockhausen tape loops, ululating Iglut shaman [sic] chants, mime, Dada word rebuses," or to scream messages such as "Fuck sanity, go crazy!"[81]

We should pause here to note that within such countercultural projects to free your mind, rock music often proved more incidental than integral. Electrified guitar music paired easily with these deep dives into the human mind, but so too did Western art musics (from the Baroque period to the present) and traditional musics (from non-Western art music traditions to orally transmitted ones the world over). Thus much of the experimentation at these emancipatory multimedia events happened alongside recordings of Bach and Beethoven, or Smithsonian Folkways LPs, not the Beatles or Bobby Dylan. And here we come to a key issue, often overlooked. The music did not bring its political values meanings to such events. Rather, utopian democratic values fused to rock during these events. In the telling and retelling of these stories, this point often gets overlooked.

Through the mass media, white rock music would, however, disseminate these values far and wide, and well beyond their original contexts. At the time, certain commentators saw this relationship clearly. In *Ramparts*, Walter Hinckle noted how rock coincided with the emergence of what he calls "acid culture." "What was happening, Mr Jones, was that folk music, under the influence of early acid culture, was giving way to rock and roll," Hinckle wrote. "Rock spread the hippie way of life like a psychedelic plague, and it metamorphosed in such rapid fashion that a very suspicious person might ask if seemingly safe groups like the Kingston Trio were not, in fact, the Red Guards of the hippie cultural revolution."[82]

If this really was a cultural revolution, how democratic was it in practice? To some, the practices of self-discovery proposed by Leary the Liberator seemed too reliant on the top-down figure of the psychedelic guide. And as was increasingly the case in the postwar American imagination, the utopian play of liberation had a dark flipside, an equally strong fascination with bondage and control, spiritual or otherwise. Warhol's superstar Gerard Malanga stalks the stage with his big black bullwhip; the Merry Pranksters blare from their bus not only Baez and the Beatles, but also Carl Orff's *Carmina Burana* (1937); countercultural intellectuals become fascinated with leather-clad outlaw biker gangs; the Merry Pranksters hold aloft at a peace rally an ironic placard identifying themselves as the "Hells Angels Vietcong Birch Society."[83] And arising from the center of the dancefloor at the Big Beat Club in Palo Alto is "a tower made of scaffolding from which radiates lights, color wheels, movie projectors, speakers, cameras, tape recorders, slide projectors, and fans to keep the equipment from overheating." Perched at the top, "Captain Kesey is at the controls."[84]

To participants at such events, the traditional politics of the New Left seemed increasingly irrelevant. Student activists were "all too cerebral and talky and dialectical," Rock Scully thought in 1967, "and with the advent of acid the rational thing is dissolving (fast)."[85] The key question raised at these events, as Michael Kramer puts it, asked "when explicit systems of control were lifted away but the technologies (from electronics to drugs) of military-industrial America remained, what sorts of social formations might emerge?" Jerry Garcia believed they might find "the real order" of things. In any case, Kramer concludes, attendees "were willing to enter into chaos in the name of discovering freedoms."[86]

Not everyone agreed that ecstatic practices of self-discovery were even all that progressive, never mind liberatory. To some detractors on the left, hippies promoted a dangerous, reactionary politics based on an unexamined individualism. Hinckle scorned these young "men who, except for their Raggedy Andy hair, paisley shirts and pre-mod western Levi jackets, sounded for all the world like Young Republicans. They talked about reducing governmental controls, the sanctity of the individual, the need for equality among men. They talked, very seriously, about the kind of society they wanted to live in, and the fact that if they wanted an ideal world they would have to go out and make it for themselves, because nobody, least of all the government, was going to do it for them."[87]

Nostalgic retellings of the Sixties notwithstanding, the 1960s were, in many ways, profoundly conservative. The actual Young Republican organization had four times as many registered members as did Students for a Democratic Society in 1967; a *Newsweek* poll found that 35% of students described themselves as "doves" on Vietnam, with 49% "hawks."[88] Historian Gerard DeGroot argues that when we wrote the history of groups like the VDC, we need to emphasize their *impotence*, how their failures helped accelerate the breakdown of a postwar liberal consensus and the rise of a new conservative one.

We'll soon need to discuss Nixon and the mobilization of a variety of groups—from libertarian, to evangelical, to supremacist, to lapsed liberal—that began congealing into a powerful new base for the Republican Party. For this emerging New Right, the rock counterculture provided a compelling talking point. Campaigning for governor of California in 1966, one of its new leaders, the actor Ronald Reagan, read aloud from the Burns Report. Drafted by the California State Senate's Subcommittee on Un-American Activities, the report had examined the dangers of rock 'n' roll "dances" in the state university system. "Three rock-n-roll bands were in the center of the gymnasium playing simultaneously all during the dance, and all during the dance, movies were shown on two screens at the opposite ends of the gymnasium," Reagan explained to the conservative crowd. "These movies were the only lights in the gym proper. They consisted of color sequences that gave the appearance of different-colored liquid spreading across the screen, followed by shots of men and women, on occasion shots were of the men's and women's nude torsos, and persons twisted and gyrated in provocative fashion." Even worse, the rock 'n' roll also seemed to inspire drug use and actual hanky-panky. "The young people were seen standing against the walls or lying on the floors and steps in a dazed condition of being under the influence of narcotics," Reagan continued. "Sexual misconduct was blatant."[89]

Are these the freedoms most hard-working Californians wanted their sons and daughters to be experiencing? Reagan beat incumbent Pat Brown in a landslide. The law-and-order candidate handily won a second term four years later, besting a field that included, at least briefly, Timothy Leary.

"All healthy Americans over the age of fourteen should take at least one trip in order to preserve the New Wilderness of machine America as it really was," Leary had stumped. "If there be necessary revolution in America, it will come this way."[90] But what if a revolution of the mind was not enough? What if society was so sick, so fucked up, that we needed to destroy it and start over?

The only problem was that for many middle-class Americans, things didn't seem all that bad. Herbert Marcuse had anticipated this, writing in *One-Dimensional Man* (1964) that "a comfortable, smooth, reasonable, democratic unfreedom prevails in advanced industrial civilization." Is a comfortable and smooth unfreedom really that bad? "My generation has made America the most affluent country on earth," complained one middle-aged professor and father sick and tired of being "blamed, maimed, and contrite." Through Great Society programs, the United States had manfully addressed its problems with race, he continued, declared a "war on poverty," even put a man on the moon—"it has presided over the beginnings of what is probably the greatest social and economic revolution in man's history."[91]

And these kids wanted to destroy all that progress for the sake of some revolution in the head? "Fuck work—we want to know ourselves," Jerry Rubin

Figure 6 "Three rock-n-roll bands were in the center of the gymnasium playing simultaneously all during the dance, and all during the dance, movies were shown on two screens at the opposite ends of the gymnasium," from the Burns Report, released by the California State Senate's Subcommittee on Un-American Activities (June 1965). Collage "Hippies," the Group Image c. 1967, National Portrait Gallery, Smithsonian Institution

confirmed. "The goal is to free one's self from American society's sick notions of work, success, reward, and status."[92] If violence were to come, which side would prevail?

* * *

Uniformed police at the Chicago Civic Center pushed aside members of the Youth International Party, interrupting their presidential candidate's speech, read aloud by Jerry Rubin in accepting the nomination. The cops arrested Rubin and several other political organizers, and hustled their candidate—a massive grunting hog, Pigasus J. Pig, purchased a few days earlier by folksinger and activist Phil Ochs—into a waiting police wagon.

Spearheaded by Rubin, Abby Hoffman, and activists connected to both the East and West Coast scenes, the Youth International Party (its members, "yippies") had formed nearly a year earlier. These men articulated the serious, directed play of the more politically engaged fringes of the counterculture with the activism of the New Left in staging guerrilla theater interventions: "levitating" the Pentagon, throwing cash onto the floor of the New York Stock Exchange, or occupying Grand Central Station. Borrowing ideas liberally from other movements, they wanted to create an alternative, free society, a "New Nation" for educated white young dissenters and dropouts. (Contrasting themselves with newly formed liberation groups such as the Black Panthers, for instance, Rubin called YIP a "white revolutionary movement," arguing that "someone who takes off from middle-class American life is an escaped slave crossing the Mason-Dixon line.")[93]

At the 1968 Democratic National Convention in Chicago, the group planned "a cultural, living alternative to the Convention," a Festival of Life. "We want all the rock bands," Rubin said, "all the underground papers, all the free spirits, all the theatre groups—all the energies that have contributed to the new youth culture—all the tribes—to come to Chicago, and for six days we will live together in the park, sharing, learning, free food, free music, a regeneration of spirit and energy."[94] Thousands of protesters flocked to Lincoln Park (but only one rock band, Detroit's MC5). Would there be violence? As long as "people stayed in the Park and played the role of the good niggers," Abby Hoffman told an ABC News reporter, then everything should be fine.[95]

Richard Nixon handily beat the liberal Democratic Party candidate, Hubert Humphrey, with segregationist Democrat George Wallace receiving surprisingly strong support as the candidate for the American Independent Party. The election had been a referendum on the Vietnam War, but also on the antiwar movement itself. It demonstrated the growing power of so-called cultural issues in electoral politics, especially regarding who speaks for "Americans" and who does—and doesn't—belong in "America." The success of a third-party segregationist platform foreshadowed the coming realignment between the two major parties, with the Republican Party now beginning to siphon off blue-collar voters in the South from the Democratic Party. But so too did the Democratic ticket's pitch to an imagined moderate, middle-class center, exemplified by Humphrey's milquetoast "politics of happiness, politics of purpose, politics of joy" that had pointedly sidelined the revolutionary liberationist fringes of would-be supporters both black and white, Left and further Left.

In hindsight, that messaging seems especially narrow considering how mainstream the idea of "revolution" had become in the three years preceding Humphries' ignominious defeat. And for commentators, rock music had provided a key symbol not only marking the revolutionary shifts that the United States seemed to be undergoing, but also generating real change. In an essay titled "Chuck Berry Brings You the Free Speech Movement," Stewart Kessler outlined what he viewed as the source of rock's power. Musicians communicated not only their own perceptions about reality, Kessler claimed, but also how they believed others should think. Since anyone could start a band, this represented "a sense of real democracy." But it also foisted on rock musicians new responsibilities, an "unbelievable power": "because what, say, 'Bob Dylan' *says*, other people are gonna *be*."[96]

You can hear a bit of what Kessler's talking about in Jefferson Airplane's "Volunteers" (1969), where singers Grace Slick and Marty Balin instruct listeners directly: "gotta revolution, gotta revolution!" But rock didn't even need to be explicit, and in fact, explicit sloganeering often detracted from the message. "Anyway, straight doses of heavy street politicking just aren't too good for music," James Lichtenberg wrote in "Up Against the Amplifier!" for the *East Village Other*. "This in no way is to put down the politicking, but the real effectiveness of music is on a much deeper, spiritual level, when it comes to changing heads. *Surrealistic Pillow* is for me the most revolutionary album the Airplane has done, and along with *Bringing It All Back Home* and *Revolver* and just about all the Stones albums (it's late so I may be leaving something out) one of the most revolutionary albums ever."[97] Other commentators agreed. Maybe rock's "most important political purpose," Robert Christagau wrote, "is to keep us human under fire." (Lennon and Dylan, he notes, "are often better at keeping us human than trusty propagandists like Phil Ochs.") Yet rock's increasing popularity had, at least for Christgau, resulted in "the final irony of rock 'n' revolution": "The political value of rock is a function of how many people it reaches, yet as rock becomes more political, it reaches fewer people."[98]

By 1968, some political activists did not just doubt the political importance of rock, but saw the political pretensions of certain musicians (like Lennon's "newfound status as a pompous shit," as Christgau put it) as working at cross-purposes to theirs. Consider debate over the equivocation of Lennon's "Revolution" (1968). "Count me out—in," Beatle John croons, telling listeners to "free your mind instead." Paul and George's back-up shooby-doo-wops (are they ironic?) and "don't-you-know-it's-gonna-be-s" (in girl-group falsetto) receive a hoarse confirmation. We *are* going to be okay. But is that true? We aren't fighting bad vibes or "nasty people," radical activist John Hoyland chided the Fab Four in "An Open Letter to John Lennon" published in British leftist paper *Black Dwarf*. "What we're confronted with is a repressive, vicious, authoritarian SYSTEM. Now do you see what was wrong with your record 'Revolution?'"[99] Do you, John?

Increasingly radical groups believed that the stakes of this struggle demanded serious action. "Up against the wall, motherfucker!"—the "magic words" taken from a 1967 poem by radical black liberationist Amiri Baraka—became the rallying cry of groups such as the Motherfuckers. Their first direct action had sought to highlight the hypocrisy of American society by hauling garbage up from lower Manhattan to dump in the fountains at Lincoln Center. Memorializing this guerrilla action in their manifesto, they wrote, "AND WE PLAY AS WE MAKE OUR GARBAGE / BEETHOVEN BACH MOZART SHAKESPEARE."[100] Would symbolic violence beget actual violence? A year later, the Motherfuckers rallied to support Valerie Solanas, the radical feminist author of the SCUM Manifesto who shot (and nearly killed) the Velvet Underground's erstwhile manager, Andy Warhol. In 1969, a splinter group from Students for a Democratic Society declared war on the United States government, the newly formed Weathermen taking their name from the finger-pointing Dylan lyric in "Subterranean Homesick Blues" (1965).

For sure, most rock fans were not building homemade bombs. Why not? Had the market co-opted rock's revolutionary potential to free their minds? If so, did the musicians themselves care? In the same issue as Hoyland's "Open Letter," *Black Dwarf* approvingly published the lyrics of the Rolling Stones' "Street Fighting Man" (1968). Wary of inciting violence, disk jockeys in Chicago refused to play the song during the Democratic National Convention. But Mick Jagger didn't care. "The last time they banned one of my records in America," he told the *London Evening Standard*, "it sold a million." And anyway, it's not like it really mattered: "It's stupid to think you can start a revolution with a record."[101]

And that's the crux of the problem. In *The Lonely Crowd* (1950), sociologist David Riesman had used the word "revolution" to describe the "whole range of social developments associated with a shift from an age of production to an age of consumption." And *this* revolution, it seemed, had planted the seeds for rock's integration into American society. "I traded my rock-critic drag for tie-dyed T-shirts and tatty jeans," Richard Goldstein recalls in his memoirs.

"That's what pretty much everyone my age wore. It was part of a larger rebellion against consumerism and the false sense of self created by mass-produced goods. Only handmade products were truly authentic, even if that meant an incongruous patch of velvet sewn onto bell-bottoms, or a shirt that someone had soaked in goat urine to make the colors stick. Beads were everywhere, a symbol of membership in one or another 'tribe'—that is, a loosely arranged affinity within the Nation of the Young."[102] As this memory suggests, membership could paradoxically be realized mainly by acquiring the right things. You are what you wear, and no wonder "Aquarian Robber Barons"—specialists in separating would-be citizens of the Nation of the Young from their money in the name of rebellious self-expression—cottoned quickly to this reality.[103]

"You will only find the best hi-fi sets in hippie flats," Hinckle had noted, identifying the flower children as "frantic consumers" and Bill Graham as a salesman who exploited "the hippie bread and circuses concession."[104] Even some of the music, others claimed, was pure hype. Carl Franzoni thinks the Grateful Dead were "a publicity stunt," a product of Graham's savvy marketing of the San Francisco Sound. (Though you couldn't sell just anything. MGM's marketing campaign for "the Bosstown Sound," featuring Boston-based psychedelic garage bands such as Orpheus, Ultimate Spinach, and Chamaeleon Church, failed miserably.) The Mothers satirized rock's financial success with *We're Only in It for the Money* (1968), its cover a spoof of *Sgt. Pepper's*, even as Zappa funneled his earnings back into a label, Bizarre Records, that released records by the likes of comedian Lenny Bruce and street performer Wild Man Fischer, an unhoused person diagnosed with bipolar disorder and schizophrenia. But to be heard, rock depended on markets, required consumers. "Zappa is a fucking capitalist," Fischer correctly pointed out to the *Berkeley Tribe*. "He promised me all sorts of promotion on my record and I never got it [and] threatened to call the cops on my because I wanted to sleep in his garage."[105]

And as this complaint suggests, here, there, and everywhere, the violence seeping into so many corners of the rock counterculture remained more often pathetic in the usually predictable ways than revolutionary. Freedom of communal living required women do the bulk of the cooking and cleaning, for instance, while shifting boundaries around what constituted socially acceptable sexual mores resulted in rampant exploitation. "We want freedom!" demanded the White Panther Party, home to the MC5, even as its leader (and their manager) John Sinclair said, "the groups who journey to Ann Arbor to fuck the 5 act as energy carriers, disseminating the revolution (and the crabs?) all the way from Lansing to Grosse Pointe."[106]

Some of the violence was exaggerated, or visible only in hindsight. News stories about so-called acid casualties, individuals jumping from windows while tripping on LSD, were by and large media creations. The drug-influenced withdrawal from public life of musicians such as Beach Boy Brian Wilson or Love's Arthur Lee only entered rock mythology years later (though the overdose deaths of Jim, Jimi, and Janis proved immediately sobering to many at the time). And in its persistence, the violence of the American state proved increasingly numbing, with only spectacularly grim events such as the My Lai massacre of nearly six hundred civilians breaking through to many Americans by 1969. And even then, not to all. Plantation Records could not keep up with demand for Terry Nelson's "Battle Hymn of Lt. Calley" (1971), a country song praising the only person convicted for My Lai, and one of only twenty-three Americans total to be convicted for the hundreds of documented war crimes in Vietnam.[107]

And whether revolutionary or counterrevolutionary, violence manifested in ways that eluded the ability of musicians and listeners to frame, to make sensible in any enduring, coherent way. Two weeks after announcing his gubernatorial campaign, for instance, Timothy Leary visited John and Yoko's Bed-In For Peace, singing along to "Give Peace a Chance" (1969) and commissioning a song with the slogan, "Come Together, Join The Party." While Leary abandoned the campaign, Lennon completed the song, released as "Come Together" on *Abbey Road* (1969). The political assassinations of this period appear in the singer's perverse imperative, "shoot me!" (the "me" almost entirely swallowed up in the final mix by Ringo's kick drum). Just two weeks before Woodstock, a group of "slippies"—neither hippies nor yippies, but a commune of dropouts who believed they had "slipped through the cracks of society"—marked the walls of their grisly crime scenes with references to songs by the Beatles. Charles Manson's so-called family had traveled the West Coast in a bus painted black, a perverse inversion of Furthur, the Merry Prankster's Day-Glo transportation; they had ties to rock musicians such as Dennis Wilson, Neil Young, and (allegedly) many others.

The actual rock revolution quickly passed into history, its invocation soon to be, depending on your politics, either an exercise in cloying liberal nostalgia or conservative scaremongering. At the time Wild Man Fischer saw its demise most clearly, his plans for a new album titled *Love/Hate* appearing in hindsight quite prescient. The back cover, he told the *Berkeley Tribe*, would show him handing John Lennon a flower. But the front cover would depict him murdering all four Beatles. One song had been finished. Its lyrics in full read:

> John—POW!
> Paul—WOW!
> George—POW!
> Ringo—POW!
> Dylan—POW!
> I'm the meanie / I'm the meanie!
> I'm wicked and vicious and stingy![108]

* * *

In December of 1969, Albert and David Maysles arrived at the Altamont Speedway in California to shoot a free concert organized by the Rolling Stones. Albert Maysles's first documentary had examined psychiatric hospitals in the Soviet Union; over the intervening decade or so the brothers had helped establish a direct, *cinema verité* style of documentary filmmaking in works on subjects from Marlon Brando to the Beatles to Bible salesmen. The truth of the Stones concert, as revealed in *Gimme Shelter* (1970), turned out to be its irrational violence: the dark underbelly of the counterculture exposed for all to see, a "Charlie Manson Memorial Hippie Love Death Cult Festival."[109]

That mock-title had been bestowed on the chaotic event by the radically communal Diggers. But it accords with another critique, this one articulated by the firebrand libertarian Ayn Rand in her lecture, "Apollo and Dionysus."[110] Juxtaposing the Woodstock Festival with the Apollo 11 moon landing, Rand saw "a literal dramatization of the truth: that it is man's irrational emotions that bring him down to the mud; it is man's reason that lifts him to the stars." Not only did Woodstock symbolize a turn backward—"the return of the primitive," or "the grimmest inversion of many in the course of mankind's history"—but the emergence of the counterculture itself heralded a new stage in the ceding of individual autonomy, the shedding of personal freedom in the name of political submission.

"The hippies were taught by their parents, their neighbors, their tabloids and their college professors that faith, instinct and emotion are superior to reason—and they obeyed. They were taught that material concerns are evil, that the State or the Lord will provide, that the Lilies of the Field do not toil—and they obeyed." Driven by "urges" and "intuitions," the counterculture ultimately represented "a desperate herd looking for a master, to be taken over by anyone; anyone who would tell them how to live, without demanding the effort of thinking. Theirs is the mentality ready for a Führer."

"I wasn't born to follow," the Byrds sang on a track on *The Notorious Byrd Brothers* (1968) written by Gerry Goffin and Carole King. But not everyone in the counterculture was so sure, and Rand had some unlikely allies. "Three years ago," Country Joe MacDonald said in 1968, "we were hobos singing our hearts out about the virtues of the open road. Last year, we were Indians. Now we're revolutionaries. Man, if the Revolution ever comes for real, they'll probably use Andy Warhol munitions. You throw it and this big sign comes on—Pow!"[111]

Rand and Country Joe may seem like strange allies, but they were engaging the same debate. Only now, they were in the minority. At the turn of the decade, commentators across the political spectrum had seen popular music as a means for deadening the masses—not as a vehicle for potentially liberating them. A decade later we encounter similar criticisms as dissenting views, counter-narratives offered up against a newly dominant, emerging set of ideas about rock's aptness for expressing social truths, for proposing utopian futures. Rock music seemed to reveal the workings of an anti-humanistic society, providing musicians and listeners a privileged space to diagnose and comment on this sick society. It also appeared to suggest alternatives, demanding utopian practices of listening and dancing, while sound-tracking unorthodox spaces for living (or at least experiencing) life more fully, more authentically. And this is how rock helped us dig deeper.

Let's keep this moment in mind as the contradictory political valences ascribed to rock music begin, within the next five years or so, to gain remarkable traction both among American liberals (who increasingly romanticized it) and certain conservatives (who damned it). The quest for authentic personal experience, as we will see, did not die at the Altamont Speedway—it had only just begun. This new trend began in the United States, though we can visit Abbey Road to meet one of its key protagonists in 1968. As the Beatles recorded "Revolution" in Studio Two, the first artist on their Apple recording label was laying down tracks for his eponymous debut just one room over. As a tax haven for the Beatles' earnings, Apple Corps funded far-out projects while never turning a profit; it was "a kind of Western communism," Paul told credulous journalists. Its sole success as a label was signing a sweet-singing hippie from North Carolina by way of Martha's Vineyard.

James Taylor (1969) sold poorly, in part due to the singer-songwriter's failure to promote the album because of his ongoing problems with drugs. It took a demo recorded at these sessions, but released on his sophomore album at Warner Bros, to catapult Taylor to fame. That song's spare arrangement deepened its reflective, deeply personal subject matter—on the suicide of a close friend, on struggles with addiction and mental illness, on hours spent just talking on the phone, on the personal journey that had brought the singer to this point. Its raw intimacy helped usher in a new, confessional politics of the personal.

For sure, we all want to change the world. But as rock fans soon learned, real change comes from within. Because Lord knows when the right song comes along, it'll turn your head around.

5
How Songwriters Revealed Our Inner Truth

It's a muggy July evening in San Francisco, and *Rolling Stone* editor Jann Wenner is paging through *The Primal Scream* (1970). John and Yoko had gifted the Beatles super-fan this thick paperback, a method for exploring—and exorcising—individual trauma. The singer and performance artist were on a weekend break from its author's Hollywood clinic. They had just watched the Beatles' swan song, *Let It Be* (1970), weeping together at the film's conclusion. Now Wenner flips to the title page, where John had scrawled an inscription.

"After many years of 'searching'—tobacco, pot, acid, meditation, brown rice, you know it—I am finally on the road to freedom, i.e., being REAL + STRAIGHT."

John and Yoko first encountered primal therapy in early 1970, when psychotherapist Arthur Janov's publisher mailed them (as well as James Earl Jones, Mick Jagger, and other celebrities) an advance copy. Western society organizes human beings in ways that prevent them from tuning in to their "real" selves, Janov theorized, giving rise to a psychological condition he labelled "Pain." Talk didn't work. To pierce the protective bubble our psyches create to deal with this internalized Pain, we must "feel" or "primal," howling and weeping as we regress to a child-like state. Only then can we access our truth, can we free ourselves from society's constraints.[1]

The therapist visited Lennon's estate outside London for private consultations, staying nearly a month. John and Yoko then travelled to California for intensive group sessions. They ultimately broke with Janov, suspecting his motivations for filming their private sessions. But by then, each had recorded an album inspired at least in part by the therapeutic experience: Ono's *Yoko Ono/Plastic Ono Band* and Lennon's cathartic *John Lennon/Plastic Ono Band* (1970), two sides of deeply personal, confessional lyrics that he howled and screamed his way through in confronting a lifetime of personal traumas.

"I like first-person music," Lennon later told Wenner in a wide-ranging interview to promote this first full-length post-Beatles release, an interview that spanned two issues of *Rolling Stone* in early 1971. "But because of my hang-ups and many other things, I would only now and then specifically write about me. Now I wrote all about me, and that's why I like it. It's me! And nobody else. That's why I like it. It's real, that's all."[2]

Me, me, me, me, me! I, me mine! Truth and realness, immediacy and intimacy, rawness and the songwriter's personal quest of self-discovery: from the early Seventies, these values came to comprise the measures by which rock's significance as a form of meaningful, authentic political expression would be assessed.[3] The emergence and subsequent consolidation of this collection of values allowed critics and fans not only to identify what was real, but also to criticize and dismiss what was fake. That stark dichotomy ushered in a final split between rock and pop in the critical imagination, generating the critical discourse of rockism itself.

This shift unfolded alongside a broader set of post-Woodstock debates about individualism, liberation, and political freedoms. Had the "Now Generation" transformed itself into the "Me Generation?" Had the communitarian spirit of the Sixties give way to a "culture of narcissism?" Had the rock revolution been betrayed? And if so, by whom?

Shifting our vantage point, let's for a moment forget that rock music expresses deeply felt personal truths. Forget too that certain kinds of songwriters hold a monopoly on authentic personal expression. Rather than ask whether songwriters really *did* express their personal truths, or parse how they did so, we instead need to examine the conditions that allowed critics, listeners, and musicians themselves to *believe* that meaningful political truths might be located within a song, a recording, or a performance.

So setting aside the conviction that popular musicians matter *because* they express important truths, let's ask: how did certain songwriters come to reveal these politically significant truths in the first place?

* * *

"She's an ex-junkie, an ex-hooker, and she's still perverse," a short feature in *Rolling Stone* explained. She's twice married, unlucky in love. She's a plucky pessimist, "a double Libra with moon in Gemini, Venus in Scorpio and Saturn in mid-heaven." "If you see a miracle, don't believe it," her debut album's jacket instructed in girlish, loopy handwriting. "Your friend, Judee Sill."[4]

A month later, Judee Sill landed the cover of *Rolling Stone*. Interviewer Grover Lewis largely keeps out of her way, interjecting only to sketch a few key details: "the small gold cross she wears at her throat" and the "edge of metal" in her voice, or how she "brushes a swatch of butterscotch-colored hair away from her face," stares "gravely at the palms of her hands resting in her lap," "titters girlishly." He allows the songwriter to expose the rubbed red-raw autobiographical details in a disarmingly matter-of-fact tone. "I remember tryin' to numb myself when I was a real little kid," Sill remembers. An alcoholic stepfather abused her and her mother; dysfunction reigned. "I always had scars on my knuckles," she says. "We had such violent fights at our house that the police and newspapermen would come." She moves out, the reader learns, only to plumb new depths: addiction, prostitution, then an overdose. "Right after that, I got so sick I couldn't even put on makeup to go out and turn a trick."[5]

To experience how uncomfortably intimate the interview feels you need to read it in full, remembering that Sill was not just some protagonist in a fictional story about artistic self-expression but a real human being. If this is difficult, it's because we have become accustomed to the confessional portrait of the recording artist, so inured to this post-Woodstock genre of writing that we forget it *is* a genre. We take for granted its guiding assumption: that only by understanding a musician's unvarnished biography, accessing their past in all its painful immediacy, will we begin to understand their music. That this assumption emerged only in the late 1960s and 1970s no longer registers. As David Brackett suggests, "the idea that there exists some correspondence between the biography of the singer-songwriter and his or her songs seems unquestionable."[6]

For many rock fans, Jann Wenner's *Rolling Stone* made that correspondence commonsense. Born in 1946 in New York City, Wenner—"a Kennedy-worshipping preppy whose thwarted ambition to attend Harvard diverted him to Berkeley"—tried on several roles before dropping out of the university.[7] He first dipped into the Free Speech Movement, and then began hobnobbing with the children of the Bay Area's social elite, who were dabbling not in politics but in the emerging counterculture. Wenner soon began writing for the *Daily Californian*, filing his weekly column under the pen name "Mr. Jones." He had a front-row seat for the West Coast scene. Yet describing the acid-soaked sights and sounds at one of Ken Kesey's Acid Tests, the East Coast transplant reported feeling non-plussed by the utopian experience. "Once the music stops," Wenner wrote, "it becomes very dull."[8]

Publishing did turn Wenner on, and he soon began writing for the *Sunday Ramparts*, the weekend spin-off of Walter Hinckle's daily. It was one of that literary magazine's contributing editors, the legendary jazz critic Ralph Gleason, who in late 1967 encouraged Wenner to establish *Rolling Stone*. The *Stone*'s inaugural cover featured an image of John Lennon decked out in military gear during his role in the Richard Lester's black comedy, *How I Won The War*; its main feature explored "The High Cost of Music and Love: Where's the Money From Monterey?"[9]

Wenner's magazine filled a yawning market gap that had emerged with rock's elevation to the status of serious music for serious listeners. "To speak to the kids who understood that the revolution had arrived in 1967—to speak to the kids *who got it*—required a voice in the same register and cryptography as Bob Dylan's stoned telegrams," writes Wenner biographer Joe Hagan.[10] Wenner recruited young writers such as Jon Landau, Greil Marcus, and Langdon Winner to realize that voice, filling the pages of his magazine with their analysis of the music and its social significance. From its first issue, the magazine's politics encapsulated the tensions inherent in rock 'n' roll as it transitioned from mass culture to art, and from reactionary to revolutionary in the American imagination. "Because the trade papers have become so inaccurate and irrelevant, and because fan magazines are an anachronism, fashioned in the mold of myth and nonsense," Wenner wrote in *Rolling Stone*'s opening mission statement, "we hope that we have something here for the artists and the industry, and every person who believes in the magic that can set you free."[11]

If that politics of freedom sounds a bit hazy, well that's because it was. Wenner's emphasis on "the music," for instance, led to criticisms that *Rolling Stone* ignored the black liberation and student movements. (His writers often placed their more politically charged pieces in underground outlets, with Jon Landau writing for Liberation News Service and Greil Marcus, the *San Francisco Express Times*.[12]) Wenner's own articulation of the political power of rock often wallowed in overly broad platitudes. John Lennon, Bob Dylan, and Jerry Garcia represented the "de facto spokesmen of the youth," he wrote after Chicago, because they brought "new ideas, new approaches, new means, new goals." Yet the editor also praised them for correctly rejecting, in his mind, "political exploiters."[13]

A bromide so broad, so general, could mean anything. (Count me out—in?) Still, from its first issue *Rolling Stone* contrasted sharply with other 1960s approaches to the big beat. Middle-brow publications from *Life* to *Newsweek* to *Time* had often highlighted the general social significance of rock to "the youth" movement, their coverage superficial, if not plain goofy. (The lede to one May 1965 cover story illustrates this tone: "On campus, where it once was squaresville to flip for the rock scene, it now is the wiggiest of kicks."[14]) And while pioneering fanzines, such as Paul Williams's *Crawdaddy!* (est. 1966), took rock as seriously, if not more so, than *Rolling Stone*, they lacked its production standards and circulation (not to mention its editor's ambitions).

Even more significantly, record companies took Wenner's magazine seriously—and so did rock musicians. Wenner gave them a platform, as well as the space to expound at length. An early interview with Pete Townsend, for instance, ran across two issues to about sixteen-thousand words. "Eager for fame and legitimacy," Hagan writes, "rockers were flattered."[15] And one of those rockers was the magazine's 1969 Man of the Year, chosen to acknowledge that "the Beatles have been the single dominant force in the new social thought and style for which the Sixties will be forever remembered."[16]

Lennon's interview to promote his first solo album, which appeared not only in *Rolling Stone* but also as *Lennon Remembers* (1971), the first stand-alone book published by Wenner's imprint Straight Arrow Publishing, shows how the magazine gave musicians opportunities to bundle together ideas about honesty, authenticity, and a new politics of self-discovery. Lennon says "good" songs should express directly personal experiences; too many studio effects hamper truthful self-expression. By expressing such experiences, songs can communicate "real" or "honest" values—and "simple rock" provides the best vehicle to articulate these values.

"Because it is primitive enough and has no bullshit, really, the best stuff, and it gets through to you with its beat," Lennon tells Wenner. "Go to the jungle and they have the rhythm and it goes throughout the world and it's as simple as that. . . . And the thing about rock and roll, good rock and roll, whatever good means, is that it's real, and realism gets through to you despite yourself. You recognize something in it which is true, like all true art. Whatever art is, readers, OK? If it's real, it's simple usually, and if it's simple, it's true, something like that."[17]

For sure, this very particular vision of the politics of rock depended on pre-existing ideas, locating rock's authenticity in its African-American forebears as well in the body, and framing its expressive capacities as "art." While articles in *Rolling Stone* represent this way of talking about rock music in its purest, unadulterated form, critics and commentators writing elsewhere contributed, too. "For the last five years any rock performer worth his pretensions has written his own songs," critic Robert Christgau had explained in the *New York Times* the previous year. "Song interpretation has been relegated by both performers and audiences to that phony adult world of nightclub theatricality which rock has been striving to destroy for 15 years."[18] In less critical hands than Christgau's, an auteur theory about rock soon began taking shape. "In popular music," John Cawelti wrote in a 1971 essay published in the recently founded *Journal of Popular Culture*, "one can see the differences between pop groups who simply perform without creating that personal statement which marks the *auteur*, and highly creative groups like Beatles who make of their performances a complex work of art."[19]

These ideas indelibly shaped how fans viewed, evaluated, and consumed rock. In the pages of *Rolling Stone*, Jon Landau increasingly emphasized that a songwriter should mature creatively over a series of albums; this characterized the more significant voices in rock, he claimed, such as the New Jersey-born "rock and roll future," Bruce Springsteen, whom Landau would manage (alongside acts such as the MC5 and Jackson Browne). The explosion of serious writing about rock created a canon of artists, with founders and exemplars. Jonathan Eisen's two compilations, *The Age of Rock: Sounds of the American Cultural Revolution* (1969/1970), focused on highly poetic, white musicians such as the Beatles, Dylan, and Pink Floyd; Michael Lydon's more diverse *Rock Folk: Portraits from the Rock 'n' Roll Pantheon* (1968), organized chronologically, begins with Chuck Berry, Carl Perkins, and B. B. King, and ends with Smokey Robinson, Janis Joplin, the Grateful Dead, and the Rolling Stones. The new rock writing produced also-rans and false prophets, usually by juxtaposing them with "real" voices: Dylan versus Phil Ochs, or even John versus Paul. (As a longtime Paul apologist, I just have to remind us here that what became *Let It Be* had been a self-conscious exercise in "getting back" to liveness and authenticity, and that *McCartney* [1970] was recorded eight months before Lennon's first full-length solo album, purposefully lo-fi, and—let's just admit it—nearly as raw.)

Wenner and *Rolling Stone* played a key role in valorizing, institutionalizing, and of course monetizing the turn toward self-discovery, "selling intimacy," as Joe Hagan writes, through revealing photo-essays and tell-all profiles: "a fusion of the countercultural imperative to liberate oneself and good old-fashioned show business."[20] But this could happen only with the splintering of the post-Woodstock rock counterculture into new styles and scenes. And with these new styles and scenes came a new ethos—a turn toward the confessional, the personal, and the intimate that resonated with many musicians who, "at the turn of the 1970s," as Ann Powers writes, were "beginning to think that the impetus for cultural change might not be communal effort, but individual revolt."[21]

* * *

Over the bustle of the front bar, patrons heard a commotion at the back of the West Hollywood club. Some drunk, it seemed, was engaged in the worst kind of individual revolt. Founded by promoter Doug Weston in the late 1950s, the Troubadour began booking folk rock acts in the mid-1960s.

Buffalo Springfield played their first gig here; it quickly became a hangout for members of both the film and music industries who lived in sprawling homes across the nearby hills. Tonight the patron heckling singer Ann Peebles, however, proved that even the therapeutic balm of an entire confessional album had not salved his debilitating personal wounds.

A messy John Lennon's drunken ejection from the Troubadour that night is just one of the many nearly unbelievable moments comprising the story of a venue steeped in rock myths.[22] The Troubadour sits a block south of the Sunset Strip, just a short drive from nearby Laurel Canyon (not to mention the infamous 10050 Cielo Drive in nearby Benedict Canyon). Cass Elliott of the Mamas and the Papas, Joni Mitchell, and Neil Young lived for shorter or longer periods in the Canyon, as did Frank Zappa and his group's groupies. John Mayall memorialized the neighborhood on *Blues from Laurel Canyon* (1968), just two years before Mitchell released her classic *Ladies of the Canyon* (1970). Appearances at the Troubadour helped catapult figures such as Elton John and Jackson Browne to stardom, serving as an incubator for the sound of the Seventies.

"What sense is there in talking about the music?" James Taylor asked in a recent documentary. "A large part of the value of it is that it transcends talking about itself, it communicates directly without people needing to make decisions or analyzing it."[23] Unfortunately for Taylor, we'll need to talk about the intimate sounds making up what came to be called the singer-songwriter movement. Singer-songwriter emerged as a label in the late 1960s, an indication of the premium placed on writing and performing your own music in the wake of the Beatles. But as Christa Bentley has pointed out, from the start it meant much more, gathering "layers of meanings based in audience perceptions of intimate performance, story-telling, displays of artistic vulnerability, and a sense of immediacy between the listener and the artist's persona."[24]

On stage at the Troubadour in July 1969, Taylor even looked physically vulnerable, hunched over his acoustic guitar, his stringy long brown hair hanging down to hide his face. His debut album, the first release by the Beatles Apple label, had recently fallen flat, the overproduced arrangements swallowing up his plaintive voice and spare finger-picking. The singer-songwriter had gone to London for a change of scenery following a few false starts: a derivative single with the Corsairs, the duo he formed with his brother, as well as a failed rock band called the Flying Machine, but also a nine-month stint at a psychiatric hospital after a breakdown at a tony prep school in Massachusetts. (Oh, and there was also his post–high school problems with heroin.) But his sophomore effort on Warner Bros, *Sweet Baby James* (1970), and its smash single,

"Fire and Rain," an intimate meditation interweaving elements from his personal life, would soon make him a national star.

Readers would have found the contours of the story I've just related in *Time*, which in 1971 called Taylor (this "brooding, sensitive 22-year-old rich man's son") "the face of new rock." The new rock was quieter, introspective. It could be interpreted as either a maturation of the genre, *Time* suggested, or as "a tragic slide from activist rage into a mood of 'enlightened apathy.'" But Taylor's popularity could also be explained through his appeal to a broad swathe of fans who identified with someone who also felt "those pains that a lavish quota of middle-class advantages—plenty of money, a loving family, good schools, health, charm and talent—do not seem to prevent, and may in fact exacerbate." (To emphasize the point about his privileged background, the article even included the annual tuition at his former prep school, as well as the average fees for a private psychiatric hospital.) His fans "feel instinctively that the anguished outlines of his private life . . . could be their own."[25]

If listeners did have the sense they were accessing the unmediated, inner truths of these songwriters, this in part had to do with how the musicians presented themselves: a smoldering Taylor peering out from *Sweet Baby James* (1970), chin almost resting on an arm; a domestic Carole King, shoeless and sitting in soft focus at home with her cat on *Tapestry* (1971), illuminated only by the gauzy morning sun shining in through her lounge room windows. And then there's the songwriter movement's signature sound. Each instrumental track separated, the voice pushed forward in a mix engineered, in the case of Taylor and many others, by Henry Lewy. Born Heinz in Germany in 1922, Lewy emigrated to the United States with his family on the cusp of World War II. After graduating from Hollywood High in 1945, he worked as an audio engineer first at local radio stations, and then at several recording studios. He recorded the early novelty records by David Seville and the Chipmunks (but had moved on before their 1964 smash *The Chipmunks Sing the Beatles Hits*). He soon recorded Joni Mitchell's *Ladies of the Canyon*, and the sound he crafted—intimate, close, warm—would suffuse releases by Judee Sill, Leonard Cohen, and Neil Young. Lewy produced Young's country-rock smash *Harvest* (1972), the laconic mix complemented perfectly by the gatefold image, a stylized image of the singer's fuzzy reflection in a doorknob, as well as the record's contents, acoustic songs with deeply personal lyrics about bittersweet love, loss and addiction, aging and mortality.

Activism and a communal spirit versus the disinterested apathy of navel-gazing individualism: mainstream and underground commentators alike had previously juxtaposed these two sides of the counterculture. By the early 1970s, the latter side had seemingly triumphed, and this indicated a major social problem for liberal and progressive commentators. Tom Wolfe portrayed the triumphant individualism as a betrayal of the Sixties in his acerbic takedown of "the Me Decade" published by *New York* magazine in 1976. (He had first pitched this think-piece to *Rolling Stone* in 1972).[26] "The saga of the Me Decade begins with one of those facts that is so big and so obvious (like the Big Dipper), no one ever comments on it anymore," Wolfe wrote. "Namely: the 30-year boom." Postwar affluence had made possible liberation, albeit in a form unrecognizable to the utopian socialists of the nineteenth and early twentieth centuries. Self-determinacy had resulted in the self-help movement, and self-actualization—even "the common man was also getting quite interested in this business of 'realizing his potential as a human being' "—had gone mainstream. And this, Wolfe argued, had a key consequence. "If I have only one life to live," Americans now said, "then let me live it as _____." (It's your life—you fill in the blank.)

White, middle-class Americans no longer viewed their lives as a series of stages culminating in "adulthood" (or "father-" or "motherhood," or even a career), Alex Honneth summarizes, but had instead begun "to think of the various possibilities for personal identity as being the stuff of experimental self-discovery."[27] This shift helps explain the popularity of the "new rock" with listeners who "instinctively" (as *Time* suggested) responded with recognition to songwriters' journeys of self-discovery. That's not to say the music industry didn't have a lot to do with the commercial success of this music. Figures such as David Geffen intuited the confessional turn, moving quickly to sign up artists such as Judee Sill and Jackson Browne to his label, Asylum Records, and (as Barry Hoskyns puts it) "to sell anti-capitalism to the kids, the longhairs, the dropouts."[28] And if it had seemed gauche to strive too hard in the still-warm afterglow of the post-Woodstock communalist zeitgeist, that too soon changed. "There was *absolutely* an agenda going on," one scene participant remembered, describing the Eagles' Glenn Frey's hustle at the Troubadour. "He was very, very career-oriented—they *all* were. Anyone who pretends they weren't doing that is fooling themselves."[29]

Shifts in radio programming also opened up new spaces for softer, more introspective sounds. An effort to reach beyond young white male rock fans pushed radio executives to craft new formats, from "middle-of-the-road" (MOR), to "album-oriented rock" (AOR), to "blended play," to "easy listening," to "soft rock."[30] This shift followed radio's discovery of the "lonely housewife" demographic (and its purchasing power that advertisers coveted). "If I played Alice Cooper or Black Sabbath at 10 in the morning," one programming executive said, "100,000 women would find another station [and] I'd be looking for another job."[31] Others justified this shift in programming as dictated by radio's function, to "communicate" with listeners; one programmer urged deejays to play "communication music," meaning "records whose lyrics communicate an adult message with total emotional commitment by the artist."[32] Finally, still others pointed to the inevitable maturation of listeners who, by the 1970s, had simply grown up. (One journalist accurately, if a bit uncharitably I think, attributed the popularity of middle-of-the-road artists to "baby boomers' metabolic meltdown."[33])

These changes occurred alongside a tectonic shift in first the economic, and then the political, organization of the world. The collapse of the postwar liberal consensus cleared space for new forms of capital accumulation, glossed variously as "disorganized" or "flexible" capitalism or (later) "neoliberalism." And this coincided with a major change to political critique. Historically speaking, two major forms of critique have, sociologists Luc Boltanski and Eve Chiapello claim, been pursued in capitalist societies.[34] Artistic critique has focused on capitalism's relationship to values such as creativity, freedom, and autonomy: its idealists try to understand how capital disempowers individuals' capacity for experiencing "freedom." In contrast, social critique has emphasized the structural violence wrought by capitalism, its propensity to exacerbate inequality and foment competition among individuals who come to perceive themselves as autonomous actors, all while breaking down the bonds (social, familial, and otherwise) that might connect people but elude its grasp.

Boltanski and Chiapello suggest that after the 1960s powerful actors in the West moved to suppress the latter form of critique while not only validating, but ultimately institutionalizing, the former. This is one suggestive way to think about the elevation of a "politics of the personal" in Seventies soft rock. "It was so easy then, never takin' any stands," Carly Simon sings on a nostalgic paean to childhood on *No Secrets* (1972). "It was so easy then, holdin' hands." (Easy for whom? Simon and her cowriter had bonded during the dog days of summer 1968—not in the streets of Chicago or Detroit or Los Angeles, but as counsellors at a posh summer camp in the lily-white Berkshires.)

Returning to West Hollywood, we can see another example of the institutionalization of artistic critique in a rock 'n' roll passion play about liberalism, freedom, and the project of "America." The music licensing for *Easy Rider* (1969) cost three times the film's entire production budget, just north of a million dollars (or about $7.5 million today). Director and star Peter Fonda had wanted Crosby, Stills, Nash, and Young to write the soundtrack, but a rough edit that used preexisting songs had stuck. Its opening is easily one of the most iconic scenes in New Hollywood cinema.[35] Fresh from smuggling cocaine, Wyatt (played by Fonda) stuffs tightly rolled hundred-dollar bills into a plastic

Figure 7 "Of course, don't ever tell anybody that they're not free, 'cause then they're gonna get real busy killin' and maimin' to prove to you that they are. Oh, yeah, they gonna talk to you, and talk to you, and talk to you about individual freedom. But they see a free individual, it's gonna scare 'em.'" Lobby card, *Easy Rider*. Copyright 1969, renewed 1997 Columbia Pictures Industries, Inc. All rights reserved. Courtesy of Columbia Pictures

tube that he secrets inside the gas tank of his chopper before roaring down the road alongside Billy (played by Dennis Hopper). The camera pans slowly over Wyatt's gas tank, emblazoned in an American flag that matches his stars-and-stripes motorcycle gear; Billy is dressed in standard-issue buckskin togs of the late Sixties West Coast hippie. As their choppers roar to life, Steppenwolf's "The Pusher" (1968) fades out, and Wyatt and Billy hit the open road to "Born To Be Wild" (1968).

New Hollywood scenesters shared direct connections to the rock counter-culture. Dennis Hopper and Michelle Phillips (of the Mamas and the Papas), for instance, married on Halloween 1970, though this union lasted only eight days; Jack Nicholson's *The Trip* (1967) had been filmed throughout the Sunset Strip and Laurel Canyon, where he and other member of the scene lived, worked, and partied. But the main focus had now become the musicians—and this was a major change. "A company town, Hollywood demands deference," Michael Walker writes, "and for years musicians, like writers, were glorified handmaidens to the moviemakers, necessary craftspeople of a lower caste who kept the business humming but didn't overstep their station." All at once this changed: "Movie stars wished *they* were rock stars."[36]

The crux of *Easy Rider* comes at the film's midpoint and is accompanied only by the sound of silence (or less poetically, of chirping crickets). In a symbolic reversal of the conquest of the American frontier, Wyatt and Billy wind their way east, their destination New Orleans and Mardi Gras, that final carnivalesque debauch preceding the traditional Christian season of penance and sacrifice. Along the way they meet lawyer George Hanson, an ACLU lawyer played by Jack Nicholson, in small-town jailhouse. George personifies the moderate, open-minded American, society's politically temperate vital center. (Though ironically, he's being held for his intemperance, public drunkenness; Wyatt and Billy had been jailed on charges trumped-up by a few small-town squares.)

The hard-drinking George is the kind of liberal with whom sympathetic audience members might identify; Wyatt and Billy represent the counterculture they must learn to understand. Chased out of town by narrow-minded roughnecks in rural Louisiana, the three make camp and share a joint.

"You know, this used to be a helluva good country," George says. "I can't understand what's gone wrong with it." Wyatt replies that people are scared; too scared, even, to allow the three to spend the night at a local motel.

"But they're not scared of you," the liberal George muses. "They're scared of what you represent to 'em."

"All we represent to them, man, is somebody who needs a haircut."

"Oh, no," George replies. "What you represent to them is freedom."

"What the hell is wrong with freedom?"

"Oh, yeah, that's right," George replies. "That's what's it's all about, all right. But talkin' about it and bein' it, that's two different things. I mean, it's real hard to be free when you are bought and sold in the marketplace. Of course, don't ever tell anybody that they're not free, 'cause then they're gonna get real busy killin' and maimin' to prove to you that they are. Oh, yeah, they gonna talk to you, and talk to you, and talk to you about individual freedom. But they see a free individual, it's gonna scare 'em."

* * *

Spoiler: the narrow-minded town-folk prove George right. As the camera pans across the stars-and-stripes motorcycle helmet, hillbilly toughs sneak into the campsite. Wyatt and Billy survive the beating. But liberal George dies, murdered in his sleep by the rednecks without waking. Wyatt and Billy press on eastward; they don't report the crime. Because what would the newspapers report if they did? *Extra! Drug-Crazed Hippies Murder Lawyer!*

It's another George who, in retrospect, turned out to represent the last gasp of America's postwar liberal consensus. Born in 1922, George McGovern was too old for rock 'n' roll. The Democratic Party's presidential candidate in 1972, McGovern had served first as a congressman and then senator in South Dakota. He had earned a PhD in history with a dissertation on coal strikers; he served in the Second World War as a bomber pilot. (As a sophomore at Dakota Wesleyan University in 1941, McGovern had been making notes on a Sunday afternoon broadcast of the New York Philharmonic for a music appreciation course when a speaker interrupted to announce the Pearl Harbor attacks. The first piece on the program was by Shostakovich, that "active cog in the Soviet machine" according to the Phil's program notes. McGovern recalled handing in "strictly B.S." for this compulsory humanities class.[37])

McGovern briefly mounted a challenge for the 1968 nomination after Robert F. Kennedy's assassination, coming a distant third in Chicago. But despite entering the 1972 race a longshot, he won the nomination in no small part due to his success in mobilizing younger voters on the campaign trail. In April 1972, McGovern spoke to eighteen-thousand of these young voters at the Forum in Los Angeles. Organized by New Hollywood maverick Warren Beatty, "3/4 McGovern"—"Three For McGovern"—enlisted major star power to raise money for the antiwar, pro-amnesty candidate. Those in the upper levels paid $4 to $10 per ticket, while attendees on the floor paid $100 (and were served by celebrity ushers including Jack Nicholson, Mama Cass, and Michelle Phillips). Carole King, James Taylor, and Barbara Streisand performed their current hits. And then McGovern spoke.

"You know there's an old French proverb that says gratitude is the heart's memory," the forty-nine-year-old liberal senator told the roaring crowd. "A couple of years ago there was a song, 'Here comes the sun—it's all right.' Well, we're going to see the sun again. Things can be all right again. With great effort '72 will be a great year."[38]

Beatty helped organize three more concert fundraisers over the next few months.[39] Major recording artists donated their time to support McGovern's campaign: singer-songwriters such as King, Taylor, Joni Mitchell; folkies such as Judy Collins, Simon and Garfunkel, and Peter, Paul, and Mary; and soul singers such as Dionne Warwick and Tina Turner. In part, these events addressed a pressing need for candidates to raise funds as budgets for election campaigns ballooned. "Those damn Republicans," Maureen Orth, reporter

Figure 8 "Good ole George, honest and bland, is being transformed into sexy George, George the Hip, George the Magnetic, all because of a powerful new magic weapon in his campaign," according to Maureen Orth in the *Village Voice*. Concert poster *McGovern: Carole King- Barbara Streisand- James Taylor: In Concert* (1972)

with the *Village Voice* quoted a McGovern aide as saying. "Before Warren came along with his Glamor Brigade there was no way we could compete with their $1000-a-plate Agnew-Reagan sit-down dinners." But the concerts also addressed an increased focus on cultivating a candidate's personal image. "Good ole George, honest and bland," Orth noted sardonically, "is being transformed into sexy George, George the Hip, George the Magnetic, all because of a powerful new magic weapon in his campaign."[40]

To many young voters, McGovern did seem to be a very different kind of candidate, so much so that *Rolling Stone* even sent Hunter S. Thompson out on the campaign trail. ("Jesus Christ! That's weird," a friend of the self-proclaimed *Rolling Stone* National Affairs editor supposedly exclaimed. "The *Stone* is into politics?"[41]) In a historical quirk, McGovern had not been the first presidential candidate to invoke the messaging power of rock musicians, albeit inadvertently. "The youth of today can change the world," Nixon had intoned over a 1968 television ad that featured a slightly psychedelic-sounding backing track (and a slightly stoned-looking Jerry Garcia, uncredited, in an Uncle Sam top hat).[42] But McGovern's ascendancy points to the role of "the youth" as both a newly important demographic group and cultural symbol within the political imaginary of American liberalism.

This emphasis on young people had to do in part with sheer numbers, the Democratic Party's bet on an inexorable push leftward due to the country's changing demographics. Fifty years later, centrist Democrats are still waiting for some version of this bet to pay off. But in 1972, it seemed commonsense that the next generation would vote Democrat. The previous year, the twenty-sixth amendment lowered the voting age to eighteen, with Congress acceding to the antiwar movement's common-sense proposition that "old enough to fight, old enough to vote." Democratic Party officials expected first-time voters to support them in droves, injecting a shot of adrenaline into the party base. "[I]t has been twelve years since I could look at a ballot and see a name I wanted to vote for," Hunter S. Thompson affirmed. "In 1964, I refused to vote at all, and in '68 I spent half a morning in the county courthouse getting an absentee ballot so I could vote, out of spite, for Dick Gregory."[43]

To attract young people, some party operatives sought to harness the messaging power of rock stars. "Put the power of your vote in your hip pocket," a slightly stoned-sounding Dennis Wilson told listeners in a radio spot aimed at first-time voters. But this occurred at a time when American politics had also been undergoing a large-scale realignment, when it was not always clear what distinguished one party from the other. In 1964, Republican Barry Goldwater ran on a pro-civil rights but anti-government platform; four years later, Democrat George Wallace ran a surprisingly successful campaign on a pro-segregation platform. In between these two campaigns, Allen Ginsberg reminded William F. Buckley on *Firing Line* that they both shared a belief in "greater individuality" and "freedom"—which was not untrue.[44] And at Wellesley's graduation in 1969, a former Goldwater Girl-turned-Democrat rallied her fellow students with a call for freedom. "We know that to be educated, the goal of it must be human liberation," Hillary Rodham told her classmates. "A liberation enabling each of us to fulfill our capacity so as to be free to create within and around ourselves."[45]

North versus South, Democrat versus Republican, liberal versus conservative—the political meanings of these categories had seemingly come unstuck. What role would young people have in rearticulating these terms of debate to the political landscape? A professor at Yale Law School who taught both Rodham and her future husband, a Southern boy named Bill, believed they would play a decisive role. "There is a revolution coming," announced the cover blurb to Charles Reich's bestselling *Greening of America* (1970). "It will originate with the individual and with culture, and it will change the political structure only as its final act."[46]

Countercultural truths permeated the forty-two-year-old Reich's analysis. Institutions such as public schooling ("a brutal machine for destruction of the self") made people into cogs that would fit into the social machinery of American society.[47] But there was a way out. Culture and art—including, for Reich, popular music—created a "way of life" for the individual who "creates his own life and thus creates the society in which he lives." Of course, this process had contradictions. "While consciousness is the creator of any social system," Reich wrote, "it can lag behind a system, once created, and even be manipulated by that system."[48] And here things get even hazier: "The new consciousness is also in the process of revolutionizing the structure of our society. It does not accomplish this by direct political means, but by changing the culture and the quality of individual lives, which in turn change politics and, ultimately, structure."[49]

If certain kinds of "culture" manifest new ways of life, then it stands to reason that other kinds can reinforce a reactionary status quo. Here we find the roots of the idea that your parents' record collection might not just be embarrassing. It might be, if not counter-revolutionary or even fascist, then at least anti-progressive. (The limits of this idea should be obvious. A hi-fi enthusiast, Nixon had showed Duke Ellington his "expensive stereo machine with many records and tapes" during a White House visit in 1969. But while he had tragically middle-of-the-road taste, with a record collection that included Rodgers and Hammerstein, Mantovani, the Boston Pops, even Lawrence Welk, that was probably the least of his sins.)[50]

This raises a few questions. Should a vanguard of particularly hip young consumers be charged with remaking our society's consciousness? Who decides what culture is "right" and what is "wrong?" Could someone have good taste—but bad ideas? And what about, as one of Nixon's campaign advisors called them, the "children of the silent majority?"[51] Like McGovern's campaign, Nixon's 1972 re-election bid also cultivated youthful supporters, Young Voters for the President, mounting a sophisticated marketing campaign not only to curry their votes, but also to demonstrate the candidate's broad appeal to all Americans.

The "Nixon Youth Shows" that he mounted were admittedly not very hip. Sammy Davis Jr. was the headliner.[52] But speaking at a YVP concert the night before formally accepting the Republic Party's nomination, Nixon had told young supporters that "nobody has the youth vote in their pocket."[53] And he turned out to be right. "Everywhere we've been going lately, we've been talking a little bit about power," Beach Boy Carl Wilson had told young listeners in a radio spot leading up to the election, "the power each of us eighteen or older now has to try and get things on the right track in this country." Yet the McGovern revolution did not just fizzle, it spectacularly imploded. Nixon soundly beat the senator in an embarrassingly lopsided affair. The youth candidate carried only one state, the deeply liberal Massachusetts. (When I was growing up in a Boston suburb fifteen years later, some people still proudly displayed the Seventies' versions of "Believe Science" or "Coexist" slogans, smug bumper stickers reading, "Don't Blame Me, I'm From Massachusetts.")

Nixon would not long remain in office. Few voters initially seemed to care that Republican operatives had broken into the Democratic National Committee's offices; a Harris poll in late 1972 showed most believed *all* politicians played dirty tricks. But his subsequent resignation, coupled with the resounding defeat of McGovern's platform at the polls, helped accelerate the ascendancy of a new brand of conservatism. Openly virulent racism? This no longer worked, at least in public. Politics now turned to struggles over culture born from the dizzying changes to American social mores over the previous decade. And rock played an increasingly important role as a symbol of artistic critique in these incipient culture wars.

* * *

In late 1970, President Nixon received a knock at the White House front door. Quite literally, in fact: the visitor from Memphis hand-delivered a letter offering his services in fighting the administration's recently announced war on drugs. Intrigued, Nixon invited Elvis Presley into the Oval Office to discuss the drug problem. The Beatles had been a force for anti-government sentiment, Presley said, for spreading values antithetical to the American way of life. He could help counter that influence—but only if he were named an honorary officer with the Bureau of Narcotics and Dangerous Drugs, precursor to today's Drug Enforcement Agency. Thanking him for the offer, Nixon posed for a photograph.

In her memoirs, Priscilla claimed that Elvis believed a bureau badge would allow him to board airplanes with handguns, as well as the pills he was now ingesting by the handful.[54] (It wouldn't have.) Nothing came of the meeting. But the image of Elvis and Nixon shaking hands is not just the National Archives' most-requested image. It also reminds us how the federal government approached drugs as a pretext for responding to the counterculture's role in reshaping social values in the United States. And rock more so than any genre, as both Elvis and Nixon recognized, represented a potent symbol for conservative reformers.

Hearings that examined the relationship between the white rock counterculture and the so-called drug culture had begun in the late 1960s. In Indiana, Theodore Sendak pushed through laws banning rock festivals, arguing that their promoters were often entangled with drug trafficking. The attorney general was too zealous; he had to insert loopholes into a law that had accidentally banned the Indianapolis 500 stockcar race.[55] At the federal level, Republican Senator James Buckley organized hearings, which resulted in a report published in 1973. Inspired by a *Times* editorial by William Safire, the congressional hearings sought to discover if rock music was contributing to rising levels of drug use in the United States. Rock needed to be regulated, Buckley contended, because it fundamentally reshaped young Americans' attitudes. Tremendously powerful, it was thus tremendously dangerous.[56] He cited at length a report published by the United Nations' Department of Economic and Social Affairs in late 1969. "Sooner or later, when an urban child, who lives in the ordinary world, not in the pop world where a drug conviction can be shrugged off, is offered a marijuana cigarette or a dose of LSD," that report's authors had stated, "he will remember them not as something his health and hygiene teacher spoke warnings about, but as something Mick Jagger, or John Lennon, or Paul McCartney had used and enjoyed."[57]

Here we find the roots of another new way of talking about rock music, a conservative perspective that, as we will see, reached its full, mature form only a decade later. Rock should be regulated, these commentators claim, and the music industry has a "responsibility" to the young people of America. This position depended on two assumptions. The first linked youthful consumption to young people's attitudes and perspectives, suggesting that the records you bought, the lyrics you parsed sitting on your bedroom floor, the music that you danced to, had real-world effects at the level of consciousness. This conservative assumption is remarkably similar to countercultural claims about each individual's capacity for "freeing" their mind, for eluding the institutionalizing effects of American social structure by consuming recorded music. The second, closely related assumption attributed to musicians a powerful status: the ability to shape young Americans, to change how people think. Again, this new conservative truth aligned surprisingly well with how critics and the musicians themselves had been talking about rock since the mid-1960s.

Congressional hearings about rock music, of course, did little to affect the actual course of the music. We might view such hearings as a symptom, not the driver, the discovery by a new class of conservative thinkers of a new front in the ideological struggle for the heart and soul of the United States: young people and their "culture," especially as disseminated by the mass media. A year after Elvis's visit to the White House, one such thinker, on the cusp of being named to Nixon's Supreme Court, drafted a letter to the US Chamber of Commerce. The Powell Memorandum, as Lewis Powell's report came to be known, crystallized the tenets of a still inchoate movement that fit neatly into neither the Democratic nor the Republican Party at the time. It called for corporate leaders to take an activist role in lobbying for smaller government and fewer regulations, and it identified "the free market" as the only legitimate arbiter for economic, political, and social life in the United States. It provided a blueprint, historian David Harvey suggests, for neoliberalism as a political project.[58] And it had been inspired by the proto-culture wars struggle between Nixon's "silent majority" and student activists, public intellectuals, left-wing artists, and the mass media.

Why should the most *economically* powerful men in America, Powell asked, cower before the most *culturally* prominent? The latter included "Communists, New Leftists and other revolutionaries who would destroy the entire system, both political and economic." And while they are "minorities," their spokespersons "often are the most articulate, the most vocal, the most prolific in their writing and their speaking." They are savvy, Powell argued. They know how to use the mass media, which "now plays such a predominant role in shaping the thinking, attitudes and emotions of our people." And that's the crux of the problem. "One of the bewildering paradoxes of our time," Powell concluded, "is the extent to which the enterprise system tolerates, if not participates in, its own destruction."[59]

It's worth pausing here to examine this larger claim. On the one hand, the "system" (in this case, free-market capitalism with American characteristics), found itself under attack from "minorities" (here meaning predominantly white antiwar activists, liberal media elites, politically minded artists and musicians). The enterprise system appears remarkably passive, for some unknown reason tolerating the hijacking of its television and radio airwaves, and submitting to the commandeering of its editorial pages and glossy magazines. These media products reflect the worldview of a radical fringe, not the values and beliefs of ordinary Americans. This claim coincided with the invention of novel terms for describing these ordinary or "real" Americans. We have already encountered Nixon's "silent majority," a label for the mass of Americans who did not see their "traditional" values represented in mainstream media. The terms "heartland" and "middle America" also emerge during this period, reorienting debate, as historian Kristin Hogansan traces, over who "counted"—and who didn't—within the political imaginary of the United States, and purging overt class- or race-based language from the political speech of conservatives (and later, liberals).[60]

The state and its violence also disappear. Atrocities in Vietnam, but also covert campaigns throughout Europe, Latin America, the Middle East, Indonesia, Africa, and Southeast Asia, do not fit into this scheme. And this despite the fact that, from the late 1960s onward, Americans were increasingly aware of not only the global reach of the military-industrial complex, but also how the United States turned its powers of surveillance, harassment, and violence on its own citizens. Beginning in 1953, the CIA had undertaken a broad experimental program of psychological warfare; in 1975, the Rockefeller Commission revealed the scope and tactics of Project MKUltra, which included LSD trials that introduced figures such as Allen Ginsberg and Ken Kesey to psychedelics. In 1971, the Citizens' Commission to Investigate the FBI revealed the existence of COINTELPRO, an FBI counterintelligence program launched fifteen years earlier that targeted leftists, civil rights leaders, black and brown power organizers, and antiwar activists. A CIA program, Project CHAOS, more specifically targeted the antiwar and student movements from 1967.

Such programs did not specifically target music, though white and black folk musicians felt the effects of government programs to stifle dissent. Intelligence agencies investigated folk musicians in the 1940s and 1950s, even planting informers in the folk revival. "The words 'freedom' and 'justice': only Commies talked about things like that," said Pete Seeger, a key target who found himself blacklisted from the entertainment industry, explaining the government's justification for its actions.[61] Such activities continued into the 1960s. The FBI began its surveillance of Phil Ochs in 1963; it only closed its file on Woody Guthrie when he died in 1967.[62]

The most extensive investigation of a rock musician began in 1971. John Lennon had planned a series of concerts to register voters and galvanize protesters; eleven months of surveillance yielded little actionable evidence, which didn't prevent immigration officials from ordering his deportation in spring 1972. The political sloganeering of Lennon's music during this period, however, demonstrates an unhappy truth: bad rock songs don't actually mobilize anyone. *Some Time In New York City* (1972, with Yoko Ono and Elephant's Memory) flopped, its overwrought lyrics about prison reform, sexism, and racism a bit too on-the-nose. "Woman Is the Nigger of the World" (1972) would be Lennon's worst-charting single; he himself later disavowed the more successful "Power to the People" (1971) as misguided pandering to the political radicals who had been critical of him.

So did the United States government ever seek to control rock musicians because their messages could actually be harnessed for significant, real-world political work? There's scant evidence demonstrating a cause-and-effect relationship between political messaging on the one hand, and direct political action on the other; there's less evidence that musicians were specifically targeted for their music-making; and there just aren't cases of direct interference. Notwithstanding the many books and articles written about Lennon and the FBI, the case remains an outlier, probably best explained by the personal animus of figures such as Strom Thurmond, who initiated the surveillance, or Richard Nixon, who approved it. What the amount of ink spilled over this case does reveal is what someone like Lennon represents within the post-Woodstock liberal imaginary—it shows how we tend to retrospectively valorize the musical taste of a certain kind of white, middle-class listener not as mere consumption, but as a meaningful form of political resistance.

Could this be why the records consumed by blue-collar listeners in America's suburbs, especially heavy metal or hard rock, have occupied so little space in the larger story about popular music and freedom? (Not to mention the records—soul, funk, R&B, disco, salsa, and later hip-hop—consumed by black and Latino listeners.) Their consumption cannot easily scan as "resistant," as a form of politically significant artistic critique, within a post-Sixties liberal imaginary that centers the listening experiences of Dylan fans over those of Def Leppard fans. Yet while much has been written about the cultural politics of the Republican Party's "southern strategy," a pivot toward cultivating white resentment against blacks and the advances of the civil rights movement, we tend to overlook the cultural consequences of the Democratic Party's rejection of their former base of urban white ethnic working-class voters, a rejection that explains why Lennon (but not Led Zeppelin) figures so prominently in stories about the political significance of rock.

The rejection was a conscious decision. In *The Changing Sources of Power* (1971), Frederick Dutton had argued that Americans' ever-rising standard of living meant that Democrats should turn away from an emphasis on making appeals to blue-collar voters. (Dutton had been a party power broker in the 1960s. He served in Jack Kennedy's cabinet, and he was with Bobby at the Ambassador Hotel in Los Angeles, even riding with him in the ambulance.) But if blue-collar voters no longer constituted the party's symbolic center, who would take their place? White college students, Dutton wrote, who had demonstrated their ability to "rescue the individual from mass society," to "refurbish and reinvigorate individuality."[63]

From this point forward American liberals would assume, as Thomas Frank writes, that the "great players on the stage of history were all from the Now Generation."[64] These players would have to wait for their turn at the actual levers of power. An eighteen-year-old who started college in 1968 would be eligible for the presidency only in 1985. But for now, the elevation of these players within the American liberal imagination initiated a key shift: the privileging of the symbolic over the material in the realm of politics. As depicted in the satirical political comic strip *Doonesbury*, Democrat Jimmy Carter recognized the importance of this battlefield by creating a new cabinet post, the Secretary of

Symbolism. Cartoonist Garry Trudeau rendered the fictional politico, Duane Delacourt, with a moustache and blue jeans. From March 1977, he slouched in an armchair, working the phones to ensure that White House events included enough "plain folks" or asking President Carter to hand out trophies to recognize those nations that "still cherish human dignity."[65] "Funny," historian Rick Perlstein writes, "but serious: symbols mattered."[66]

This implied a new theory of politics, a theory that viewed political power as deriving not from class-based movements or material conditions, but from the harnessing of cultural symbols and the winning of hearts and minds not only abroad, but at home. With this shift toward artistic critique, certain kinds of cultural expression began acquiring outsized political significance. From the start, liberal thinkers articulated the significance of the new style of critique by applying this theory to white rock musicians.

"If the Marx they emulated was Groucho, not Karl, if their world was a playground instead of a battleground," Jeff Greenfield wrote in a 1975 *Times* op-ed summarizing the legacy of the Beatles, "they still changed what we listened to and how we listened to it, they helped make rock music a battering ram for the youth culture's assault on the mainstream, and that assault in turn changed our culture permanently."[67] A staunch McGovernik, Greenfield claimed awesome powers for the Fab Four, even if "their behavior as a group reflected cheerful anarchy more than political rebellion." They matured the overly commercial, overly sexy, overly black music, he suggested, proving its "energy could be fused with a sensibility more subtle than the 'let's go down-to-the-gym-and beat-up-the-Coke machine' quality of [early] rock." But more significantly, they brought individual listeners together, cohering them into a group with a common purpose: "millions of people began to regard themselves as a class separate from mainstream society by virtue of their youth and the sensibility that youth produced."

And that, he concluded, had been their true power. "They changed rock, which changed the culture, which changed us." At last, the truth about the power of rock has becomes clear: it had been a revolution in the head all along.

* * *

"The dream is over, what can I say?" John Lennon intones at the conclusion of "God" on *Plastic Ono Band* (1970). In popular memory, the Sixties usually end in a single, cataclysmic moment: Sirhan Sirhan in Los Angeles, Charles Manson's slippies at Cielo Drive, the National Guard at Kent State (though not the police at Jackson State), the Hells Angels at the Altamont Speedway. Each moment, the story goes, the placid surface of a generation's guilelessness breaks, allowing the rushing release of contradictions that had been building up within American society. "A demented and seductive vortical tension was building in the community," Joan Didion famously wrote in *The White Album* (1979), "a time when the dogs barked every night and the moon was always full."[68]

This sort of narrative asks us to think about "the Sixties" as more homogenous than it really was; it also suggests we think about the period that comes "after" the Sixties as, if not a betrayal, then at least a loss of innocence, however inevitable that loss may have been. But with that loss came an opportunity: for seeing things as they really are, for more fully discerning the personal politics shaping our lives from the inside out. And that's how rock helped reveal our inner truths.

At this point, our unified narrative about rock will split, and we'll explore two contrasting sets of plot points that shaped how listeners and musicians alike made and then assigned political meanings to rock as a privileged form of artistic critique in the late Seventies and Eighties. The first extends key elements we've just been exploring: about the music's capacity for truth-telling and self-expression, about its ability to articulate a romantic vision of freedom, individualism, and rebellion. This is Peter Fonda and Dennis Hopper skinny-dipping with two lithe hippie chicks in *Easy Rider* (1969) as "I Wasn't Born to Follow" plays; it's the slow helicopter shot after two white hillbillies kill Hopper's character, with Roger McGuinn singing the film's epitaph, "Ballad of Easy Rider," making sure we didn't miss the moral of the film, that "all he wanted was to be free."

If the Sixties represented our innocence, and the Seventies its betrayal, then what might come next? "John has talked about the Sixties and how it gave us a taste for freedom," Yoko Ono told *Playboy* magazine in an extended interview that appeared on newsstands in the days before Lennon's murder. But this glimpse of what-could-be had been subsumed and overwhelmed, subjected to individual egos and social pressures, to child-rearing, careers, divorce. "I really think that what happened in the Seventies can be compared to what happened under Nazism with Jewish families," Ono continued. "Only the force that split them came from the inside, not from the outside. We tried to rationalize it as the price we were paying for our freedom."[69] What would happen in the Eighties? Would a new kind of freedom be reclaimed?

We'll need to wait to see. Because before we find out how mainstream rock became fully institutionalized, its capacities for personal liberation and real social change stylized and common-sense, we need to examine a second set of plot points: the emergence of an important counternarrative about rock and freedom. The proponents of this counternarrative saw the Sixties and their immediate aftermath not as an Eden to be reclaimed—but as a site of betrayal to be annihilated. For them, rock had lost its way. And the music's truth resided not in self-indulgent concept albums, or at the Fillmore, or in upstate New York, but on the goofy, scratchy 45s of the Fifties and the suburban garages of the early Sixties.

"Hate to come on like a Nazi," one wrote in 1971, "but if I hear one more Jesus-walking-the-boys-and-girls-down-a-Carolina-path-while-the-dilemma-of-existence-crashes-like-a-slab-of-hod-on-J.T.'s-shoulders song, I will drop everything (I got nothing to do here in California but drink beer and watch TV anyway) and hop the first Greyhound to Carolina for the signal satisfaction of breaking off a bottle of Ripple (he deserves no better, and I wish I could think of worse, but they're all local brands) and twisting it into James Taylor's guts until he expires in a spasm of adenoidal poesy."

"EXTRA! TRAGEDY STRIKES ROCK! SUPERSTAR GORED BY DERANGED ROCK CRITIC!! 'We made it,' gasped Lester Bangs as he was led by police away from the bloody scene. 'We won.'"[70]

6
How Rock Got Real Again

"I just think of it as rock and roll, because that's what it is," Eugene sneers at the start of Penelope Spheeris's punk documentary, *The Decline of Western Civilization* (1981). "I like that it's something new, and it's like reviving old rock and roll and it's like rock and it's for real. . . . And it's not bullshit, there are no rock stars, you know?"[1]

Somewhere between the Fifties and the late Seventies, rock lost its way. This time, the story comes from entirely within rock itself, from a particular group of musicians and the critics who promoted them. Some blamed the counterculture, and especially the hijacking of its program for radical social change by self-interested, navel-gazing hippie drop-outs and ex-activists. "Everybody's out for themselves," Jello Biafra, frontman for Dead Kennedys, told an interviewer in 1981, "and the people who were saying something in the Sixties now just want to sit around and get stoned."[2] Tom Wolfe had anticipated this critique in "The 'Me' Decade," roasting former radicals such as Rennie Davis and Jerry Rubin, two-sevenths of the Chicago Seven, for exchanging their former activism for the meditation-heavy pieties of the self-help movement. "It is entirely possible that in the long run," Wolfe had concluded, "historians will regard the entire New Left experience as not so much a political as a religious episode wrapped in semi-military gear and guerrilla talk."[3]

Others claimed you could hear this betrayal in the dulcet tones of the easy-listening, album-oriented Seventies. Those post-Woodstock musicians had betrayed the true spirit of rock 'n' roll, stripping the music of the political heft it once had. Soft, wimpy, girly, maybe even a bit queer: the Eagles, Linda Ronstadt, James Taylor, and their ilk all but demanded a counter-reaction. "Can you imagine the frustration, 'when's it gonna by my turn,'" Mike Watt of the seminal hardcore band, Minutemen, later recalled, "and you get there, and it's Peter Frampton's 'Do You Feel Like I Do?' [*sic*]—and he's in a kimono?"[4]

Were the Sixties a failure? What did its movements, and its music, ultimately mean? Popular accounts of punk and hardcore often frame the music's emergence as a reaction to the material conditions of the Seventies, that "decade of nightmares" (in the felicitous phrasing of historian Philip Jenkins) created by fear-mongering tabloids, economic crises, and a new pessimism about Americans' prospects at home and abroad.[5] But the bands making these claims and their partisans had a historical consciousness that merits closer examination.

And that's why we'll take this detour to examine punk and hardcore music. After all, groups with names like Dead Kennedys or their later tour-mates, the Crucifucks, did not (for a few obvious reasons) curry much mainstream success. Yet the emergence of punk scenes in the late Seventies and their expansion in the Eighties helped articulate key offshoots about the political potential of rock 'n' roll. This music eluded corporate control. It was real, and it was democratic. Its proponents spun from their photocopied zines, cut-and-pasted fliers, pin-pricked tattoos, and chaotic performances an entire ethics, a moral universe explaining how to live authentically—to live free (even if this ethics took until about 1991, "the year punk broke," as filmmaker Dave Markey puts it, to become commonsense for most rock fans).[6]

So bearing in mind that those most invested in arguing that rock had foundered were the same individuals who saw themselves as righting the ship, we'll cast a skeptical eye on claims that rock had once been real, and that by the distorted, aggressive guidance of certain kinds of bands it was becoming real again—though as someone who fell in love with rock at the height of post-1991 grunge earnestness, I probably can't promise full objectivity.

Shifting focus, let's explore *why* some people thought that rock had lost its way. And then we can ask: How did rock get real again?

* * *

As preparations for the United States Bicentennial ramped up to their star-spangled zenith, Danny Fields found himself across the Atlantic, snapping photographs of sneering British teenagers with bad DIY haircuts and worse attitudes. The American band he managed had cut its teeth at a small club just ten miles from their home in Forest Hills, Queens; their first album, released on Seymour Stein's independent label, Sire Records, had appeared in April to lukewarm sales. But the thirty-six-year-old Fields foresaw a bright future for the group.

This industry veteran knew a trend when he heard it. As a jack-of-all-trades at Elektra Records, he had hyped Jim Morrison to teenyboppers and helped sign the Stooges and MC5. (Though as a muckraking editorial assistant at *Datebook*, he had also nearly gotten Beatle John assassinated by digging up those ill-put remarks about Christianity.)[7] So as Americans back home tuned in to watch KC and the Sunshine Band and singing cowboy Roy Rogers fete the United States on Paul Anka's pre-recorded special, *Happy Birthday,*

America! (1976), a band of scrappy revolutionaries from Queens launched a much-belated response to the British Invasion in the United Kingdom.

The British rag *Rock Scene* headlined their feature "Ramones Blitz London."[8] Surviving footage of "Judy Is A Punk" from the Roundhouse gig demonstrates the group's raw appeal: Joey's screamed "1-2-3-4," Johnny's machine-gun guitar staccato, Dee Dee's sweaty, sinewy sneer, and the whole thing lasts maybe ninety seconds. Nationalistic American writers sometimes portray the Ramones' visit to London as the catalyst for punk's explosion in the United Kingdom. That's a myth. But for Fields, the band's reception confirmed his gut feeling after seeing the boys at CBGB, a seedy club in NYC's Bowery. That while the Ramones might have difficulty reaching the radio airwaves, their live act demonstrated a fanbase existed, hungry for this music. "We always played some place where no band had ever played before," Fields later recalled. "They left a legacy of fans, kids—'no future' people, 'no future.'"[9]

That sobriquet comes a line in "God Save the Queen" (1977) by the Sex Pistols. The American label for these "'no future' people" had been proposed the same year by Richard Hell and the Voidoids: "Blank Generation" (1977). If the Sixties had produced the Now Generation, what would come of the Seventies? "I belong to the ____ generation," Hell squawks, leaving a fill-in-the-blank space, "but I can take it or leave it each time." The Pistols arrived with the United Kingdom's sharp turn rightward that culminated in Margaret Thatcher' election (and her implementation of the nihilistic, atomizing ideology that there's "no such thing as society"). Back with Richard Hell in New York City, disorienting economic adjustments there had preceded an equally sharp conservative turn in the United States. So-called economic stagnation pushed New York to the brink of bankruptcy in 1975, while racist housing practices, systemic disinvestment, and "white flight" contributed to the razing of entire neighborhoods. President Gerald Ford told the city, as interpreted by the *Daily News*, to "drop dead."

As America's largest city neared ruin, the nightmares seemed to accelerate, and Americans celebrated the nation's bicentennial haunted by myriad specters. The United States formally withdrew from Southeast Asia the previous year, bringing to an end an incredibly unpopular war that saw the deaths of over fifty-thousand Americans, and upward of three million total soldiers and civilians in Vietnam, Laos, and Cambodia. Wearing a red robe just a few months later, Manson follower Squeaky Fromme pointed a loaded gun at President Ford in Sacramento; it jammed. Seventeen days later, a woman fascinated by the Symbionese Liberation Army got off a single shot in San Francisco, and the president began appearing in a bullet-proof trench coat. Meanwhile, a parade of events badly shook Americans' confidence in what had previously seemed to be an ever-expanding economy: gas lines and rationing, growing unemployment, wage stagnation coupled with runaway inflation, dubbed "stagflation" by dumbfounded economists who had not believed it theoretically possible.[10]

These nightmares suffused popular culture, reaching their apotheosis (or is that nadir?) in the gritty anti-hero films of 1970s Hollywood. Based on a true story, *Dog Day Afternoon* (1975) told the story of desperate bank robbers laid siege by the police, examining how two losers become heroes to a growing mob of onlookers following their failed heist. There is no music in the film; its soundtrack suffocates you with smothering silence. But it was Martin Scorcese's *Taxi Driver* (1976) that provided the most harrowing depiction of the new anti-hero. Oppressed by the empty, banal violence surrounding him, Robert DeNiro's returned Vietnam veteran descends into violence, murdering a robber, stalking a presidential candidate, executing a pimp and then a john, shaving his hair into a (punkish?) mohawk. Wimpy Jackson Browne's "Late for the Sky" (1974) is the only song in the film, played as DeNiro's character mindlessly watches *American Bandstand* on a small, flickering television in his rathole apartment, the soft rock superstar's mewling underscoring his crippling loneliness, the asocial emptiness of his existence.

If Americans' best days were behind them, others asked, then why not return to the warm, safe embrace of the Fifties? Up-and-coming auteur George Lucas's *American Graffiti* (1973) absolutely drips with feel-good nostalgia. Though set in 1962, this coming-of-age story about a group of teenagers draws heavily on original doo wop and early rock 'n' roll recordings from the late 1950s (as well as a few soundalike recordings by the retro act Flash Cadillac & the Continental Kids). Suddenly rock 'n' roll's past seemed to be everywhere: in the camp homage of the band Sha Na Na (formed in 1969), in the birth of a Golden Oldies radio format, in the revival tours of artists such as Bill Haley, Chuck Berry, and a Las Vegas–bound Elvis Presley.

Historical consciousness about a golden age of American popular culture had diverse sources. Nostalgia coincided with some musicians' efforts to discover roots, musical or otherwise: the Band forsaking paisley for farmer drag on the back of *Big Pink* (1968); Dylan recording in Nashville; the entire phenomenon of country rock. It resonated with rock's autobiographical turn. Recorded in homage to childhood heroes (and to settle a lawsuit with Morris Levy, the copyright holder of Chuck Berry's 1956 "You Can't Catch Me," over the similarity of "Come Together" to that song), *Rock and Roll* (1975) featured thirteen oldies "relived" (as the liner notes put it) by John Lennon.[11] The album cover showed a leather-clad Lennon from his Hamburg days; the photograph by Jurgen Vollmer had been found at a nostalgic Beatles convention.

Figure 9 "We gots just one thing to say to you fuckin' hippies, and that is: 'Rock 'n' Roll Is Here To Stay!'" Sha Na Na's Bowser, introducing track D2, "Rock 'n' Roll Is Here To Stay." Album cover, *The Golden Age of Rock 'n' Roll* (1973) Kama Sutra KSBS 2073-2

But nostalgia also foreshadowed a new critical stance toward the Sixties counterculture. "We gots just one thing to say to you fuckin' hippies," lead vocalist Bowser mock-snarls on Sha Na Na's *Golden Age of Rock 'n' Roll* (1973), "and that is: 'Rock 'n' Roll Is Here To Stay!'"[12]

But what exactly *were* Americans returning to? Formed at Columbia University from an acapella group called the Kingsmen (but not *those* Kingsmen), Sha Na Na performed a campy parody of Fifties music in all its greased-back, streetwise, retrospectively imagined glory. The group had played Woodstock on the recommendation of Jimi Hendrix in 1969; a crack touring outfit, the band later hosted a television variety show from 1977 to 1981. Their repertoire drew heavily on white rock 'n' rollers like Elvis and Jerry Lee Lewis, as well as black doo wop groups such as the Silhouettes, whose nonsense syllables in "Get A Job" (1958) had inspired the group's name.

Their hairstyles, costumes, and stage names, however, suggested a kind of white ethnic stereotyping, which at least a few observers saw as problematic. Some "see the Sha Na Na phenomenon as a manifestation of reactionary decadence, as an expression of an unhealthy desire to return to a less complicated era, or as an idealization of white hoodlumism," an unnamed author had acknowledged in the Columbia College yearbook. "But to those less easily alarmed, Sha Na Na seems to be a loving look—part tribute, part spoof—at rock's origins."[13]

In its heyday, rock 'n' roll had been resolutely presentist, if not forward-looking. Sha-la, la-la-la-la, live for today, and all that. Now rock would begin looking backward. All of a sudden, its history mattered.

* * *

Picture yourself back on campus, eavesdropping on two friends hanging out at the student union.

"You know, they should teach a course in rock 'n' roll," one begins.

"Yeah, it'd be a lotta fun."

"There'd be problems . . . it'd have to be a year, maybe a two year course."

"Come on . . . they teach the whole history of European intellectual thought of political theory in one year—that's 2500 years of material! Rock's fifteen, at most."

"Well, seventeen, if you count *Sixty-Minute Man* by the Dominoes, in 1951. But the thing is, people really *care* about rock 'n' roll, it's part of them, even if they only know it subconsciously, or when it hits them. I mean, who really cares if you leave out Marsilius of Padua. But everyone has their greatest song, and they'd scream if you left it out, and they should. Two years."[14]

This passage comes from *Rock and Roll Will Stand*, one of three books reviewed by Barry Gewen in the June 1970 issue of *Commentary*. At the time, Gewen worked at an anticommunist advocacy group, the International Association for Cultural Freedom, revealed to be a CIA-funded cultural front organization just four years earlier; he would later serve as editor at the *New York Times Books Review*. Two of the books he reviewed were collections of essays, *The Age of Rock: Sounds of the American Cultural Revolution* (1969) edited by Jonathan Eisen and *Rock and Roll Will Stand* (1969) edited by Greil Marcus. The third was a standalone history by Carl Belz. (We encountered the Marcus volume earlier in the prologue, even reading it as Gewen suggests, deriding its substance while proposing that "future historians, after all, will find it useful as an artifact of the youth culture."[15])

Book-length treatments of rock 'n' roll began appearing in the late 1960s. Some were paperback compilations of previously published essays, rushed out quickly with basic prefatory materials and little editing. A few were the products of rock obsessives such as A. J. Weberman, whose pamphlet *Dylanology* first appeared in 1969. (Not only a Dylanologist, combing carefully through the American Yevtushenko's works for hidden messages, Weberman was also a self-described "garbologist" who harassed the singer and rifled through his trash cans. He also served as the self-appointed minister of defense in the Dylan Liberation Front, which sought to "free" Dylan and his message from the capitalist music industry before later evolving into the more general Rock Liberation Front.)[16] The more influential and widely read books, however, attempted to situate rock within a deep social and historical context.

It's this final group of works that most deeply influenced the stories that critics would later write about rock lions such as the Beatles and Dylan. And the most influential voice among these critics would be Greil Marcus. Born in 1945, Marcus majored in American Studies at the University of California at Berkeley. His first music writing appeared in the college newspaper; he later became the first reviews editor at *Rolling Stone*. To Gewen, Marcus and his collaborators represented an "intuitionist" approach to rock: that you just gotta feel the music's true meaning in your gut (though that feeling requires scores of words to imperfectly express). A history of rock following accepted academic practice, as Marcus had written, cannot be possible, because rock "was, is and will be a basic part of the experience, of the growing up years."[17] As an experiential force, the whole of its semantic parts must always be greater than their sum; to properly assess a piece of writing, the reader of rock history should know the historian's personal relationship with the music. (Here's where I admit that my own conflicted, love-hate relationship with rock hagiographies provided an early motivation for writing this book.)

"Can the intuitionists be right—is rock destroyed by the written word?" Gewen asked.[18] *The Story of Rock* by Carl Belz suggested otherwise. An art historian at Brandeis University, the Princeton-trained Belz was thirty-two years old when Oxford University Press published his stylistic overview. It is straight history: basic biography, clear and simple and straightforward in its attempt to introduce the reader (and who exactly is the audience for such a book?) to the major figures in this genre's development. Rereading this bloodless, chronological "story" (it seems even Belz was wary of using the word "history"), the work still feels stale, square. And indeed, this style of writing rock history did turn out to be a dead end. Marcus and the intuitionists won.

By the mid-1970s, intuitionist takes on rock had begun not only expressing their authors' (increasingly middle-aged) enthusiasms, but also building a canon of artists and works. Published in 1975, Marcus's monumental *Mystery Train: Images of America in Rock 'n' Roll Music* wove together radically subjective, idiosyncratic readings of rock's "ancestors" (Robert Johnson, of course, but also the lesser-known Harmonica Frank) and the "inheritors" of their tradition (from the Band, to Sly Stone, to Randy Newman, to Elvis) with snatches of imagined scenes and flights of literary description. In one such fictional passage, Elvis covers Bob Dylan's "I Threw It All Away," a legitimately beautifully bittersweet track off *Nashville Skyline* (1969). In another, Marcus asks us to apply novelist Herman Melville's understanding of the mystery of American democracy to Presley. But really, you can only get a true sense for this approach's virtuosic, literary quality through extended quotations: "Elvis takes his strength from the liberating arrogance, pride, and the claim to be unique that grow out of a rich and commonplace understanding of what 'democracy' and 'equality' are all about: No man is better than I am. He takes his strength as well from the humility, the piety, and the open, self-effacing good humor that spring from the same source: I am better than no man."[19]

The next year, Wenner's imprint Straight Arrow published *The Rolling Stone Illustrated History of Rock and Roll*, a massive tome anthologizing works by dozens of writers. Editor Jim Miller penned its expansive introduction organized around an intuitionist reading of Bob Dylan's recent comeback tour, Rolling Thunder Revue. "It was all there: the social statements (again), the drug anthems, the personal confessions, the evocation of an heroic American past, and this kaleidoscope of folk music past and future, amplified through the medium of rock epitomized for me the music's magic."[20] And yet Miller cannot help but feel cynical, realizing that "this tour had been lofted in a mass of hype and hot air; that Dylan loved indulging in self-conscious mythologizing; that he revealed in the obsequious prose pumped out by such latter-day acolytes as Allen Ginsberg; that the whole tour had been conceived, at least in part, as a glorified scare and mis-en-scene for a movie that would finance itself."

"As for the question: is this for real, for fun, or for money—well, it was for all three, and that's rock and roll. It was *all* there."[21]

Here Miller's narrative shifts abruptly to tell the story of a Polish émigré in West Germany for whom "rock represented a total release from the constraints of the old country." In another context this would be a jarring shift, but the intuitionist approach enables the reader to accept all sorts of connections that a more straightforward history disallows. "A music 'above ideology,'" Miller writes, presumably channeling the teenaged Pole, "it promised fun, immediate gratification, instant glamour and for these reasons, he and his friends, while despairing American imperialism, followed rock avidly: it seemed a bright moment in an otherwise bleak reality."[22]

There are a few threads we can begin taking in hand to make sense of the peculiarly ahistorical kind of historical consciousness at play. History matters, because for rock to assume its full significance, these writers imply, we need to situate it within a longer chronology. And yet the trajectory that really matters is, in some sense, ideological—not stylistic. These authors want to uncover an unbroken line stretching back from the present to a prior condition of liberation. In this reading, rock 'n' roll demonstrates a kind of political continuity: the music is endowed with an intellectual honesty through its commitment to freedom, a commitment that sometimes waxes and sometimes wanes, especially under the stresses of the capitalist music industry, but never completely disappears.

Yet in reading Miller, we can sense some ambivalence. Rock once had a golden period—but has that period now ended forever? Does the music's political power still free Americans in the same way, for instance, it might a young Polish defector? And what's even the point? Why translate into words an expressive form that moves you in non-rational ways, that functions outside language as a feeling, an experience, an urge?

The idea that rock has always had this political constancy—as an expression of authenticity and realness, albeit churning beneath the level of explicit ideology—drives the historical imagination of the intuitionists. But what if they had it all wrong? What if there had not been a smooth trajectory from the Fifties to the Sixties to the present? What if the political purpose of rock had been betrayed? And what if this happened when Dylan started making rock poetry, and the Beatles, rock art?

* * *

In 1972, Jann Wenner called in critic Lester Bangs for a meeting. Born in 1948, Bangs had grown up in a lower-middle-class family in Southern California. His first freelance gigs had been with *Rolling Stone*, where he quickly became notorious for his scathingly sharp barbs, such as describing Black Sabbath as "like Cream! But worse." (Well that's just nitpicking, isn't it?) He'd later claim to have never fit in at a magazine where, as he remembered it, he'd argued (correctly, I should interject) that "*Anthem of the Sun* by the Grateful Dead and *Sailor* by Steve Miller were pieces of shit and *White Light/White Heat* by the Velvet Underground and Nico's *The Marble Index* were masterpieces."[23] Wenner delivered the bad news swiftly, firing Bangs for being "disrespectful" to musicians. The final straw had been a mocking essay about Canned Heat.[24]

Bangs soon moved over to *Creem*, a new rock mag that like its brethren, *Flash*, *Who Put the Bomp?*, *Fusion*, *Cheetah*, or *Back Door Man*, sometimes trod the line between fanzine and something just a smidge more professional. Reviewers in these magazines often slayed the sacred cows of the Sixties and post-Sixties rock establishment, praising the less cerebral hard rockers of the

Seventies with articles (according to the tagline of *Back Door Man*) "for hard core Rock'n'Rollers only!"

The stereotype is that *Rolling Stone* completely missed rock's harder, faster punk turn, their writers' soft-focus emphasis on singer-songwriters and arena-rocking Sixties geriatrics rendering them incapable of hearing the good news. Their coverage of more straight-ahead bands did sometimes get it right, at least according to the new critical standard emerging at their upstart competitors. Writing in the *Stone*, critic Ed Ward correctly assessed the significance of a 1969 debut album from a Detroit-based quartet calling themselves the Stooges. "They are a *reductio ad absurdum* of rock and roll that might have been though up by a mad D.A.R. [development of artists and repertoire] general in a wet dream," Ward wrote. "They suck, and they know it, so they throw it back in your face and say, 'So what? We're just havin' fun.'"[25] But describing the fast, aggressive new style that would come to be called punk in late 1977, another *Rolling Stone* critic whiffed, calling it "music that could not stand the test of time [as had] Presley, Berry, the Beatles, Dylan and many, many more."[26]

Now the Ramones didn't describe their music as "punk," but as "real rock 'n' roll," and Sha Na Na could be jokingly described in 1972 as "punk music," invoking the American sense of the word suggesting juvenile delinquency.[27] Despite being this genre label's foremost champion, Lester Bangs himself applied the term "punk" in pretty idiosyncratic ways. Reviewing a live show by the Guess Who (the *Guess Who*, for chrissakes!), Bangs called the Canadians "real punks without even working too hard at it." He once even praised James Taylor as "a real *punk*" (a tongue-in-cheek usage, for sure), because "he just sits around and gets fucked up all the time, just like most of us, and I betcha when he's not being a Sensitive Genius he's a getdown dude who don't give a shit about nothin'."[28]

It is difficult to overestimate the influence of Bangs on how we came to talk about rock from the mid-Seventies onward. His style inspired a generation of young, male critics. His writing spoke directly to readers who gagged at the "prehistorically pretentious rockwriting" by "counter-culture totalitarians," as one follower wrote in a retrospective remembrance, people like "Jon Landau expending thousands of words to explain why *Dr. Byrds And Mr. Hyde* was just a so-so album, or Ralph J. Gleason wheezing old-left phlegm over The Band's Daguerreotypes of American life."[29]

Bangs theorized that the power of rock resided in the loud and the untutored, in bands that best expressed—unmediated—their members' collective id in visceral, first-take recordings and stripped-down, shambolic live performances.[30] Describing the Stooges, Bangs praised "music that was totally impossible to ignore and successful on its own aboriginal terms: hypnotic repetitions of a single thunderous chord at a volume that would reduce dogs to agony, over which Iggy would croon and bark and shriek improvised gut-level ditties about adolescent torments in a voice rather like some henbane mutant shade of Mick Jagger." Unselfconsciously primitive and raw, repetitive and amusical to a fault, and not only that, but slavishly imitative to prior models of rock-as-body music: "identity-crisis music on a perhaps too-basic level, it was as extreme in its aggressive neurosis as everything else about the Stooges," Bangs continued. "If ever there was a band predicated upon extremism on all levels, this was it."[31]

The sound cannot be separated from the ethos, Bangs claimed, with each gaining meaning through that mutually constitutive "extremism." It changed you, affected you, something recognized early on by members of legitimate artistic circles. Andy Warhol and his retinue, for instance, hung out at CBGB, where bands like the Ramones "just played really short, and really fast songs," remembered photographer Roberta Bayle, who worked the doors, "but they were really serious about it, it was almost like conceptual art or something."[32] "Fer me, it's all food," Bangs himself said in a 1974 interview with Metal Mike Saunders, a fellow critic who had earned this sobriquet by christening bands like Humble Pie ("27th-rate heavy metal crap") or Lord Baltimore (a band that "seems to have down pat most all the best heavy metal tricks in the book").[33] Bangs continued: "Rock is art, art is rock, rock is cock, rock is sock hop jukejoint moptop pud blood."[34]

Now if a definition of rock as sock-hop-jukejoint-moptop-pud-blood only makes sense at a sub-cerebral level, well that's because rock itself only made sense at that level. The new critics recognized this, even theorized it. "Unlike rock & roll, rock criticism was born genteel, the product of kids who attended Dartmouth, Brandeis, Swarthmore and Berkeley," Dave Marsh wrote in an "Obituary of Rock and Roll" published in *Rolling Stone* in 1979. "That's always been the contradiction between the music and what's written about it: while rock is most natural when it's most vulgar, in criticism vulgarity inevitably seems a pose."[35]

We'll touch briefly on the second part of this idea a bit later by meeting a few critics, Bangs included, who gave up the artifice of *writing* about rock for the authenticity of *making* it. But first, the music's natural state: vulgarity. "The truth of the matter is this: The Dave Clark 5 deserve a place in Rock & Roll Heaven right along there beside Question Mark & The Mysterians, the Standells, Count Five, the Troggs, and the Music Machine," Metal Mike Saunders wrote in *Flash* (1972). "And they had more good songs than any of these groups too! So you have to start from the beginning—the first good song of the DC5's endless many—which puts us back in early 1964."[36] Nineteen-sixty-four: the Beatles had not yet gone folk, Dylan had not yet gone electric, rock 'n' roll had not yet shed its status as trash to become art. The bands that Saunders cites represent a counter-canon, a golden age cut short by LSD and sitars, by the Summer of Love, by just plain seriousness.

But what if the music had never grown up? What if rock 'n' roll never became rock?

To excavate this alternative history, critics such as Saunders or Bangs or Marsh visited two sites. The first included the rhythm and blues and early rock 'n' roll of black recording artists such as Chuck Berry. We encountered nostalgia for this music just a few pages back; we have already heard John Lennon (*Beatle John*, fer chrissakes!) claim that "the thing about rock & roll, good rock & roll . . . is that it's *real*." But that first site would not be nearly as fruitful as this second one: white garage rock bands from the early Sixties. The most conscientious curator of this music, Lenny Kaye, began assembling *Nuggets: Original Artyfacts from the First Psychedelic Era 1965–1968* (1972) for Elektra as a record store clerk in New York City. Across four LP sides, Kaye's compilation introduced listeners to regional guitar bands that, despite never quite making it, had now begun to enjoy a second life as cult favorites: the Amboy Dukes, the Barbarians, the 13th Floor Elevators, the Count Five. A superfan, Kaye had wanted to release eight LPs, or sixteen sides. His liner notes, ascribing scant political significance to the music, instead focused on its inchoate, intuitive feeling for rebellion. The groups were "young, decidedly unprofessional, seemingly more at home practicing for a teen dance than going out on national tour," Kaye wrote. And here he pastes on the new genre label: "The name that has been unofficially coined for them 'punk-rock' seems particularly fitting in this case, for if nothing else they exemplified the berserk pleasure that comes with being on-stage outrageous, the relentless middle-finger drive and determination offered only by rock and roll at its finest."[37]

For Kaye, the music represented pure nostalgia, unmarked by questions of race and social class. The compilation helped you "remember that bittersweet moment when you first decided to let your hair grow / take up a picket sign / wonder what a deadly toke would feel like, or just welcome yourself into some surprisingly fine and memorable music, well, that's 'your trip.'" For Bangs, the music's transcendence had serious real political weight. He could sound positively Greilian, and at his most earnest could out-Greil even Marcus. He described a Munich-based commune's first album, for instance, as "an organic expression of certain young Germans learning, as their peers all over the world are, to relate to themselves and their own freedom in totally new ways, to translate that freedom into a new free music like nothing heard on the planet heretofore, and to totally oppose anyone or anything that stands in the way of the attainment and ongoing sensation of that freedom."[38]

Yet Bangs swaddled his analyses so tightly in layers of irony and gauzy, gonzo prose that for a moment it makes you wonder whether it isn't all a shuck, a goose in the anus. In a letter to British radio presenter Charles Gillett, author of an early serious rock history, *The Sound of the City: The Rise of Rock and Roll* (1970), for instance, Bangs imagines an extended scenario starring *Nuggets* darlings, the Count Five. You should read the entire piece, published only posthumously. But here are the highlights: The CIA bans the Count Five's album, *Psychotic Reaction* (1966), for political subversion, forcing Columbia Records president Clive Davis to destroy all unsold units; American soldiers are purchasing "Japanese pressings available in Bargain Bins throughout Southeast Asia"; the Vietcong "plays the shit out of all the Count Five albums, since they're such perfect fodder for Communist propaganda" (read: anti-American propaganda); the author advises readers to write Pyongyang's Foreign Publishing House for copies ("I can't think of a better Christmas gift than copies of *Psychotic Reaction, Carburetor Dung, Cartesian Jetstream* [by the Count Five] and *The Democratic People's Republic of Korea is the Banner of Freedom and Independence For Our People and the Powerful Weapon of Building Socialism and Communism* by Kim Il Sung").[39]

All that said, we actually don't need to read between the lines to understand Bangs's theory of freedom. He outlined it in his most celebrated essay, "Of Pop & Pies & Fun: A Program Of Mass Liberation In The Form Of A Stooges Review, or, Who's The Fool?" (1972).[40] The essay is unabashedly anti-rock star. Bangs praises Stooges singer Iggy Pop, "a preeminently Amerikan kid, singing songs about growing up in Amerika, about being hung up lotsa the time (as who hasn't been?), about confusion and doubt and uncertainty, about inertia and boredom and suburban pubescent darkness." He mock's the singer's inspiration, Mick Jagger, for being "a fake moneybags revolutionary, and in general for acting smarter and hipper and like more of a cultural and fashion arbiter than he really is."

"A Brief History Lesson" frames this critique. In the beginning there were groups like Lenny Kaye's favorite group, ? And the Mysterians, a band who to many commentators "seemed to represent everything simpleminded and dead-endish about rock." British mods thought they had found one path forward. Ex-folkies ("a buncha fuckin' effete snobs") thought they had found another. They "all got electric guitars and started mixing all the musics stored in their wee-educated little beans up together, and before we knew it we had Art-rock." Drenched in acid and bloated by artistic pretension, that's where things stalled.

So how could the music progress? Avant-garde free jazz represented one way. A few rock groups, such as the Velvet Underground with their experiments in noise, suggested another. "What was suddenly becoming apparent," Bangs concluded, "was that there was no reason why you couldn't play truly free music to a basic backbeat, gaining the best of both worlds." Bands such as the Stooges did this and, in making this "truly free music," suggested "The Outline of Cure." Their sound "comes out of a primal illiterate chaos gradually taking shape as a uniquely personal style, emerges from a tradition of American music that runs from the primordial wooly rags of backwoods bands up to the magic promise eternally made and occasionally fulfilled by rock: that a band can start out bone-primitive, untutored and uncertain, and evolve into a powerful and eloquent ensemble."

But once you had seen the light, what were you supposed to do? Bangs offered one solution, an option he believed the "smug post-hippie audience, supposedly so loose, liberated, righteous and ravenous, the anarchic terror of middle American insomnia" were too scared to take: get up on stage yourself. "And how many times have you heard people say of bands: 'Man, what a shuck! *I* could get up there and cut that shit.'" Bangs did this in the years preceding his early death, cutting a single, "Let it Blurt/Live" (1979); recording a chaotic session with Mickey Leigh (brother of Joey Ramone) as Birdland, released posthumously as *"Birdland" with Lester Bangs*; and briefly fronting an Austin punk band, the Delinquents, on *Jook Savages on the Brazos* (1981). Critic Richard Meltzer, too, would form a band, VOM (that is, "vomit"). Metal Mike Saunders would have the most success, though I guess that's relative, with a group we'll meet later called the Angry Samoans.

The remainder of the review, and it's all-told a whopping nine-thousand words, subjects the Stooges album, *Fun House*, to a track-by-track close reading. "In Desolation Row and Woodstock-Altamont Nation the switchblade is mightier and speaks more eloquently than the penknife," Bangs concluded. "But this threat is cathartic, a real cool time is had by all, and the end is liberation."

* * *

If to some rock music potentially provided a program for liberation, its practice radically democratic, not everyone agreed. The new bands had "a raucous, mock violent sound," *New York Times* columnist William Safire wrote, that "rapes the eardrum," and the "brief and meteoric emergence of punk is rooted in a satiric reminder of the potential for brutality that lurks in every one of us."[41] Would this "faddist fascist fashion," Safire asks, endure? Fascism—surely that's an exaggeration that could only be dreamed up by a deeply conservative mind.

"What we're going to do is get lots of—what do you call them? . . . allies—in key positions and um, if you get somebody that works for the post office, I mean somebody that's just even a mail clerk, you can really screw the post office up bad," Darby Crash told one zine in 1980. "If you go to the newspapers and they have those big machines, you know, that print them and you shoot a rubber band into it . . . it rips the paper; it ruins the whole day's edition. So if you can get enough people to do that, you can go to the government and say, 'Well, you've got the armies, but we can just stop this country from working.'"

"We're trying to get Reverend Moon to back us to go over to China . . . so he'll just say, 'I'll show them how decadent America is, we'll put these people up here to play on this wall and they'll make fools out of themselves.' And after that we're going to play the Berlin Wall, right? Is that the next one? Any more walls we can play?"[42]

Born Paul Beahm in 1958, Crash never played the Berlin Wall with his influential Los Angeles punk band, the Germs. He died of a lethal heroin dose nearly nine years to the day before it fell. Crash had met bandmate Pat Smear (né Georg Ruthenberg) in an alternative program at University High in Hollywood in the mid-Seventies. The school's program sounds like something straight out of a Tom Wolfe satire. Influenced by both est, or Erhard Seminar Training, as well as Scientology, the program attracted "weirdos and drug addicts," one former student remembered, who took classes in everything from English to Tai Chi.[43] The motto of its founder, Caldwell Williams, was "Find yourself—find your frame."[44] A veteran counsellor, Williams cut his teeth in a late-Sixties afterschool program, DAWN (Developing Adolescents Without Narcotics), which emerged from the post–Summer of Love drug panic with a West Coast twist. "The basic emotional needs of humans," Williams's colleague had told the Congressional sub-committee convened to tackle youth drug use, "are two in number: (1) love; (2) self esteem."[45]

Smear/Ruthenberg and Crash/Beahm had a different perspective. "The teachers were attempting to brainwash us, while teaching us brainwashing techniques," Smear recalled. "Meanwhile, we were taking *tons* of acid and acting out as wannabe-rock stars."[46] Beahm's personal journey to love and self-esteem first manifested in an obsession with David Bowie. He dressed like him and wrote poems about him; he worshiped him, even making a shrine to the British glam rock star. "He looked at *Ziggy Stardust* as the *Mein Kampf* of pop," a friend claimed, a blueprint for total (rock) domination. David Bowie, then deep in his Thin White Duke persona, might have agreed. Promoting *Young Americans* (1976), the glam rock star slammed the average American's "plastic soul." Postwar US politics represented a "ghost force liberalism permeating the air in America," he said, which had run its course. The United States now required "an extreme right front [to] come up and sweep everything off its feet ... [and] you can get a new form of liberalism."[47]

Cocaine may be a hell of a drug, but its effects only heightened, did not invent, the dark dreams of domination haunting proto-punk's glitter-infused turn. "Whip me, hurt me," Iggy Pop screamed during an infamously bloody performance at Rodney Bingenheimer's Los Angeles club in 1974, egging on a whip-wielding Stooge, guitarist Ron Asheton, at the time wearing his Nazi dress uniform; the singer ended up in the hospital after carving into his own chest a ragged X.[48] In retelling how he dodged the Vietnam draft, Alice Cooper frontman Vince Furnier too tapped into dark fantasies of control. Asked about his professional goals, Furnier told the board he daydreamed about locking listeners in a darkened hall, shocking them with electricity, blinding them with strobes, even dosing them with semen. "At that point you suggest an action," Furnier said. "For instance, 'fuck' or 'dance.' Mass hypnotism."[49]

For the teenaged dropouts, runaways, and burnouts in punk scenes bubbling up throughout the United States, the flipside to these reveries of domination were fantasies of freedom, with punk music, fashion, and dancing representing a compelling program for emancipation. Los Angeles punks initially met at the Masque, a West Hollywood club that opened in August 1977. "The fashion was amazing, the music loud and crazy and pretty much like nothing I'd ever heard before," Ann Summa, a participant and photographer who documented this scene later recalled. "It felt like a revolution."[50] This revolution naturally found expression in young people, recalls Exene Cervenka, singer in X, the scene's most commercially successful band: "we were all the same freedom-loving rebels, doing our job as young people do—changing and destroying, creating and rebuilding culture."[51]

Rebellion, revolution, and liberation have become the tropes that early punk participants lean on in interviews and memoirs telling and retelling (and re-retelling) the music's origins. No style of postwar American music has been so heavily documented through the genre of oral history, and especially in collections such as Legs McNeil and Gillian McCain's *Please Kill Me: The Uncensored History of Punk* (1996). Between 1976 and 1979, McNeil helmed fifteen issues of the early fanzine *Punk*. His retrospective accounts have helped formulate one dominant narrative about punk and hardcore music in the United States. "I mean the great thing about punk was that it had no political agenda," McNeil claims in *Please Kill Me*. "It was about real freedom, personal freedom. It was also about doing anything that's gonna offend a grown-up.

Just being as offensive as possible. Which seemed delightful, just euphoric. Be the real people we are. You know?"[52]

How did this "real freedom" work in practice? From scene to scene (and even month to month, it sometimes seems in perusing early fanzines), ideas about punk's revolutionary potential for freedom-making could shift quite radically. Staying in Los Angeles to read *Flipside*, one of the earliest and longest-running punk zines, we can sketch some typical (rather than exceptional) ways that participants raised problems about "freedom" on the West Coast. A few high school friends in Whittier, California, a predominantly white suburb about a thirty-minute car ride east of Los Angeles, founded *Flipside* in 1977. By the early 1980s, the fanzine had more than doubled in size from its first issue's twenty black-and-white typescript pages to include record reviews, advertisements, semi-regular columns, and reader letters. It's this last category that in DIY zines takes up the most space; through countless page and often across multiple issues, readers argued, shared information, complained about their lame high schools, and invented and policed norms of conduct.

Flipside 39, as the editorial by founder Al puts it, represents "6 years since we started in the summer of hate, 1977."[53] "1st off I'll say I've kind of been in the scene since the Masque days," one letter-writer begins before listing off the bands he's played in, "so I guess I'm qualified to have an opinion. I also am a definite individual (never having really gotten into the trendy social fun) so my opinion could be wrong." Then comes his question to the scene at large: "You seem to think that Punk is in someway failing in its purpose, what is its purpose?"[54]

And what is its purpose? "In my mind punk is and always has been a chosen lifestyle in which your very existence is making the statement that you won't be one of the system's little disco-clones and that you will be exactly who you want to be," the author writes. "To me it seems that being a punk means you gotta believe in Individualism (isn't that what Anarchy is) and I think most of us do (in social [terms] at least)."[55] This question of purpose generates conflicting answers. A few pages later, a reader using the handle Gail Butchette poses the opposite view. Anarchy works only if everyone is peace-loving, she writes, but that is not the case. What should happen if a mentally ill person murders your mother? Or with the "morbid idiot" who tortures animals? "We have to remember that not 'all cops are bastards,'" Gail says. "The USA may not be perfect but if you truly think about it, it's the best country in existence."[56] Hmmm.

Taken as a whole, the letters and editorials and polemics seem to suggest there's really no way out. "Alot of punk bands out there sing about Big Brother and 1984 and Government control and all that shit. How many times have you seen 'Please Fuck The System Now,'" editor Al writes in another of his opening editorials. "Well what are you going to do about it?"[57] He tells readers to stop sending checks, a financial instrument of the surveillance state, and start sending cash. "Fucking the system starts at home," he concludes, before repeating himself. "One more thing I must dwell on again briefly—that is the fact that we are individuals."[58]

In giving these debates a forum, the founders of zines such as *Flipside* sought to cohere their scenes, to build community. And in a way that really could be democratic: everyone (potentially) has a voice. But in practice, scenes were not always paragons of inclusion. Available only to those who knew better than the brainwashed "disco clones," membership itself rested on a principle of gendered and racialized exclusion. And while the earlier, artsier Los Angeles scene provided spaces for women, people of color, and queer punks, its expansion across Southern California whitened performances, fueling them with testosterone, the aggression infusing the dancing, the speed, the volume, the lyrics.

And as theory, the do-it-yourself imperative often slipped into foregrounding a post-Sixties truism: that politics was personal, an individual responsibility that you either opted into or not. The potential for countercultural change, in the sense of creating an alternative from the mainstream status quo, comes from the overall accretion of small, quotidian practices. "Anarchism was not just utopian," historian Kevin Mattson writes, "but also prefigurative, that is, the act of writing the future in present-day activities."[59] But did that future ever arrive for these no-future people?

The interminable navel-gazing may have in some ways inhibited the consolidation of durable political meanings in these scenes. Debate could become an end in itself, an opportunity to express your individuality in ways that proved counterproductive. Arguing about "correct" behavior, indeed, could even splinter scenes. Adherence to norms, meanwhile, ensured a measure of conformity, with all people sharing the impulse to rebel in ways that made sense to the group. I saw three guys "walking around cocksure with shirts with anarchy signs on one side of their shirts and swastikas on the other," one *Flipside* letter-writer reported. "The dumbfucks seem to think fascism is anarchy."[60] Don't you think that maybe they're just trying to upset you? responded an editor. "I think there's a new breed of kids who are trying to irritate the old punks, fuck, they know what they're doing . . . it's what you call Shock-value . . . in other words, I don't think they believe in anything."[61]

What are you rebelling against? What do you got? "En masse, they are scuttling like lemmings to their idea of individuality," William Safire had mocked, "that is, the uniform of the nonconformist, in the regiment of the unregimented."[62] And this is the problem with individualizing political responsibility in general. But luckily, not all scenes left organizing up to the lemmings.

"If more people thought the way you do, this scene would be a lot better," Michelle and Lynn wrote to Tim Yohannon at San Francisco's *Maximum Rocknroll* in 1982. "People go around talking about anarchy and freedom, those same people don't think about the responsibility that goes along with it."[63] Could punks really organize into a political movement able to take the reins of state power in Amerikkka?

* * *

A disheveled crowd clustered on the steps of Town Hall in downtown San Francisco. Their candidate had just arrived, as he put it, for "shaking babies and kissing hands." One supporter held a placard that read "Apocalypse Now, Vote Biafra," and another, "Vote Jello, Because Conformity is Death." In a field of ten, his main opponents were Dianne Feinstein, the wealthy Democrat serving out George Moscone's term following his assassination, and Quentin Kopp, a long-serving conservative on the Board of Supervisors. Despite the first-time punk candidate's inexperience, his campaign literature claimed that "Jello Biafra is no more a joke than anyone else running this year."

Of course, the Dead Kennedys singer's platform really was a joke, a put-on in the classic American tradition of radical dissent. Biafra promised to make businessmen wear clown costumes to work. He pledged to erect a statue of Dan White, the killer cop who had assassinated both Moscone and Harvey Milk, so the Parks Department could sell eggs and rotten fruit for people to hurl at it. When Feinstein took a broom to the streets to figuratively sweep them clean, Biafra took a handheld vacuum to her wealthy neighborhood. When Feinstein promised to enact tough new vagrancy laws, Biafra promised to legalize squatting.

Jello Biafra's stage name juxtaposed the sickly-sweet American consumer product with the short-lived war-torn West African nation and its humanitarian crisis. The band's name, of course, referenced those martyred white liberals, Bobby and Jack. Read together, they evoked the symbolic death of the Sixties: the foreclosed dream of American liberals for a prosperous peace and unbridled economic growth. Dead Kennedys' first single, "Holiday in Cambodia" (1979), indicts an ineffectual, lame-duck Seventies liberalism. Biafra imagines sending to the killing fields of Cambodia a coddled white college student, a post–New Left wimp reveling in his discovery of the dispossessed by sitting in his dorm room listening to "ethnicky jazz" and telling anyone who'll listen that he understands "how the niggers feel cold / and the slums got so much soul."

Biafra's gift as a lyricist lies in how deftly he articulates the bland vacuity of post-Woodstock liberalism with so many other, more obvious horrors. Dead Kennedys' *Fresh Fruit for Rotting Vegetables* (1980) juxtaposes the softer ugliness of liberal pieties with their more muscular conservative counterparts, the banality of quotidian experience in the United States with the spectacularly overt violence of the American state. Each carefully chosen word packs maximum satirical punch. We're not going to just kill landlords, we'll lynch them. Then we'll spray mustard gas, stolen from a US Army depot, over a posh country club ("watch 'em die chokin' shakin'"). Serial killers, assassinations, and the rolling dirty wars of post-Vietnam American imperialism suffuse this 12-inch nightmare. And its album cover, a car burning at the San Francisco riots following assassin Dan White's acquittal, reminds us that the rot has come home.

If Biafra's Dead Kennedys stirred the Northern California scene's political energies, then Tim Yohannan' *Maximumrocknroll* zine channeled them. Born in 1945, Yohannan was a decade or so older than most punks on the West Coast. He had caucused with the New Left in the Sixties before defecting; Fifties West Coast Beat legend Lawrence Ferlinghetti funded several of his early ventures. The first issue of *MRR* appeared in 1982. Its cover featured Dave Diktor of MDC ("Millions of Dead Cops") as well as a rough collage of Klansmen alongside Ronald Reagan drawing back a white hood. Its opening manifesto posed Tim Yo's mission statement in the form of a riddle:

Q: "What has two legs, hangs out on street corners, panhandles, sells dope, says 'That's cool, man', is apolitical, anti-historical, anti-intellectual, and just wanted to get fucked-up and have a good time."
A: "A Hippie? Nope, a punk!"

In Yohannon's historical narrative, punk emerged as a rejection of the "failures" of the Sixties counterculture and its "hipeoise," a class "decimated by drugs, cults, and greediness" in the Seventies. But the movement had failed to learn from the recent past. "The co-optation," Yohannon suggests, "is well under way." To be truly free requires us to challenge dominant social structures by demonstrating our ideological unity. "If the system stresses anti-intellectualism," Yohannon argues, "we must become intellectuals. If it stresses isolation and ignorance of each other, then we must learn to trust. If it stresses individualism, we must collect ourselves." And what role would music play? "Unfortunately, in a basically illiterate society such as ours," Yohannon concludes, "music is one of the only ways new ideas get disseminated, and it is within this sphere that the real battles for minds are being fought."[64]

How would collective action work in practice? Complaining that not enough punks attended demonstrations (maybe they were turned off by "the decidedly 60's cultural atmosphere"), *MRR* suggested the zine could organize "punk contingents." Because even the direct action that had been taking place needed to expand. A column titled "Know Your Weapon" acknowledged that the San Francisco scene was political from the beginning, holding local benefits for striking blue-collar workers, raising money for the Black Panthers, even participating "in a direct assault on the state" during the riots following White's acquittal. But the fight had grown larger, had gone global. (The example used here is genocide in Palestine, funded by American tax dollars siphoned from domestic programs at home via "capitalist austerity.")[65] What is to be done?

Many punks agreed with *MRR*'s general analysis. One wrote a letter listing all the things he "hates": money, Bank of America, and "the media and the mind control for which it stands," but also "Patriotism, Communism, Capitalism, Catholicism, Protestantism, Judaism, Socialism, Democracy, Totalitarianism, Monarchies, Sentimentalism, and all other -isms and -cies and un-'s and suffixes and prefixes that move our minds on an Orwellian chessboard with that sham of a language." (*MRR*'s response? Find a therapist—or a girlfriend.)[66] But others found the sloganeering stifling, a form of oppressive political correctness. Hardcore singer Dave Smalley, active with East Coast bands in the Boston and Washington DC scenes, for instance, called the West Coast political punks "fascists of the left" and *MRR* a "horrible, hatemongering, isolationist, left-wing fascist magazine."[67]

Internecine struggles could be exacerbated by the incestuous structures of these scenes. In retrospective accounts, participants often fondly recall sitting on grungy apartment floors stuffing singles, or photocopying and distributing zines. And for sure, some people were remarkably supportive of other acts. In Los Angeles, the fanzine *Slash* (1977), which championed local groups like Bags, the Screamers, and the Weirdos, led to Slash Records (1978), which released albums by Germs and X. From this DIY platform, X even made it onto *American Bandstand* in 1982, with Exene gifting a vintage button reading "I Love Dick Clark" to its ageless host. But good luck if, like critic-turned-punk-rocker Metal Mike Saunders and his SoCal band Angry Samoans, you found yourself on the outs. After their single "Get Off The Air" (1980) crudely mocked Los Angeles scene-maker Rodney Bingenheimer, radio stopped playing their records. Venues even boycotted them, Saunders has claimed, after larger bands such as X told promoters they wouldn't play clubs that booked the Samoans.

Yet when bands looked beyond their local contexts, they did find a network of like-minded activists ready to be organized. At the national level many punks found a common enemy following the ascension of the Moral Majority and the election of Ronald Reagan. Released by Biafra and East Bay Ray's Alternative Tentacles label, *Let Them Eat Jellybeans!* (1981) featured punk and hardcore bands from across the United States. Its cover features a smiling Reagan (he famously loved jellybeans) giving the thumbs-up in front of the stars-and-stripes. Its subtitle, *17 Extracts From America's Darker Side*, and its insert, a near-exhaustive list of North American bands, suggested the country's conservative turn as the primary context that made punk make sense as a political movement.

The most organized mobilization of this movement at the national level happened in 1984. The Rock Against Reagan tour shadowed the president's re-election campaign, rallying protesters and raising money to register voters. Dead Kennedys, as well as bands such as MDC, the Dicks, and Dirty Rotten Imbeciles, provided the strongest draw, though they also booked local bands at each stop. (The Dallas concert featured G-Spot, for instance, a Tulsa band that claimed they'd arrived a year or so earlier to stage a re-enactment of JFK's assassination.)

Figure 10 "And there was a seven-hour punk concert, 'Rock against Reagan,' featuring such artists as The Dead Kennedys. *I left my heart in San Francisco*... But that was the kind of effluvium that is to be found, in more diluted form perhaps, in half a dozen other large American cities," in *National Review* (10 August 1984). Concert bill, *Rock Against Reagan* (1984)

Rarely were the political messages at these events subtle. The Crucifucks from East Lansing, Michigan, taunted local law enforcement with songs like "Cops for Fertilizer" (1984). "Hinkley Had a Vision" (1984) namechecked the president's would-be assassin, a man who had sought to impress the actress Jodie Foster after becoming obsessed with her character in *Taxi Driver* (1976). Its lyric mocks Reagan's evangelical supporters, the "superstitious spastic fools" who "live for everlasting life / and ruin my life here on earth." In its final verse, these Christian supporters open a trash bag to find the president's severed head.

Such sentiments brought the Rock Against Reagan campaign notoriety, even if local news stations refused to broadcast the bands' performances. And this raised a problem. How shocking was too shocking? In 1983, MDC retired the meaning of their acronym, "Millions of Dead Cops," in response to the objections of pacifist punks; they'd later cycle through variations such as "Mega-Death Corporation" or "Millions of Damn Christians" (used on 1987's *This Blood's For You*, which even featured a Cream cover). How many Americans agreed with their song, "John Wayne Was A Nazi" (1982)? Even if you agreed with the first two-thirds of the chant on "Born to Die" (1982), what about the last third? "No war! No KKK! *No fascist U.S.A!*"

Of course, none of this is to suggest that hardcore music was inherently antifascist, never mind enlightened. Some punks wore swastikas as part of the ultimate put-on, an immaturity and political dead-end challenged by DK's slogan-song, "Nazi Punks Fuck Off" (1983)—though the misogyny and, especially, homophobia deployed in the service of shocking listeners rarely received such immediate, resounding condemnation. Hardcore music also increasingly provided the soundtrack for fringe white nationalist, skinhead, and neo-Nazi movements during the 1980s, both in the United States and abroad.[68]

Still, events such as Rock Against Reagan did foster the kind of political solidarity that Tim Yohannan envisioned for punk. But others worried, as one punk told *MRR*, that guerrilla theater functioned as "a sort of pacifier, in the sense that people participate, release their anger concerning the topic at hand, and return to their normal lives without having accomplished anything."[69] That's the real function, a cynic would say, of artistic critique. It's why some conservatives didn't lose much sleep over the punk rock protests. William F. Buckley's *National Review* viewed the Rock Against Reagan shows at the Republican National Convention as merely part of the general anti-Reagan "effluvium," dismissing the bands along with an "All Species Parade" featuring people in silly costumes, a "pair of radical lesbian feminists" who disrupted a conservative family values meeting with a long passionate kiss, and "a bunch of transvestites in nun costumes [who] performed an exorcism of Jerry Falwell."[70]

A few pages later, *National Review* noted with a healthy measure of smug self-satisfaction that "Ronald Reagan receives his strongest support from the same demographic group that has grown up with rock 'n' roll." The mainstream media has ignored this fact, however, perhaps because for liberal journalists, "rock is institutionally rebellious." But change was in the air. "The leftist anthems of teenage rebellion that Led Zeppelin, The Who, and the Rolling Stones churned out a decade ago now sound silly and pretentious," the *National Review* continued.[71] With the "trendy leftism of the late Sixties and Seventies" fading, toward what political projects might rock turn?

* * *

Now it's 1978, and Jello Biafra is goose-stepping around the stage of the Mabuhay Gardens. Formerly home to a Filipino Elvis impersonator, the Mab had just started booking bands playing this faster, louder, more aggressive style. But Reagan isn't yet on Biafra's radar. He's raising his arm in a mock-Nazi salute to a future President Jerry Brown.

The liberal California governor had finished third at the 1976 Democratic National Convention; he would challenge the Democratic incumbent, Jimmy Carter, for the nomination in 1980. Brown was suave, so West Coast—he was even dating soft rock singer-songwriter Linda Ronstadt. And in "California Über Allës" (1979), Jello Biafra painted a harrowing portrait of his coming liberal dystopia. President Brown forces children to meditate. His stormtroopers (the "suede-denim secret police") spirit away the unhip to concentration camps. He murders citizens using "organic poison gas." And most chillingly, in my view, he makes everyone jog.

As usual, Jello Biafra was both dead wrong—and completely right. Brown failed to primary President Carter; a Senate defeat two years later torpedoed his political career. But the sick vision of a world in which liberals shift all responsibilities onto citizens—to meditate and to jog, to help themselves first because the public sector has been completely hollowed out—sounds a lot like today's United States.

It's too easy, too facile to divide rock into "good" and "bad" politics, with the "good" championing liberal causes and challenging conservative ones, and the bad doing the opposite. In part, that's because at their core, post-Seventies politics—both left and right—depend on an unexamined, radical foundation of individualism. That's not to say that conservatives and liberals espouse the same ideas, but that each side has come to share in common an emphasis on personal experience and individual agency. "Exponents of sixties liberationism had stressed that the personal was political," the historian Philip Jenkins summarizes. "Conservatives accepted this equation and carried it much further: the realm of personal moral choice was indistinguishable from that of national politics, law and order, defense and diplomacy. And in each of these areas, good and evil mattered."[72]

Of course, rock got real again in part by refusing to take itself all that seriously. "All of us liked music a lot; we just didn't *care* that much about it," an editor at *Creem* recently reminisced. "Everyone thinks they've got to treat this like they're honest to God reviewing the works of Mark Twain, or something. This stuff is disposable. It comes and it goes. For people to sit around and pontificate about it . . . I've never understood that."[73] This stance represented a reaction against countercultural liberationism, against a kind of liberal politics that in the Seventies had begun arguing that rock was politically significant insofar as it had changed how we think.

Political struggles are not won in the realm of ideas alone, something liberal heirs to the vital center of the Fifties have misunderstood since the Seventies as they increasingly channeled their energies toward fighting the good fight for the right kind of symbols, language, ideas. If only we could change people's heads, they have the audacity to hope, then a better world would be possible. This fatal misrecognition of the power of artistic dissent, this over-emphasis on the realm of the symbolic has elevated "culture"—the books we read, the films we watch, the albums we listen to, the music we play—to a political status it maybe never deserved.

The punk alternative counter-history of freedom should remind us that any post-Sixties story about rock's capacity to free our minds always had critics. In the *Decline of Western Civilization* (1981), Penelope Spheeris's camera pans across the ramshackle Church, a communal punk squat that housed early incarnations of Black Flag. We get a glimpse of graffiti scrawled next to the cubbyhole where singer Ron Reyes sleeps. It's only in the frame for a few seconds, and you need to squint to make out the slogan: "Remember the Altamont."

Sunnier days, however, were coming. Dawn would once again break in Eighties America over those seeking to rekindle the emancipatory hopes of the past, as precursors to the transcendent promises of the future.

7
How We Taught the World to Sing

On a sweltering afternoon in July of 1985, over 150,000 music fans packed John F. Kennedy Stadium. Via satellite nearly two billion people worldwide would watch portions of this event, the most ambitious experiment in global broadcasting ever attempted. At nine a.m. Eastern Standard Time, Joan Baez stepped up to the microphone. Addressing the masses, she framed the concert in terms Americans would be sure to understand.

"Good morning, children of the Eighties and others," Baez told listeners at home and abroad. "This is your Woodstock—and it's long overdue."[1]

The biggest megaconcert of its time, Live Aid raised over a hundred-million dollars for hunger relief in sub-Saharan Africa. Nearly eighty artists performed in Philadelphia and at Wembley Stadium in the United Kingdom. Organizers nixed an intercontinental duet between David Bowie and Mick Jagger at the last moment due to technical difficulties, but Phil Collins did play both venues (boarding the quintessential symbol of the Eighties, a supersonic Concorde jet, after his set in London). Artists worldwide got involved, too, with parallel benefit concerts in Australia, Japan, Austria, and Germany, as well as Yugoslavia and the USSR. The entire event concluded with Paul McCartney leading a star-studded singalong to "Let It Be" (1970), the mere presence of a real live Beatle, organizers believed, granting the event a measure of global legitimacy.

Spearheaded by Scottish musician-activist Bob Geldof, this particular initiative had its immediate origins in a handful of fundraisers staged over the previous eighteen months in the United Kingdom. But the roots of megaconcerts such as Live Aid stretched back to the Sixties. Geldof's co-conspirator, San Francisco legend Bill Graham, had not only managed the Philadelphia concert, but called in favors (and twisted arms) to get the impossibly complex set of concerts to air worldwide, while the roster included not only Baez and McCartney, but also Santana, a reunited Crosby, Stills, Nash, and Young, and the Beach Boys, among other Sixties acts.

Like Baez, many commentators in the United States viewed this event as part of as a longer, American story—as the fruits of the rock revolution.

Rocking in the Free World. Nicholas Tochka, Oxford University Press. © Oxford University Press 2023.
DOI: 10.1093/oso/9780197566510.003.0008

Once upon a time, Samuel Freedman wrote in a *Times* think-piece titled "Live Aid and the Woodstock Nation," a few hundred thousand people took over a muddy dairy farm in upstate New York.[2] Those numbers had shocked organizers back then; the estimated hundreds of millions of spectators watching Live Aid now seemed almost unfathomable. The event's sheer scale demonstrated how "rock-and-roll has moved from the turbulent fringe into the vast middle ground of American culture and commerce."

So what had changed? We can begin by comparing the two events, Freedman suggested. The former had been defined by the ingestion of consciousness-raising hallucinogens; the latter, by watered-down beer in plastic cups. The former attracted gate-crashing skinny-dippers; the latter, a relatively well-behaved ticketed audience who "had short hair and waved the Stars and Stripes." A bit of flag-waving jingoism in Philadelphia notwithstanding, however, this was not strictly an "American" affair. The telecast represented "Marshall McLuhan's 'global village' prophecy come to pass," Freedman argued, and "rock-and-roll was the Esperanto of the 'global village.'"

So here we come to our final challenge. From a form of expression that might be considered un-American, to America's most successful export, and from an expression of adolescent angst to a truly global lingua franca: rock had shed its parochial origins, becoming a universal language for freedom and dissent worldwide. Even if we grant that rock really did once represent a kind of global language, today it certainly does not. If anything, American hip-hop has proven more easily spread and absorbed, able to be combined and reinvented on a worldwide scale in ways rock never was. So today that notion seems quaint, the product of a triumphalist period that would generate over a decade's worth of wrong-headed intellectual takes, from Frances Fukuyama's *The End of History* (1992) to Thomas Friedman's *The Lexus and the Olive Tree* (1999).

Indeed, the past three decades have done much to sour that triumphalism, so we may no longer need to suspend our disbelief about the global role of a United States that, for many, is no longer marked by its altruism, but by its hypocrisies, whether in the form of a militarized humanitarianism deployed in the name of "democracy" or the promotion of individual choice and market logics in the service of "freedom." To turn back the clock on these twilight hours, we'll need to once more experience that guileless optimism of morning in an America on the cusp of winning the Cold War, its technologies promising peace, its confidence broadcast globally through celebrity sing-a-longs to songs by Bob Dylan.

So we'll ask just one more question: how did Americans teach the world to sing?

* * *

There won't be a repeat of what happened at the last year's Fourth of July celebrations in Washington DC, Interior Secretary James G. Watt told reporters. Drinking and antisocial behavior had marred that event. Rock groups attracted "the wrong element and you couldn't bring your family, your children, down to the Mall."[3] So in 1983, Watt banned rock.

The ban stemmed, in part, from Watt's own political ambitions. He had been Reagan's most controversial cabinet pick: rabidly anti-regulation, he spoke publicly about how his fundamentalist religious beliefs shaped his understanding of government policy. As he eyed a future campaign run, Watt thought he knew which symbolic buttons to press in burnishing his reputation both with evangelical Christians and thought-leaders in the New Right. Unfortunately for him, the musicians he targeted—past-their-prime rock luminaries such as the Grass Roots, Ringo Starr, and the Beach Boys—had fans in the White House.

Criticizing Watt's ban, Ronald Reagan's chief of staff called the Beach Boys "an American institution." Members of the Reagans' California-heavy inner circle reacted with "a mixture of humor and disgust," Beltway wags reported; Nancy Reagan was reportedly "angry." "I like the Beach Boys," she said. "My children like the Beach Boys. I wouldn't let my children go to a hard rock concert." She even called Mike Love. In reversing the ban, President Reagan gave Watt a curious gift: a plaster foot with a bullet hole in it, not a mob threat but rather a joke that he'd "shot himself in the foot." Holding the plaster cast and speaking to reporters, Watt sounded suitably chastened. "We need to stress patriotism in America," he said. "The Beach Boys will help bring us patriotism, I'm sure."[4]

The new patriotism of the Reagan administration stressed sunny optimism, a muscular star-spangled vision of a United States back on track after Seventies. "It's morning, again, in America," the incumbent's 1984 campaign ad stressed, an America made great once more through low interest rates, low unemployment, low inflation. "Why would we ever want to return to where we were, less than four short years ago?"[5] While his predecessor Jimmy Carter had merely used symbols, the former actor Reagan mastered them, portraying himself during the 1980 campaign as a counterweight to the killjoy Democrat's nagging pessimism.

This represented a remarkable turnaround. As a presidential candidate, Reagan had initially been pegged as a gaffe-prone lightweight. At the beginning of his career, pundits believed him to be too extreme, with the *New Republic* in 1966 calling him "anti-labor, anti-Negro, anti-intellectual, anti-planning, anti-20th Century."[6] But that last part, "anti-20th Century," had resonated in some important ways with voters. His law-and-order anti-drug and anti-hippie messaging, focused on returning to an idyllic pre-Sixties past, elevated him to national prominence and the governorship of California.

In the Eighties, the Reagan administration's relationship to rock 'n' roll would be somewhat less straightforward. In part, this was due to the changing status of rock as well as a large-scale shift in conservative politics. We have already noted cleavages in the conservative movement, the move to elevate cultural wedge issues in order to peel off socially conservative blue-collar workers from the Democratic Party, as well as the shift toward championing a more extreme free market ideology from the late Sixties into the Seventies. These changes helped foster the political emergence of evangelical Christians, vaulting a group that once as a matter of policy (and faith) had not engaged in politicking to a newly prominent position in the national conversation. By the Eighties, this new Moral Majority even had the power to reshape presidential elections.

Founded in 1979 by evangelical preacher Jerry Falwell Jr., the group found its political voice in articulating the social and political interests of the faithful with those of the post-Goldwater Right. Their traditional bogeymen included sex, drugs, and sometimes rock; their pamphleteering deployed scare tactics developed in the Sixties to demonize "the drug culture" and bemoan the breakdown of "the traditional family," with tracts by activists such as cartoonist Jack Chick raising awareness about, for instance, secret Satanic messaging in rock lyrics. Formerly extreme positions became mainstream by the mid-Eighties, institutionalized at the national level through campaigns such as the Parents Music Resource Center hearings on popular music or the War on Drugs.

Reagan strategically engaged with new conservative projects, elevating some of their architects to positions of power in his administration while selecting particular issues to rally his base. For conservatives, these cultural issues fit together, albeit sometimes uneasily, under a larger ideological umbrella stressing the importance of American "freedoms." This gave rise to some contradictory positions, such as a fiercely held commitment to freedom of speech, for instance, that did not extend to heavy metal bands who wanted to turn your children on to Satanism. But significantly, this messaging appealed to an increasingly large number of Americans across the political spectrum, as the meaning of "freedom" narrowed to focus on the rights of the individual.[7] "A restored ideal of freedom from restraint was both an effective demagogic tactic," historian Greg Grandin writes, "and a moral appeal to a greater good, a way to conjure an inclusive, boundless Americanism, organized around an inexhaustible horizon, or frontier."[8]

Reagan intuited the power of this restored ideal. He imbued the presidency with a near-filmic weight, and his administration carefully stage-managed a sense of boundless Americanism from the start. His first inauguration staged concerts featuring works by American composer Aaron Copland alongside those by Mendelssohn, Ravel, and Schubert; star conductor Mstislav Rostropovich led the National Symphony Orchestra in selections from Erich Wolfgang Korngold's score for *Kings Row* (1941), the film that featured a young Reagan's breakthrough performance.[9] The president had not personally selected the programs (aides had been asked only "to avoid music that was highly esoteric and to provide performances of the highest quality"). But over the next eight years, his administration would use music to support policy. Awarding Ukrainian-born Vladimir Horowitz the Congressional Medal of Freedom, for instance, Reagan praised the pianist for promoting "peace and freedom" during a recent tour of the Soviet Union.[10]

As a symbol, rock proved trickier to use than classical music. During the 1984 elections, both Reagan and his Democratic challenger, Walter Mondale, tried to use songs by Bruce Springsteen on the campaign trail. When Springsteen balked, Mondale doubled down on linking his campaign to rock musicians, choosing "Teach Your Children" (1970) by Crosby, Stills, and Nash for one television advertisement. The spot intercuts a couple of tow-headed white kids with a retiree and factory worker talking about their lives. It ends with an ICBM launch, suggesting that Sixties dropouts-turned-parents need to think about the message they are sending the next generation with their votes. The words Mondale-Ferraro appear, but not before the missile has faded out—and not to an American flag, perhaps too clichéd, but to an image of the whole earth from space, a knowing nod to the counterculturally hip.

In trying to draw on the messaging power of rock, liberal commentators pointed out gleefully, conservatives had apparently simply missed the memo about Springsteen's politics. "No one sings more passionately about the working-class victims of Reagonomics than Bruce Springsteen," Jon Wiener wrote in the *Nation*. "If Reagan could use Springsteen, imagine what he might do with Elvis: taking 'Don't Step on My Blue Suede Shoes' as inspiration for standing up to the Russians. Or Muddy Waters: 'Got My Mojo Workin'' as an example of black capitalism. The whole thing leaves the rest of us singing 'Help!.'"[11] (Not the most current references, given that this election also heralded the upstart MTV's inaugural campaign imploring young people to "Rock the Vote.")

Despite being based in California nearly five decades, Reagan had better luck linking his image to country music. "This feller, Mr. Reagan, has put our country back in order where it should be," Roy Acuff told a capacity crowd at the Grand Ole Opry. The incumbent entered to "Wabash Cannon Ball," but name-checked another Acuff song, "We Live In Two Different Worlds," to contrast his America, a "strapping young adolescent beginning to flex its muscles in the technological age," with Mondale's, a United States frail, its economy "an old and quivering thing," its global role something for which Americans must apologize.[12]

Having secured a second term after soundly defeating the hapless Democrat, Reagan and his conservative culture-war fellow travelers began more freely inveighing against moral turpitude in popular music and film. In 1985, the Parents Music Resource Center elevated sex and violence in so-called porn rock into a pressing issue; the Senate held hearings, with Dee Snyder, Frank Zappa, and John Denver (who compared the censoring of lyrics by pearl-clutching politicians' wives to book-burnings by Nazis), testified. Two years later, Reagan reignited the anti-rock movement by suggesting that when it came to combatting drug use, the music and film industries "should be part of the solution, not part of the problem."[13] (The Gipper failed to mention that *Kings Cross* had gone through several drafts to satisfy Hays Code censors who demanded references to incest and nymphomania be cut, and a few more just consequences for immoral behavior be inserted.)

"Freedom of speech, freedom of religious thought, and the tight to due process for composers, performers, and retailers are imperiled," Zappa had told the Senate committee, "if the PMRC and the major labels consummate this nasty bargain."[14] But speaking about Reagan's War on Drugs, an unnamed music industry insider sounded a bit more sanguine. Under Nixon the anti-rock movement "was actually more dangerous," he told the *LA Times*, "when the government was actually run by people who really detested rock. Now we have people in power who grew up on rock. If the President can barely get his $100-million Contra military aid package through Congress, I can't see him getting a bill through that would advocate any rock censorship."[15] While conservatives must be seen to be fighting the good fight against rock, and liberals, to be fighting conservatives, both sides know the stakes couldn't be lower. The important thing is to engage, or at least seem to be engaged, on the right side of the struggle (as defined by *your* side).

By the time Secretary Watt lifted the Fourth of July ban back at the National Mall, the Beach Boys had taken another gig. They would headline the following year's festivities, their concert the "centerpiece" of a massive celebration that included fireworks and the National Symphony performing patriotic works (as well as Beethoven). "America still has much to celebrate on this day—unity and affection, prosperity and freedom," Reagan told his fellow Americans in that Fourth of July address. "No one emigrates to Cuba or jumps over the wall into East Berlin; those who look for freedom seek sanctuary here."[16]

Looking back at the short-lived ban, music critic Robert Hilburn marveled that Watt had "managed to transform a band that is more than a decade past its artistic peak into a national symbol." But for fans, the problem had been obvious all along—and it transcended partisan politics. "Usually the issues are so complex or politicians speak in such double talk that you don't know what's going on," a thirty-four-year-old fan said. "But here was something real simple: the Beach Boys. I don't think Watt is any worse than most of them, but he gave us an easy target."[17]

In bearing all that symbol weight, did rock have a responsibility to the people of the United States? "It's sad to see an industry with the power to do so much for Africa and our farmers hasn't the resolve to take the lead in the battle against drug abuse," one reader had written in to the *LA Times* in 1986. This activism, record men responded, actually proved the opposite. "I'm really shocked to see Reagan pointing the finger at an entire industry," Eddie Rosenblatt, president of Geffen Records, said, "especially an industry that's done so much good around the world."[18]

* * *

"Andrew Carnegie built libraries, John D. Rockefeller gave away dimes," Tom Morgenthau wrote in *Newsweek*. "Stephen Wozniak—'Woz' to his friends—has Unuson ('Unite Us in Song'), a corporation dedicated to promoting rock concerts as 'a new kind of unity.' The for-profit corporation's vaguely educational goal is to eliminate what Woz sees as a distressing national tendency to ask, 'What's in it for me?' Instead, Woz wants young America to ask, 'What's in it for *us*?'"[19]

Just six years removed from co-founding Apple Computers, thirty-two-year-old Steve Wozniak was now easing into a new role: millionaire philanthropist. How better to counteract the unbridled individualism of the Me Generation, he thought, than through the shared experience of a three-day music festival? Organized by Unuson in 1982, the US Festival drew nearly 400,000 fans to sweltering Southern California over Labor Day weekend to explore cutting-edge technology and hear music. Wozniak provided the funding. His co-organizer, promoter Bill Graham, managed the logistics. Soft-rock giants Fleetwood Mac, Jimmy Buffet, and Jackson Browne played, as did new wave groups the B-52s, Oingo Boingo, and the Cars, as well as Sixties lions Grateful Dead and Santana. Almost without exception the bands were entirely white and, with few exceptions, fronted by men; there were no black commercial genres represented, and no hard rock or metal. "They obviously wanted to attract people who could get into the computers," Robert Hilburn wrote in the *LA Times*, "not just a bunch of kids who'd be strung out all weekend on downers."[20] Or as a headline in the *New York Times* proclaimed: "the Age of Aquarius meets the Age of the Microchip."[21]

While the festival's name was pronounced like the pronoun ("us"), it also of course evokes the acronym for the United States. "The '60s were a we/they decade," Woz told journalists. "Protests. We're against things. Something is wrong in the world. And what that did to our heads was no good.... The '70s, of course, was the me decade. Take care of myself first, I'm No. 1.... Now the '80s are taking on a new kind of unity. And boy we are out there promoting that." Unuson's president, the ex-SDS activist and environmentalist Peter Ellis, agreed. "To me, this is something very basic to this nation," Ellis said. "It's not a political thing. We're trying really hard not to make it that kind of case.... We're not saying it's bad to ask what's in it for me. It's just that we're saying, hey, once in a while, ask what's in it for us first."[22]

Some idealists came to the US Festival seeking a feeling of one-ness with their fellow man. Others (as an attendee leered) sought "the music, the women, the beer and the sun—and not in that order." The heat proved punishing, sending a number of festivalgoers to the hospital. And the beer (along with some harder drugs, as suggested by overdoses on site) contributed to the more than three dozen arrests. There was even a murder, the result of a drug deal gone wrong. Had the event represented "the Woodstock of the Eighties," some journalists asked?[23] Or a second Altamont, confirmation that pathological individualism had completely and irrevocably atomized American society?

Squint hard enough, and you can see either one, though after the concert, most agreed it had been neither. "I guess I was intrigued by Woodstock—I had read about the spirituality of it," one US Festival attendee said. "I came for a sense of togetherness; I found a nice quiet concert."[24] The only artist to play both Woodstock and the US Festival, Carlos Santana, agreed. "People were scattered here, kind of like in separate tribes," Santana told reporters. "They seem to be having a good time, but they are not a unit or a family like they were in Woodstock. [Woodstock] was like another side of America—a beautiful side that said: 'Hey, there's a lot of us that feel a certain way about this country and we can make it work.' . . . Maybe the difference is that there is no Vietnam for everyone to rally against."[25]

Yet even rallying for a blandly unobjectionable feeling of togetherness had stirred divisions in the Unuson team. A vocal contingent on the board of directors, for instance, had a background with Erhard Seminars Training, which they had hoped to integrate into the event. Oblivious to the fact that most people "just want to have a good time," one person complained to the press, they butted heads with Bill Graham by trying to use the event to "preach" their New Age gospel.[26] The hard-nosed promoter, of course, just wanted to put on a good show: smooth-running, safe, with great sound and excellent sightlines.

The entire team agreed, however, on the significance of cutting-edge computer technology—a "harmonizing" force, according to Unuson's co-founder—in fostering togetherness.[27] Screens dotted the festival grounds, with some transmitting "elaborate computer graphics" and others, pre-recorded performances from the stage for concertgoers stuck in line for the watery beer, two-dollar lemonades, and overpriced food. A "technology fair" allowed visitors to examine products from Atari and Apple in air-conditioned tents, "connecting rock music," deejay Casey Kasem said, "with the scientific wave of the future."[28]

"One of the things we are celebrating, one of the things that is good about the '80s is technology," Wozniak said. "It's bringing us closer together."[29] The incorporation of rock into this kind of techno-utopian thinking marked the culmination of a transition from "counterculture to cyberculture."[30] As we have seen, part of the counterculture's critique concerned the dystopian role of technology in de-individualizing, even de-humanizing, people. But now many ex-hippies had changed their tune. "I think computers will be the cultural bomb of the '80s," Jerry Garcia told critic Robert Hilburn. "We used to fear [computer technology] because of its soullessness. But it's obviously just another human tool and kids are going to know how to make those things talk."[31]

Media theorists had first suggested technology could be a unifying force in the Sixties, and rock music had been part of their techno-utopian projects from the start. Broadcast in June 1967, the BBC's *Our World*—a two-and-a-half-hour live telecast that reached an estimated half-billion viewers globally—used cutting-edge satellite technology to connect people across the globe. Broadcasters in twenty-four countries supplied teams of translators; its symbol, a Da Vinci–esque male figure in front of a globe, represented its universalist ambitions; and political leaders were purposely excluded in favor of representatives of (apparently) non-political arts and culture such as Pablo Picasso or Maria Callas.

For the telecast's finale, a camera pans between the massive mixing console in a recording studio control room and a rehearsal hall. Beatles producer George Martin, in suit jacket and tie, directs the action via an intercom; John and Paul, looking a bit stoned in their psychedelic togs, sit patiently as orchestral musicians file in. A voice-over emphasizes the advanced recording technology, describing how the Beatles had laid down basic instrumental tracks that would be overdubbed with their vocals and "the symphony-men." The song, the BBC announcer tells viewers, will surely be a global hit. Purpose-written in simple language to reach a world-wide audience, "All You Need Is Love" (1967) has a clear, seemingly universal, message: love, love, love, love, love, love, love, love, love...

The idea that popular music could promote unity worldwide provoked strong divergent reactions. Some foresaw a "cultural grey-out," as folklorist Alan Lomax wrote in 1967, with sounds by groups such as the Beatles progressively blotting out the musical diversity of human beings.[32] Seeking new markets for English-language recordings in the Second and Third Worlds, record companies began invoking universalist language that suggested national borders mattered less and less. "If it's music, we speak your language," claimed an advertisement celebrating CBS's agreement deal to market Western recordings in Eastern Europe in 1974. "At CBS Records International, there's only one world of music."[33] Or as an industry advertisement about new international licensing agreements claimed in 1976, BMI "brings American music to the world."[34]

Popular music might even, some believed, connect human beings with extra-terrestrials. In 1977, the NASA Voyager spacecraft carried a phonograph player, engraved with instructions, and two gold-plated records, the Voyager Golden Records, bearing the inscription: "To the makers of music—all worlds, all times." Following a statement by the secretary-general of the United Nations, Kurt Waldheim, as well as greetings in fifty-five languages, future alien listeners would hear a mélange of Earth songs: from whale songs to classical works by Bach, Mozart, and Stravinsky, and from blues songs by African-Americans to a folk song from the Georgian Soviet Socialist Republic, and including non-Western art musics from Japan, China, and India as well as the music-making of indigenous groups in the Americas, Europe, and Australia. There's one rock 'n' roll song, Chuck Berry's, "Johnny B. Goode" (1958)—the only commercial track on the album. The project's cultural advisor Carl Sagan has claimed they wanted to include a Beatles song, "Here Comes the Sun" (1969). The rights, however, proved prohibitively expensive.

In Southern California, Steve Wozniak was finding out just how expensive it could be to integrate rock music into techno-utopian universalist projects here on Earth. After the first US Festival lost four million dollars, Woz shifted gears for a second event, held in May of 1983. "Much of the utopian rhetoric that attended the first US Festival has been toned down, and the founders," journalist Michael London reported for the *LA Times*, "seem to regard this year as more of a commercial than a cultural proposition."[35] The stars were bigger (though despite rumors, Paul, George, and Ringo did not reunite), and even more homogeneously white, if that were possible. The festival scheduled more commercial draws, including a heavy-metal day with Van Halen and Ozzy Osbourne, though some organizers worried the "hard-rock hordes could alter the original character of the festival . . . a forum for progressive music, futuristic technology and '80s-style togetherness."[36]

About 700,000 concertgoers needed to attend over the four nights for Woz to break even. He put more funds toward security (including temporary jail cells) to discourage gate-crashers and unauthorized vendors. The technology exhibits remained, taking up nearly as much space as the concert grounds. And a new innovation, a two-way satellite hook-up with the Soviet Union, promised to demonstrate the symbolic promise of technology as a unifying force. A conversation between astronaut Rusty Schweikart and his cosmonaut counterpart in Moscow worked. A musical exchange between American and Russian rock bands, however, succumbed to technical difficulties.[37]

This failure to rock the bloc proved to be the least of organizers' problems. They had to boot John Cougar Mellencamp after he demanded a fee hike. And they clashed with Joe Strummer, then concluding his group's final, ill-starred tour. "Everywhere you go there are Wozdogs and Wozburgers," the Clash's manager complained to the press, arguing that Wozniak should donate his millions directly to California's poor. "I doubt the Clash could spell socialism," sniped back Unuson president Peter Ellis. ("I fully support the Clash," Van Halen's David Lee Roth smirked at the opening press conference, "in their search for whatever it is they're searching for.")[38]

Only 300,000 people attended, and Woz lost an estimated ten million dollars. There wouldn't be a third US Festival. "They're talking about, 'Oh there's no spirit—it's not like Woodstock,'" Danny Elfman, lead singer of Oingo Boingo, yelled from the stage at one point. "Well, I say screw them—Woodstock's over, the Sixties are finished, and I say: Good riddance!"[39]

The dream of a second Woodstock, a renewed commitment to the politics of peace, love, and togetherness, had ended. "But then, how much cultural significance can you expect from a music festival where the primary issue seemed to be how close sponsor Stephen Wozniak would come to breaking even?"

Figure 11 "They're talking about, 'Oh there's no spirit—it's not like Woodstock.' Well, I say screw them—Woodstock's over, the Sixties are finished, and I say: Good riddance!" Danny Elfman, on stage at the US Festival '83. Photograph by Bev Davies

asked music critic Robert Hilburn. And then he made a prediction. The failure of the US Festival, he wrote, had marked the "end of the megaconcert."[40]

* * *

"Woodstock, meet MTV."[41] 160 countries. Over 1.5 billion viewers. A sixteen-hour long concert. Over sixty stars. The Live Aid "concert and telethon," reported *Newsweek*, "was a long march of superlatives: the most complicated live broadcast ever mounted (aired live throughout on MTV and ABC Radio and for 11 hours on an ad hoc network of 107 broadcast stations; ABC-TV carried it for three hours). The most satellites used in one global broadcast (14, to link JFK with Wembley and the world; last summer's Olympics used only four). The most pizzas ever delivered backstage per hour (50)."[42]

Hilburn's predictions about the death of the megaconcert proved premature. Held in July 1985, Live Aid represented the Eighties in its purest form, as a spectacle of unadulterated excess, with the lines between hype and reality, corporate sponsorship and authentic feelings, first blurred and then obliterated. The high-handed rhetoric of the US Festivals, however, remained. "All over the planet, at the same time, people will see and hear and feel the same set of emotions," the event's producer, Michael Mitchell, told the press. "We're using television to catalyze the world."[43]

The event's white-savior paternalism, shot through with a heavy dose of rhetoric about individual responsibility, had its roots in organizers' earlier projects. Nine months before, the UK-based fundraiser Band Aid had released "Do They Know It's Christmas?" (1984), organized by Bob Geldof and Midge Ure. (The single's sleeve juxtaposed two emaciated young figures with plump white children and adults cut from Victorian-style Christmas cards.) The US-based group USA for Africa then followed suit with "We Are the World" (1985), Lionel Ritchie's team of pop-rock celebrities just barely outpacing Band Aid's do-gooderism in smugness. Each raised money for famine relief efforts in Ethiopia, hit hard by drought and the anticommunist violence of their rightwing military dictatorship.[44] Westerners each have a "choice" to end world hunger, Ritchie and USA for Africa celebrities sang, betraying either rank cynicism or, more likely, a profound naïveté.

For the sake of gravitas, the Live Aid roster included a Beatle, though still more rumors of a Beatles reunion (minus John, of course) turned out to be false. All performers waived their fees. Geldof cemented his reputation as a humanitarian, as co-organizer Bill Graham burnished his legendary reputation for strong-arming rock stars and getting events to air through sheer will. But while most liberal publications praised participants' high-mindedness, some criticized its politics. Such an event could only happen in the United States, the *LA Times* pointed out, citing "good old-fashioned Jewish-Catholic-Italian-Polish-Anglo-Saxon guilt."[45] The constant, numbing recitation of statistics—money raised, stars performing, satellites used, countries broadcast—suggested that "figures become a talisman against global evil, and statistics are wielded like amulets that will draw magic contributions."[46] And what, asked *Time*, about the nearly all-white cast of singer-saviors? (Only one hip-hop group, Run-DMC, performed.) "Would a racist go to all this trouble to keep all these people alive? People who just happen to be black?" Geldof shot back, defending his decision to roster (as he claimed) artists who would sell the most tickets. "And by the way, the fact that [the recipients] are black is incidental. They could be luminous orange for all I care."[47]

On the right, the event irked William F. Buckley. Writing in *National Review*, he rolled his eyes at the event's pomposity. (He and his wife caught only the final twenty minutes of the three-hour primetime broadcast; imagine how upset he'd have been had he watched the entire thing.) Actor Jack Nicholson's introduction of Bob Dylan (as a figure who "transcended history") annoyed him, as did the recipients of the money ("Africans being systematically starved by the implementation of Marxist doctrine in Ethiopia," he wrote, incorrectly). But these problems paled next to the insinuation that the music represented a new global lingua franca: "What is being said for rock music, in effect, is that the entire world is at its feet." Yet even if the event's massive audience proved this to be in some sense true, we need not agree with the Geldofs and Grahams that rock, and rock alone, saves. "If one does not master rock 'n' roll, is one closing the door on a transformative experience? Is it the equivalent of inviting color-blindness? Deafness? Impotence?"[48]

Rock fundraisers—and some of these criticisms—were not new. In 1979, Musicians United for Safe Energy had staged concerts following the Three Mile Island disaster; the triple-LP live album that Asylum Records released, *No Nukes* (1980), went gold. Between 1977 and 1981, Amnesty International also organized a series of smaller fundraisers. Spearheaded by activist Peter Luff and comedian John Cleese (alongside his Monty Python mates), the first two broadcasts of the Secret Policeman's Ball featured actors and comedians. At the third show, Pete Townsend performed intimate, acoustic covers of classic Who songs, a successful innovation that the fourth iteration built on by featuring not only major stars past and present like Eric Clapton and Donovan, but also the younger musicians—such as Bob Geldof and Sting—who would take a leading role in socially conscious events in the Eighties. An album, *The Secret Policeman's Other Ball: The Music* (1981), spent five weeks on the *Billboard* charts, just cracking the top thirty.

The original template for rock humanitarianism had been George Harrison's Concert for Bangladesh, a fundraiser organized in collaboration with Ravi Shankar in 1972 (and exuding "an aura of a humanity reaching out to the people of Bangladesh").[49] Staged at Madison Square Garden, the live concerts raised an initial quarter-million dollars via ticket sales for an unfolding refugee crisis in what was then called East Pakistan/Bangla Desh. A single, "Bangla Desh" (1971), three-LP box set, *The Concert for Bangla Desh* (1972), and documentary film raised millions more over the next decade.

The star-studded concerts featured Ravi Shankar, George Harrison, and friends including Dylan and Ringo, Billy Preston, and Eric Clapton, as well as sarod virtuoso Ali Akbar Khan. For George, as Beatles' biographer Philip Norman writes maybe a bit too cuttingly, the crisis presented "a chance to prove the genuineness of his affinity with the Indian subcontinent and his exhortations to universal brotherhood."[50] Contemporary commentators, however, attributed the event's success to its ability to channel the political consciousness of young Americans. "At a time when the mission-oriented heavies of the rock music world were floundering impotently in the backwash of the Nixon administration's 'cooling-off' policy," Don Heckman wrote in the *New York Times*, "Harrison found a new outlet for the energy." And this following any number of "miserable peace-love music rip-offs," and after all of Lennon's "self-serving public crusades." At last, Heckman concluded, someone had made "an effective, meaningful move that would convert the high-flown musical rhetoric into genuine action."[51]

We see here threads that would be knotted together only a decade later. There is the distinction between "words" and "genuine action," between the naturally liberal inclinations of rockers and their audiences, and practice. But there's also the idea that both the (predominantly white) rock musicians as well as their (predominantly white) consumer-fans hold an individual responsibility to support causes (especially to help the impoverished Third World). If the government won't, then we will. "There was a world emotionalism about Bangladesh," one UNICEF spokesperson told an interviewer at the time. "And the American youngsters felt that what our government is not doing, we shall do and enjoy ourselves in doing it."[52]

Were the motivations of consumers attending a concert, buying an album, or watching a film so clear-cut? It's impossible to say in retrospect. But we can find out how critics assigned political meaning to these cultural events and products. Many agreed the concert film had arrived at a major inflection point in the political history of rock. "Late sixties energy has faded into early seventies lethargy," film professor Foster Hirsch wrote. "Embarrassed by causes and crusades, the country seems to be in a flaccid transitional phase, the direction and the spirit of the new decade haven't yet been formulated."[53] "It is a very good movie as such movies go (and they often go quite badly)," critic Roger Greenspun wrote in the *New York Times*. "But anyone who has seen many rock-concert movies will appreciate that in this one there are no unnecessary zooms, no lab-created light shows, almost no exploitation of the on-screen audience, no insistence that a concert of music is somehow a social revolution."[54]

Ho-hum. This is a film "which cautiously avoids political or social context," Hirsch continued, "which has no sense of event or audience, and which has neither good Woodstock nor bad Altamont vibrations, but instead occupies a flavorless, non-reverberating middle ground."[55] Woodstock's masturbatory self-congratulation had represented an authentic grasping at freedom after the "crew-cut hibernation of the fifties and early sixties." Altamont's brutal abjection had confirmed that the "Fillmores are closed, the Haight is boarded up, the Lower East Side is grim, vacant, the campus is quiet—who bothers to rebel now, and for what?" But the Concert for Bangladesh, Hirsch acidly concluded, enabled relieved observers to breathe easy, because the storm had passed and nothing had changed: "Here, they said, is a rock concert which doesn't try to masquerade as a social revolution; everybody, thank goodness, is pacified."[56]

Had Live Aid proved that this process of pacifying well-intentioned liberals had been completely, unreservedly a success? And if they had been pacified, was this a bad thing? Maybe not. The "Sleaze Age" of the Sixties and Seventies had given way to the "Nice Age," journalist Julie Burchill wrote, with rockers—surprisingly—leading the charge. "After years of being identified as rebels and mavericks in the public mind," Robert Hilburn agreed, "rock's biggest figures have finally entered the Age of the Good Guy." Thus Geldof exuded "a sense of Springsteenian integrity," and while the Boss did not participate ("a rare mistake in judgment"), major stars such as Bob Dylan and Paul McCartney "recognized their roles as symbols and responded."[57]

But toward what end? Who thought rock really could solve world hunger? Indeed, could it even solve smaller problems at home? Inspired by an off-hand comment backstage at Live Aid by Bob Dylan about the plight of American farmers, Willie Nelson with John Cougar Mellencamp and Neil Young slapped together Farm Aid three months later. The more modest event still raised just shy of ten million dollars. What did it say about "America's soul in the 1980s," a thinkpiece in *Newsweek* asked, that people only cared about a cause when rock stars got involved?[58] "I'm glad to be helping the hungry and having a good time," a twenty-two-year-old fan at Live Aid told the *New York Times*. But did it matter that corporations could make money, could "do well by doing good?"[59]

"I think this is just the beginning of a resurgence of caring for others," Mary Travers of Sixties super-folkies Peter, Paul, and Mary had said after the Philadelphia concert. "It's a dream, a positive dream."[60] Artists such as Bruce Springsteen seemed to herald a new, pragmatic patriotism: "proud of the country's musical heritage, sympathetic to the 'ordinary guy,' suspicious of big government, the arms build-up and cuts in social programs."[61] Yet the popularity of these artists portended economic success not only for their causes, but also for their sponsors. An event like Live Aid also, according to a vice president at Pepsi-Cola, showed "that you can quickly develop marketing events that are good for companies, artists and the cause."[62]

Good for the artist, especially in enabling these arena-rock moralists to self-consciously spin compelling stories about their global significance. The "real story," Bill Graham instructed journalists covering Live Aid, was "the power of musicians to literally save lives. That's a power that is unique to rock 'n' roll. Actors, poets, athletes couldn't do it on this scale. We've seen evidence of this positive power for years, but it has always been on a limited scale. This project is taking it from the community and the country to the world."[63]

Writing in the *New York Times*, Jon Pareles agreed. "Where rock in the 1960's was often adversarial—anthems of a counterculture—rock in the 1980's is part of mainstream culture and has the clout of television and radio," the critic wrote. "Performers who sell millions of records worldwide have developed a new sense of their power and influence, and have begun to see themselves as participants on a world stage."[64]

Or as Robert Hilburn put it, the mass media had "turned Springsteen into a statesman treated with a reverence unimaginable in the '60s."[65] To journalists, musicians such as Springsteen most convincingly played the role of statesman in promoting the global spread of liberal democratic values worldwide. And as the Eighties wore on, these rocker-diplomats found their music assuming world historical significance in the Second World.

* * *

In 1986, pundit Norman Podhoretz visited Prague. The self-described neoconservative bundled his luggage into the airport taxi, and pulling open the door, heard a familiar voice on the radio. Here's how he related the encounter in a *Washington Post* op-ed winkingly titled "Yes, You Can Fight the Evil Empire":

"'Bruce Springsteen,' the young driver grins. 'You like, yes?'

"'Yes,' I lie, fearing that to tell him how I really feel would be tantamount to spurning a gesture of political solidarity.

"'America very free country,'" he goes on. That he takes Springsteen's existence as definitive evidence of this makes my little lie all the whiter in my own eyes.

"But now I can be completely honest. 'Yes,' I say. 'American is a very free country.'

"He is silent for a minute or so, and then he sighs. 'Czechoslovakia is also very beautiful country. But not free, not free.'"[66]

The freedoms evinced by liberal democracy in general, and by the political-economic system of the United States in particular, assumed their fullest contours during the Eighties in contrast with the unfree system of the Soviet Union and its satellites. The most bombastic expression of this newly revived Cold War rhetoric came from President Reagan's characterization of the Soviet Union as an "evil empire," its citizens living under "a terrible political invention—totalitarianism." In that 1983 speech, Reagan committed the United States to helping foster "the march of freedom and democracy which will leave Marxism-Leninism on the ash heap of history as it has left other tyrannies which stifle the freedom and muzzle the self-expression of the people."[67]

This stance ratcheted up tensions, already high since the Soviet invasion of Afghanistan had ended the cautious steps toward détente taken under Nixon a decade earlier. For civic-minded Americans, the newly aggressive rhetoric simply provided more evidence that individuals need to bypass governments in order to foster cultural understanding. Prior megaconcerts, as we've seen in passing, had attempted to facilitate direct exchanges between American and Soviet citizens using technology. The Unuson Corporation employed so-called space bridge technology to connect its festivalgoers to the Soviet state broadcaster. "We've see each other through distorted masks," the American moderator said in introducing that exchange. "And yet, we hardly know each other, we haven't really met."[68] But technology had now thrust the United States and the USSR into "one global nervous system," he continued, and engagement was inevitable. "We're gonna talk, and we're gonna listen," the moderator concluded, "and above all, we're gonna dance to each other's music and be moved by the same rhythms."

US and Soviet broadcasters next used the Space Bridge technology for several "Citizens' Summits," hosted by American Phil Donahue and Russian Vladimir Pozner. Citizens on each aside asked each other questions in real time, an effort to "get to know" each other outside the distorting lenses of either side's government. "Eyes filled with hope, and a desire to find out about each other," a Russian responds at one point, "and I think we should try to get to know each other better and live together, I think that's the most important thing."[69] Indeed, it bears repeating (and in fact, these programs repeated it over and over again): we just need to get to know each other.

Live Aid tried to model positive exchange through the mere fact of global broadcast. "Come on, Russia let me see it!" Geldof had cried out on stage at Live Aid. "China! Germany! France! Australia! USA!"[70] Organizers even scheduled a Soviet rock group Avtograf, though not everyone in the United States understood the intended symbolism. "[Avtograf] were so boring that MTV went to a commercial," one viewer, Joanna Stingray, later recalled. Their appearance inspired Stingray to travel to the Soviet Union to discover "real" Russian rock. She released a compilation of "unofficial" bands a year later titled *Red Wave* (1986). But connecting American listeners to authentic Russian rockers, Stingray claimed, was not a political act. "It has nothing to do with politics," she told *Cashbox*, discussing the compilation, "and it's unfortunate that every time you do anything with the Soviet Union and the United States people automatically think it is political. But it's just music and I think it's a very positive album. I really think that this is going to create a better understanding between people."[71]

Not political? Stingray intended to mail copies to Ronald Reagan and Mikhail Gorbachev in order to communicate a simple message: "that Russians are like everyone else, and rock 'n' roll is the same everywhere."[72] This one-off effort to bring Soviet music to the United States, however, paled in comparison to projects focused on introducing Western rock music to the Second World. A few exchanges preceded the megaconcerts we've just discussed. The Rolling Stones played Yugoslavia and Poland in 1967, and Blood, Sweat, and Tears toured under the auspices of the US State Department in 1970. A past-his-prime Cliff Richard, trying to rediscover his rock roots after a few years in the Eurovision wilderness, played Leningrad and Moscow in 1976. (At the risk of sounding rockist, I'm not sure whether we should call that "rock." As recent revisionist historiography of the eastern bloc has shown, Soviet kids were more likely to be listening to hard rockers Deep Purple than Cliff's 1973 Eurovision hit, "Power To All Our Friends.")[73]

After Cliff, the first major tour was by British star Elton John—accompanied by two British producers, who filmed footage for a documentary later released as *To Russia . . . With Elton*, as well as *LA Times* critic Robert Hilburn. Elton John played eight dates in Moscow and Leningrad in May 1979; he traveled without a full band, accompanied only by the virtuosic London sideman, percussionist Ray Cooper.

Hilburn's dispatches from the Cold War front emphasized the event's historical significance. "Twenty-five years after Elvis Presley first excited American teen-agers," he wrote, "rock 'n' roll officially arrived in the Soviet Union and ignited immediate sparks."[74] And they amplified the Russians' difference through reporting on the food (the group worried their hosts were serving them horsemeat) and young Russians' mania for Western goods (how can they be "so primitive," lacking even chewing gum and blue jeans, he wondered), depicting the average Russian as imbued with a cartoonish fatalism. ("Someday we will have the things we want. We must be patient. We get a little bit more every year").[75] Framing John as a pioneer, he casts "the Russians" as lagging pathologically behind when measured against the yardstick of Western consumption.

There's a tension, too, between reporting on the singer's wild reception and the seemingly bleak circumstances of these listeners' lives under the yoke of totalitarianism. "Elton John Captures Leningrad!" claimed an Associated Press headline, reporting that "thousands of young people chanting 'El-ton, El-ton' went into a frenzy during the performance." Yet the concert film later portrayed a different message, foregrounding the audience's passivity while hinting darkly at an atmosphere of fear pervading young communist fans' lives. "If the kids did get up," we are told, "then there were men in navy-blue suits who would push them down again." And this is the curious thing. Both Hilburn and the documentary emphasize not the audience's reaction per se, but the reaction of government officials to the reaction of the listeners. For *their* reaction serves, Hilburn writes, as "a barometer of the Soviet Union's attitude toward Western artists."

Yet as quite a bit of recent work has shown, young Eastern European listeners were not just familiar with bands such as the Beatles, Deep Purple, and others. Many did not even necessarily see a contradiction between consuming Western rock music and holding socialist values.[76] The stereotype came from an earlier moment when socialist policy during the 1950s and early 1960s stressed prohibition and censorship. These policies largely failed, and large grey markets emerged to supply bootlegged recordings pressed onto discarded x-ray film or smuggled in from abroad. By the late 1960s and 1970s, nearly all states—including the most hard-line, such as Albania—had experimented with accommodating Western musical styles, with officials drawing youth spaces into their purview by empowering cultural workers to produce local versions of Western popular culture.

Tours by Western artists represented institutionalization, the phase that succeeded accommodation and included the import of Western cultural products—including popular music. Moscow first signed bilateral copyright agreements with its satellites after 1967, acceding to UNESCO's Universal Copyright Convention in 1973; the state recording company, Melodiia, tentatively began exploring licensing agreements with American and British companies in the late 1970s, which in turn led to agreements for tours. The tours did not always go smoothly. But the problems were usually not political, but political. Eastern bloc booking agencies imposed price caps on tickets, nearly torpedoing several agreements with Western promoters. So to recoup financial losses, musicians had to find creative ways to monetize their eastern bloc tours, leading to licensing for an increasing number of television specials, documentaries, and live albums throughout the 1980s.

By this time, the deepening financial crisis in Eastern Europe, if anything, made life easier for state-socialist rock musicians. International realist and citizen-diplomat Bruce Dickinson, lead singer of British metal band Iron Maiden, explained the popularity of the local hard rock bands he met while touring the eastern bloc to Western journalists in 1984. "I think the government tolerates them mainly because some of them tour in the West," Dickinson told *Billboard*. "And that earns foreign currency. The Polish government will tolerate anything that earns foreign currency." On why Maiden took gigs in Poland and Hungary that lost them money due to price caps, he sounded even more pragmatic. "We agreed out of curiosity, really. That, and a desire to play somewhere in August, which is bloody difficult in Europe because everybody's on holiday.... [W]e didn't want to go straight into the major markets cold."[77]

In contrast, most Americans viewed importing rock into the bloc as an incredibly powerful symbolic act. In July of 1987, an idealistic young American named Allan Affeldt organized the March for Peace, a 450-mile walk into Moscow modeled on previous peace walks for nuclear disarmament in the United States. The *LA Times* reported that Affeldt's plan—to screen American movies, give talks, visit Soviet homes, hold open forums—"read like a Kissinger wish list for détente."[78] It concluded with "the largest American-Soviet cultural exchange ever: a concert on the Fourth of July."

Bill Graham signed on to manage the show, which Steve Wozniak helped fund on short notice. Though a previous rock festival funded by the Levi's jeans company had fizzled out six years earlier, the more experienced Graham and Woz now succeeded.[79] Film crews accompanied the walkers and documented the concert, later airing the hour-long special, *Rock 'n Roll Summit*, on the cable station Showtime. The special opens with the peace walkers, transitions into a montage of the concert lineup jamming to "Listen to the Music" (1972), then introduces the performers: James Taylor, Bonnie Raitt, the Doobie Brothers, Santana, the Russian group Avtograf, and a specially formed peacenik supergroup, Collective Vision. The camera pans across the Russian fans, as a voice-over relates platitudes. "We had music everywhere we went in Russia," a young American tells the camera. "I went up to a young man, and I sang, 'Back in the USSR.' He said right away, 'Beatles!' and sang me another song. And right away we became friends."

According to the participants, it was a concert of firsts. "I betcha this is the first time a woman has done *this* in the Soviet Union," Bonnie Raitt tells the audience before starting the guitar riff launching "Three Time Loser" (1977). She says this in English, though James Taylor has just carefully introduced her in labored Russian—Raitt seems to be posturing for the cameras, not the locals. The guiding image of the concert film soon emerges. "[Rock music] is an international language, it inspires the people," Carlos Santana tells the assembled journalists at a press conference. "And it helps people understand each other. It is pure sound, through music people can understand each other; the words don't get in the way."

"Young people are the same everywhere," a young American explains to the cameras before a quick segue to James Taylor. "We want to be friends." We are all the same, and this festival demonstrates the power of popular music to build bridges, to connect us. As the bands jam and the program concludes, organizers released doves of peace that take flight in front of the stage's huge tic-tac-toe board, its X's and O's replaced by small earths and warheads.

"It's our move," the text tells us. And if understanding will be our ticket to peace, then what better way to get to know each other than through rock music—the universal language.

* * *

"I'm not here for any government," Bruce Springsteen called out to East German fans in 1988. "I've come to play rock 'n' roll for you in the hope that one day all the barriers will be torn down." Warned to avoid any "political statements," Springsteen—peeved authorities had misleadingly billed his concert as a benefit for Nicaragua—then launched into a cover of Bob Dylan's 1964 anthem, "Chimes of Freedom."

At the end of a space-bridge telecast between the USSR and the United States two years earlier, an equally peeved Russian had wondered whether dialogue and exchange was even possible. The Americans felt so sure they knew the real situation in the Soviet Union, he told host Vladimir Posner, that anything positive Soviet citizens said about their state would be dismissed out-of-hand as propaganda, shilling for the state or, even worse, coerced. By providing an impetus for Americans to think about the United States and its place in the world, for three decades rock music had contributed to an understanding of the eastern bloc as both backward and lacking freedom, without the "normal" outlets for the rebellious self-expression necessary to a functioning society. Its presence behind the Iron Curtain now heralded the belated arrival of the Second World's citizens to a world without borders.

Figure 12 "I'm not here for any government. I've come to play rock 'n' roll for you in the hope that one day all the barriers will be torn down," Bruce Springsteen in East Germany (1988). Photograph by Sandra Tiger

A transcendent and universal form of political expression—had rock become so over-determined as a symbol, both at home and abroad, that all Americans agreed on its meaning and significance? Even the music's harshest conservative critics now struggled to critique the now-middle-aged big beat, their broadsides sounding increasingly like retreads of stale old arguments, their authors treading water in a sea of rehashed morality and bad sophistry.

There's one notable exception to this trend, a minority position we have not yet encountered. And it comes from an intellectual fringe that emerged just as the Cold War ended to explain how the United States fit into the natural order of things at the end of the American century. Rebellion against society is dangerous, this dissenting conservative minority explains, because human beings require order to thrive. So if rock promotes social rebellion, no matter how stylized or contrived in its post-Sixties dotage that rebellion may be, then rock remains dangerous. In *National Review*, ex-critic-turned-conservative-firebrand Stuart Goldman thus mocked the music's "code of ethics": a foolish, naïve belief that "our 'natural' state of oneness with the Universe" is defined by "us" (teenagers, rebels, free-thinking individuals) against "them" (teachers, the government, politicians, parents, grown-ups). This belief "immunizes" rock from censure, Goldman continues, because its critics are called anti-art or even fascistic and are "branded an enemy of 'freedom of expression.'"

As a result you cannot even censure rock for being sexist, immoral, or just plain gross. The music is "junk food for the soul," Goldman concludes, promoting a "parasitic anarchism" that leads to an "anything goes" kind of society. Writing in the *Washington Post*, Allan Bloom largely agreed, highlighting a dangerous hypocrisy. "The Left has in general given rock music a free ride," he claimed. "Abstracting [it] from the capitalist element in which it flourishes, they regard it as a people's art, coming from beneath the bourgeoisie's layers of cultural repression." This leads to a peculiar situation where some people even *praise* the music for its base appeal to our lower natures. Rock is "something that speaks to the rawest of desires," and that—it probably goes without saying—is a bad thing.[80]

Who is the audience for these criticisms? Goldman and Bloom are not addressing mainstream readers. They are warning other conservatives who have, presumably, come to agree that rock represented a politically meaningful expression of individual rebellion. That such a stance garnered broad support among conservative intellectuals points to just how far dominant conceptions of "freedom" had shifted to the right by the end of the Eighties. Popular music, even *National Review* claimed, can express a positive individualism without resorting to antisocial calls for rebellion against the prevailing order. The journal praised artists such as Little Steven (guitarist in the E Street Band as well as a solo artist), for his "explicitly conservative lyrics," especially on an album, *Voice of America* (1984), featuring songs about Solidarity in Poland and the Berlin Wall, as well as "the outrage of urban crime and disorder." This conservative praise even extended to artists such as Boy George and Michael Jackson performing "songs that reflect a longing for peace and order."[81]

Let's disentangle the threads making up this largely forgotten debate one last time. Here's the claim: rock represents a universal form of culture that transcends borders; it distills the individual freedoms and spirit of dissent necessary for a normal, healthy, democratic world. In critiquing this Springsteenian position, conservatives such as Goldman and Bloom are not objecting to the claim in its entirety. They're only quibbling with the first part. There *are* forms of transcendent culture that, if we correctly choose and consume them, will lead to a better, more free, and democratic world. And the West has most certainly produced this culture. But rock, they're sorry to say, ain't it.

Outlined in his unlikely bestseller, *The Closing of the American Mind* (1987), Bloom's larger project asked Americans to look to the "classics" of Western civilization, works addressing "the permanent concerns of mankind" and enabling us to navigate "the labyrinths of the spirit of the times." It would decry the wrong-headed insistence in twentieth-century America on venerating "the democratic ideal of a pop culture out of which would grow a new high culture."[82] A stranger affirmation of Bloom's perspective can be found in the musings of Frances Fukuyama on music. In *The End of History* (1992), this political scientist was also concerned with universality, with identifying those enduring forms of human cultural expression that ensure the foundations of peace, free-market prosperity, and liberal democracy. Yet while science, he claims, "is unequivocally cumulative and unidirectional," leading us forward, the "same cannot be said for activities like painting, poetry, music, or architecture: it is not clear that Rauschenberg is a better painter than Michelangelo or Schoenberg superior to Bach, simply because they lived in the twentieth century."[83] It probably goes without saying that the Trashmen do not surpass Tchaikovsky, nor Dylan, even Debussy.

But maybe we're looking at this the wrong way around. Rather than analyzing what part of the Springsteenian claim a handful of conservative eggheads disagreed with, we should instead focus on how that claim itself reveals the essentially conservative conception of "freedom" at the heart of liberal projects in the Eighties. Built on the foundational idea that the world comprises good guys and bad guys, Eighties liberalism believed that the good guys—their faults notwithstanding—were working to extend political enfranchisement through American democracy worldwide. Such rhetoric tended to be naïve, and far too simplistic. Showtime's *Rock 'n Roll Summit*, for instance, concluded with Collective Vision, the peacenik supergroup assembled to perform Little Steven's "I Am A Patriot." The song's narrator disavows communism—but also capitalism. But what's the solution? "I only know one party, and it is Freedom."

Freedom from what? And more importantly, freedom for what? This "freedom" derived from the possession of individual, inalienable rights, the right to choose not to affiliate, to chart one's one path in the world.[84] In joining energies once aimed broadly at liberating people from a more diverse (and specifically material) set of economic, political, and social bonds, projects invoking the liberatory power of rock channeled their participants' energy toward a significantly narrowed idea of what might count as liberation.[85] That's not to say that these projects were not worthwhile. But it is to highlight just how specific the "freedoms" that rock helped us experience had become at the end of history. In 1986, Jack Healey organized a series of shows for Amnesty International to celebrate the fortieth anniversary of the Universal Declaration of Human Rights while raising awareness about the plight of political prisoners. A Conspiracy of Hope concerts featured the usual suspects from the rock world. But they also included speeches from dissidents who had been imprisoned throughout the world. At the end of the first concert, we see the Conspirators, a supergroup comprising a few members of rock's new socially conscious fraternity, inviting former political prisoners on stage.

"We have some very special guests here with us tonight, eighteen prisoners of conscience released because of Amnesty International," U2's Bono says. The guitars begin thrumming, the band gets going. On the footage later released, you can see the camera operators milling about, trying to get into position for shots that will include both the former prisoners and the current rock musicians. The opening chords of a Dylan anthem chime forth; the musicians jockey for position in front of the microphones.

A personal prayer to transcend social constraints has become a public call for action, its metaphorical prison now taken at face-value, this anti-message meditation transfigured into a finger-pointing anthem for universal rights residing outside and above the United States, if not humankind itself. "It's a song called 'I Shall Be Released,'" the rock 'n' roll liberators say. "And that says it all, really."

* * *

In December of 1989, the Berlin Wall fell, and Jann Wenner boarded a Gulfstream jet. The magazine mogul's entourage landed in Moscow twelve hours later to celebrate.[86] A bevy of rockers followed. Joe Cocker and Melissa Etheridge played the crumbling Wall, as did Crosby, Stills, and Nash. "We wanted to go there and help them celebrate, help them bring it down," Graham Nash told *Rolling Stone*. "We wanted to be part of history."[87]

The realization of what this moment meant hit journalist P. J. O'Rourke like a sledgehammer, all at once. Reporting a feature for *Rolling Stone* from Berlin, he claimed to have broken into tears. The vicissitudes of the American century—the wars in Korea and Vietnam, the nuclear arms race, even Reagan's election—now took on new meaning because "the free world won," it had once and for all vanquished "life-hating, soul-denying, slavish communism." And in the end, nary a shot was fired. (Unless you count the violence unleashed through decades of proxy wars, I guess.) "The best thing about our victory is we did it with Levi 501's," he wrote in *Rolling Stone*. "Seventy-two years of Communist indoctrination and propaganda got drowned out by a three-ounce Sony Walkman."[88]

As we come to the end of our narrative, the kinds of labels that were attached to rock earlier—as fascist or anarchic, as democratic or conservative—seemingly melt away. And that says it all, really. Rock had become the taken-for-granted symbol for the expansion of a kind of American liberalism that here veers into triumphalism, there veers into a kind of common-sense universalism.

If we Americans taught the world to sing, that's because an understanding of the world's peoples as lapsed liberal subjects had now become dominant in this emerging post-Cold War period. You no longer needed to say *why* rock music expressed certain political values, or *how* it worked to promote a politics of freedom centered on individual rights. It simply does. Hadn't history proven that this really was the American century? So it seems only natural that an American soundtrack would accompany its conclusion.

"It's been a long time comin'," David Crosby sings in "Long Time Gone" (1969), one of the songs he performed in the breach of the Berlin Wall. Indeed, it had. But at least we had arrived at the endpoint toward which the short twentieth century was striving all along. So there we were, all of us sharing in the common triumph of the American idea. All of us rocking in the free world.

Epilogue: Rocking in the Free World

It's early 2016, and a convoy of aged hippies is marching through the streets of Burlington, Vermont. They chant and bang on pots and pans. A few hack at acoustic guitars slung a bit too high against flannel-clad chests. A few months later and a political world away, two loudspeakers stand at attention on either side of a stage draped in red, white, and blue. The crowd there seethes and surges. They're chanting, too: "Lock her up!" The speakers spring to life, issuing forth the same lyrics from that chilly Vermont main street: "Keep on rockin' in the free world."

Using Neil Young's searing indictment of the failure of the American dream demonstrates the lack of imagination (and reading comprehension) of both blissed-out Bernie Sanders supporters and angry Donald Trump followers. Like Springsteen's "Born in the USA" (1984), depicting a returned Vietnam vet on the edge, "Rockin' in the Free World" (1989) doesn't quite work as a campaign song—though that doesn't stop candidates from using it. The lyrics range from bitterly sardonic to quite heavy-handed. ("We got a thousand points of light," Young sings, referencing the famous speech by George H. W. Bush speech, "for the homeless man.") But as a rallying cry, the chorus works just fine so long as your candidate reaches the dais before it ends.

If not always expert, Democrats have at least been persistent in invoking the messaging power of popular music over the past thirty years, though rock no longer dominates their means-tested playlists. On the campaign trail in 2020, for instance, Kamala Harris names her favorite living rapper, Tupac Shakur (d. 1996).[1] (Does she know something we don't?) The campaign playlist created by Hillary Clinton (or her handlers) in 2016 featured mostly upbeat pop, with a focus on Spanish-language artists and earnest young white women with acoustic guitars.[2] Michelle and Barack Obama made an art of signaling their affinity with soul music, jazz, and R&B. So did America's "first black president" (in Toni Morrison's much-misinterpreted phrasing), Bill Clinton, who famously played his saxophone on The Arsenio Hall Show in 1992.

The "right" songs that liberals choose—cool but not too cool, and diverse but not offputtingly so—can sometimes lead to surreal moments. After Trump called Hillary a "nasty woman" at their final debate in 2016, Janet Jackson's "Nasty" (1986) became the anthem for a certain kind of supporter (who might also have purchased an "I'm a Nasty Woman" tote bag). (Listen back now, and you'll recall that this song's not exactly about white feminist girlbosses.) The idea that popular music matters in this particular way can lead to peculiar claims. After Trump's surprising victory, a headline in *Forbes* suggested that "If We Voted With Our Musical Tastes, Hillary Clinton Would Have Won the Election." Can music, its author asked, change the world? "Usually no," the article quoted Sting as saying. "But it can plant a seed in someone's head."[3] What could that even mean in this specific context?

Flabby, imprecise invocations of popular music's political significance dominate center-left thinking in the United States. This liberal earnestness feeds the ironic trolling and public lib-owning so key to conservative discourse today. Rightwing pundits, for instance, reveled in reminding voters that even if a friendlier Clinton was using focus groups to craft her pitch to African-American voters in the 2010s, she still had called some of their brothers and fathers "superpredators" in the tough-on-crime 1990s. Elsewhere on the right, ideological incoherence runs rampant. After the Rolling Stones played Cuba in 2016, libertarian social media personality Matt Kibbe posted an explainer video on "freedom of expression" and rock 'n' roll. "Socialism is all about conformity," he tells viewers, "music is all about the individual, it's all about being different, it's all about expressing yourself, being free to disrupt the status quo, free to challenge authority."[4] Though when organizers at the 2021 Tokyo Olympic Games played John Lennon's "Imagine" (1971), the conservative *New York Post* decried the liberal chestnut as "a totalitarian's anthem."[5]

* * *

What does it mean that rock now represents so much and so little, that we might map onto this music political values left, right, or center, liberal, conservative, or libertarian? Form here seems to loom larger than content, pointing to a hollowing out of political discourse in the United States as well as the elevation of style over substance in our debates. And so it seems we're right back where we started. Yet having come this far over the past seven chapters, we might as well highlight several large-scale shifts, moments pointing broadly to those conditions of possibility through which the stories we've just recounted about the political significance of popular music could be told in the first place.

The first key moment saw the emergence of new forms of expert knowledge specifically about rock music, especially (but not only) through rock criticism from about 1966 to the mid-1970s. The first critics not only took rock seriously, but articulated the music they loved to a larger set of philosophical problems: about technology, the individual, and life in modern societies.

Their successors elaborated a more intuitive, albeit no less rigorous, set of ideas about how the music acted on listeners' bodies and minds. And neither group invented their approaches out of thin air. The larger problem that rock 'n' roll addressed, these commentators solemnly suggested, was nothing more nor less than the primary challenge all young people faced: the problem of *being* in a postwar world that seemed bent on stripping us of our autonomy, depriving us of our freedoms. How should we live in such a world?

The answer turned out to be the same one Cold War–era political commentators, philosophers, novelists, and visual artists in the United States had been proposing for nearly two decades. We must seek out spaces of emancipation, eluding the tight grasp of social institutions and political systems that sought to keep us from exercising our agency, realizing our full potentials, being who we want to be. Just fill-in the blank: I want to be _____. And remember that people everywhere, just want to be—*got* to be—free.

For rock music to become integrated into projects promoting these freedoms of mind and body, for its practice to become an emancipatory end in itself, what we once called "mass culture" had to undergo a remarkable transition in the United States, from an anesthetizing influence on the body politic to a form of communication to be taken seriously. It is striking just how silly so much early coverage of rock 'n' roll sounds. Assigned to gossip columnists or journalists from the culture beat slumming it, the humor often masked ugly prejudices: thinly veiled (or not) digs against young female consumers, anxieties about the effects of black sounds on white ears, and complaints about the replacement of middle-brow cultural products with working-class ones.

So for this music to be taken seriously as political expression, rock 'n' roll had to become rock, a form of music increasingly created by young white musicians for consumption by young white (and increasingly male, middle-class, and college-educated) listeners. Journalists and rock critics gave these musicians platforms that we now take for granted: lengthy interviews, critical analyses of their lyrics and recordings, deep dives into their biography and creative process. Musicians played along, viewing themselves now as self-conscious political actors engaged in serious artistic critique; an entire constellation of values—directness, rawness, literateness, honesty—emerged to help us judge the sound of their recordings, the content of their lyrics. White middle-class listeners played their part, too, helping assign value to certain kinds of musicians (and not others), expecting—even demanding—those musicians use their voices appropriately, and criticizing them when they didn't.

If this first broad shift emerged from within rock fandom during the Sixties, the second one came from outside rock, in the Seventies. A more general elevation of popular-culture symbols in national politics swept up music, too, and the invocation of rock music became the cultural messaging keystone for post-Woodstock liberals, and especially the power brokers in the Democratic Party newly focused on appealing to the young, the college-educated, the hip. For sure modern leaders had long depended on curating their public image, tailoring their words and appearances to signal larger political or ideological commitments. An intensification of these earlier trends allocated increasing power to the mass media. But while this intensification might have accelerated the use of rock music by politicians, it doesn't tell us why rock (and not some other genre) should have become so central to the political imaginary of the United States.

So why rock? Well, the music had long been associated with young people, and with the lowering of the voting age in 1972, a Democratic Party now pushing its chips onto the "youth vote" increasingly drew on popular music. But it's also important to note that as a demographic category, "the youth" is never merely a neutral label. In its narrowest conception, this category assumed a predominantly white, middle-class, college-educated group of voters in their late teens and early twenties—the very group that became the new base of the major liberal party in the United States. On the conservative side, worries about the effects of sex, drugs, and rock 'n' roll on "the youth" helped articulate a hodgepodge of groups within the emerging New Right, while at the same time paving the way for figures such as Reagan who were able to articulate the anxieties of these groups (without sliding too obviously into hate speech).

So much of rock history has focused on conservative criticisms of rock music, taking at their word musicians who claim to be struggling for universal freedoms of artistic expression or individualism. But what about the liberals who hitched their projects to certain kinds of rock music? That articulation occurred just as critical claims that the music's power derived from revealing personal truths became dominant, just as we learned once and for all that rock—as an emancipatory practice—worked by freeing our heads. It coincided with the Democratic Party shedding its traditional base of blue-collar white ethnics, betting on the continued "greening" of America as the population overall grew younger, richer, and more educated.

Unfortunately, the Democrats guessed wrong—and they guessed wrong at a really inopportune moment. Because at this very moment Americans began experiencing the profoundly disorienting rupture between two major programs for organizing political-economic life in the United States. Runaway prosperity and the expansion of the social safety net had created the postwar preconditions for new kinds of consumption and production. Young

Americans so quickly learned to take for granted the space to make or think or dream or sing, their increased comfort the result of purchasing power derived from rising wages rather than rising levels of debt. But that soon changed.

These postwar opportunities were never distributed equally among all young people in the United States. The extent to which rock musicians and listeners were able to elaborate such a robust politics of self-determination and expressive autonomy in such a short period of time may show just how unequal a share of leisure time and freedom from economic uncertainty the predominantly young, white, college-educated people who taught us how to think about rock enjoyed. Fleeting, that "extraordinary" period of postwar prosperity too soon disappeared.[6]

So across the period where rock 'n' roll becomes rock, and then rock became enmeshed with a politics of freedom, we observe a perversely complementary set of motions. On the one hand, we see the galloping expansion of postwar enfranchisement in the Fifties and Sixties, the kind of expansion that made rock—as part of an American century of consumption at home and abroad—possible in the first place. But this is followed by an equally sudden contraction that, during the Seventies and Eighties, would transform the United States—deepening inequality, and stripping away protections for the many in the service of accumulation by the few. On the other hand, we see across this entire period a rapid expansion of American deliberations on "freedom"—as not simply a political right, but a natural condition, an essential part of the American experience that's embedded in our institutions, our music, our very DNA.

* * *

Exceptionalism makes so many demands on Americans. It obligates them to live outside history. It asks them to experience their lives as defined by the many freedoms they enjoy, especially in the face of overwhelming odds, and even in the face of overwhelming evidence to the contrary.

This may help explain a key irony about rock's politics of freedom that often goes unremarked. Tolling for the rebel, for the individual, true chimes of freedom sound ever softer—even as that keyword's meaning grows. The conditions that made rock 'n' roll, that allowed so many positive political values to become stuck to this music, are long gone. They began slipping away the moment rock became real: knotted together with critical interpretations demanding authenticity and honest self-expression, with a new self-regard emphasizing both courageous self-discovery and political activism, and with formal recognition by political actors claiming that, as a social phenomenon, the music requires understanding, interpretation, respect.

It's turned out to be a bitter irony. The conditions that made possible particular arenas for postwar dissent, for exploring our capacities for political expression by making and listening to commercially recorded music, exist today—if at all—in attenuated form. What does it mean to say that such a radical expression of revolt was merely the convergence, for a brief moment in time, between a very specific set of political-economic conditions and a heady mix of hopes, myths, and anxieties?

Because that moment has passed; it won't come again. What remains? Certain ways of thinking and talking about popular music, a collection of stories about its political meanings and potentials. As the echo of those narratives resounding from the past dissolves, let's resolve to listen one final time. Then we can begin telling new stories.

Notes

Preface

1. Sanneh, "The Rap Against Rockism," *New York Times* (31 October 2004), p. AR1.
2. Austerlitz, "The Pernicious Rise of Poptimism," *New York Times Magazine* (6 April 2014), p. SM48.
3. Exemplary works in this mode include Feldman-Barrett, *A Women's History of the Beatles*; Powers, *Good Booty*; Reynolds, *Shock and Awe*; Wald, *How the Beatles Destroyed Rock and Roll*; Weisbard, *Songbooks*.
4. Roberts, *Tell Tchaikovsky the News*, p. 55.

Prologue: Popular Music as Political Theory

1. Harrington, "Rock's Induction Production," *Washington Post* (27 January 1988), p. D7.
2. Springsteen, "Bob Dylan Induction Speech," *Rock Hall of Fame* (21 January 1988).
3. Cocks, "Songs From the High Ground," *Time* (7 October 1985), pp. 78–80.
4. Loder, "Bruce Springsteen on 'Born in the U.S.A.,'" *Rolling Stone* (7 December 1984).
5. Corn and Morley, "Beltway Bandits: Springsteen Freeze-Out," *Nation* (23 April 1988), p. 559; and "Notes and Asides," *National Review* (10 August 1984).
6. Marcus, "Who Put the Bomp?," p. 24.
7. Marcus, *Mystery Train*, p. xii; emphases in original.
8. Ibid., p. 4.
9. Ibid., p. 5.
10. Ibid., p. 22.
11. Winner, "The Strange Death of Rock and Roll," p. 53.
12. Hamilton, *Just Around Midnight*, p. 7.
13. Ibid., p. 17.
14. On "articulation" as a strategy for analysis, see Stuart Hall et al., *Stuart Hall: Critical Dialogues in Cultural Studies* as well as Clarke, "Stuart Hall and the Theory and Practice of Articulation."

Chapter 1

1. "Boston Bans R'n'R," *Daily Defender* (6 May 1958), p. A4.
2. "After the Brawl Was Over ...," *Woburn Daily Times* (5 May 1958).
3. "Boston Police O.K.'d Rock 'n' Roll License," *Daily Boston Globe* (9 May 1958), p. 1.
4. Baruch, *How To Live With Your Teen-Ager*, p. 4.
5. Springsteen, *Born to Run*, p. 38.
6. Peterson, "Why 1955?," p. 98.

7. *Don't Knock the Rock* (1956), dir. Fred Sears.
8. Quoted in Carlin, *Godfather*, pp. 45–6.
9. Carlin, *Godfather*, p. 46.
10. James McGlincy and James Donahue, "Rock 'n' Roll Madness," *Daily Mirror* (23 February 1957), p. 1.
11. Edith Evans Asbury, "Rock 'n' Roll Teen-Agers Tie Up the Times Square Area," *New York Times* (23 February 1957), p. 1; "Everybody Goes Haywire At Rock 'n' Roll Premiere," *Journal American* (22 February 1957).
12. "Teen-Age Rock 'n' Roll Jams Up Times Square," *The Washington Post* (23 February 1957), p. A3.
13. Freed, "Rock 'n' Roll: The Big New Beat in American Popular Music," available at http://www.alanfreed.com/wp/wp-content/uploads/2010/07/1513-Rock-N-Roll-Program-14.pdf.
14. "Teen-Age Rock 'n' Roll Jams up Times Square."
15. See Hoch and Zubin, *Problems of Addiction and Habituation*.
16. Bracker, "Experts Propose Study of 'Craze,'" *New York Times* (23 February 1957), p. 12.
17. Lourie, "The Role of Rhythmic Patterns in Childhood," pp. 659–60.
18. Bracker, "Experts Propose Study of 'Craze.'"
19. Butterfield, "Our Kids Are In Trouble," *Life*, pp. 97–8, 100–2, 105–8. Cf. Savage, *Teenage*, pp. 393–6.
20. "Planning For Fun," p. 9.
21. Ibid., pp. 14–19.
22. Quoted in Savage, *Teen-Age*, p. 447.
23. See Marten, *The History of Childhood*, p. 86.
24. "When we have learned to discriminate and recognize the ability of each child and place upon him such burdens and responsibilities only as he is able to bear," wrote one observer, "then we shall have largely solved the problem of delinquency." Quoted in Mennel, "Attitudes and Policies," p. 182. From this perspective, programs to "cure" delinquency were deemed part of the problem: "[I]nstead of sterilizing or segregating these people," another mainstream psychologist despaired, "we are still buying them Bibles" (ibid., p. 184).
25. O.F. Lewis, *A Plan for the Reduction of Juvenile Delinquency by Community Effort*, 3ff.
26. Means, *Economic Conditions of Juvenile Delinquency*.
27. Quoted in Mennel, "Attitudes and Policies Toward Juvenile Delinquency in the United States," p. 190.
28. See David Price on how social scientists supported the war effort and worked with the US government, especially *Anthropological Intelligence* and *Cold War Anthropology*.
29. Erikson, "Hitler's Imagery and German Youth"; Benedict, *The Chrysanthemum and the Sword*.
30. Mead, *And Keep Your Powder Dry*, p. 24.
31. Adorno, *Authoritarian Personality*; for a critical perspective on brainwashing studies, see Melley, "Brainwashed!" and "Agency Panic and the Culture of Conspiracy."
32. For this argument, see Medovoi, *Rebels*.
33. Salisbury, *The Shook-Up Generation*, p. 2.
34. Ibid., p. 116.
35. Ibid., p. 117.
36. Samuels, "Why They Rock 'n' Roll—And Should They?" *New York Times* (12 January 1958), p. 16.
37. Sargant, *Battle for the Mind*.

38. Ibid., p. 195.
39. Meerloo, *The Rape of the Mind*, p. 47.
40. Meerloo, *Dance Craze and Sacred Dance*, p. 34.
41. Fromm, *Escape From Freedom*, foreword.
42. Arendt, *The Origins of Totalitarianism*, p. 455; cf. Bettelheim, *Individual and Mass Behavior in Extreme Situations*.
43. See Grogan, *Encountering America*.
44. Rogers, *Client-Centered Therapy*.
45. Maslow, "A Theory of Human Motivation," p. 384.
46. Quoted in Bracker, "Experts Propose Study of 'Craze,'" p. A12.
47. Battelle, "Presley Rocks and Money Rolls In," *Washington Post and Times Herald* (25 June 1956), p. 25.
48. Quoted in Battelle, "Rock 'n' Roll Music Is Tops With Teen-Agers," *Washington Post and Times Herald* (24 June 1956), p. F10.
49. Ricker, "Rock 'n' Roll Given Boot," *Los Angeles Times* (24 April 1957), p. A5
50. Salisbury, *The Shook-Up Generation*, p. 107.
51. Sokolsky, "Why Not Work?" *New York Herald* (8 March 1957), p. A15.
52. Ibid.
53. Roberts, *Tell Tchaikovsky the News*, p. 55.
54. Quoted in Segrave, *Jukeboxes*, p. 149.
55. Discussing the success of Jordan's group in 1942, *Billboard* suggested "the nut [i.e., guarantee] for a small unit is much lower than for a 20-piece band." Quoted in Lauterbach, *The Chitlin' Circuit*, p. 117.
56. Both Baldwin and Jacobs quoted and discussed in Lauterbach, *The Chitlin' Circuit*, pp. 272–3.
57. Lauterbach, *The Chitlin' Circuit*, pp. 272–3; p. 117.
58. See "White Rioters End Rock 'n' Roll' Show," *Pittsburgh Courier* (4 February 1956), p. 1; "Rock 'N Roll Riot Jails 9," *New York Amsterdam News* (4 February 1956), p. 1.
59. "Girl Hurt At Rock in Roll Thurs. Show," *Atlanta Daily World* (26 May 1956), p. 4.
60. "Rock 'n Roll's Sailors' Dance Ends in Riot," *Chicago Daily Tribune* (20 September 1956), p. B6.
61. "Rock 'n' Roll Riot Rocks Naval Base," *The Sun* (19 September 1956), p. 1.
62. "GI Club Wrecked in Rock 'n' Roll Riot," *Washington Post and Times Herald* (20 September 1956), p. 25.
63. "Fats Domino Rock And Roll Dance Ends In Riot Second Time," *Philadelphia Tribune* (25 September 1956), p. 5.
64. Sampson, "Rock 'n' Roll Blues Largely From Booze," *Washington Post and Times Herald* (26 September 1956), p. 17.
65. McCarthy, "America the Beautiful: The Humanist in the Bathtub," *Commentary* (September 1947), pp. 201–7.
66. Remmers and Radler, *The American Teenager*, pp. 43–4.
67. Quoted in Morgan and Leve, *1963*, p. 50.
68. Whitfield, *Culture of the Cold War*, p. 75.
69. On the fad for songs about nuclear war during this period, see Smolko and Smolko, *Atomic Tunes*.
70. Foner, *The Story of American Freedom*, p. 204.
71. Brands, *The Strange Death of Liberalism*, p. 47.

72. Levinson, *An Extraordinary Time*, p. 16.
73. Quoted in Yarrow, *Measuring America*, p. 118.
74. Orwell, "You and the Atomic Bomb."
75. Schlesinger, *The Vital Center*, pp. 2 and 9.
76. Battelle, "Rock 'n' Roll Fad Reflects Unsettled Spirit of World," *Washington Post and Times Herald* (26 June 1956), p. 26.
77. Palladino, *Teenagers*, p. 165.
78. Quoted in Morgan and Leve, *1963*, pp. 160–1.
79. Battelle, "Rock 'n' Roll Fad Reflects Unsettled Spirit of World."
80. Battelle, "Rock 'n' Roll Music Is Tops With Teen-Agers."

Chapter 2

1. Description from "Rock 'n' Roll Taking Cairo Youth by Storm," *LA Times* (8 March 1957), p. A10, and "Rock 'n' Roll Makes Friends of the Egyptians," *Chicago Daily Tribune* (20 May 1957), p. B3.
2. Caruthers, "Rock 'n' Roll Cuts Swath in Egypt," *New York Times* (23 June 1957), p. 24.
3. See Pletsch, "The Three Worlds."
4. Freed, "Rock 'n' Roll: The Big New Beat in American Popular Music," *Brooklyn Paramount* program (1955), available at http://www.alanfreed.com/wp/wp-content/uploads/2010/07/1513-Rock-N-Roll-Program-14.pdf.
5. "Blackboard Jungle out of Film Festival," *Hartford Courant* (28 August 1955), p. 17.
6. Quoted in Perlstein, "Imagined Authority," p. 414.
7. Marcus, "Rock Films," p. 390.
8. Buder, "2 Reports Clear School in Bronx," *New York Times* (17 July 1955), p. 39.
9. Exchange described and quoted in Golub, "Transnational Tale of Teen-Age Terror," p. 2.
10. Pandro Berman, quoted in Simmons, "Violent Youth," p. 386.
11. Reproduced in Simmons, "Violent Youth," pp. 385–6.
12. Tunstall, *The Media Are American*, pp. 137–8 and p. 141.
13. Fosler-Lussier, *Music in America's Cold War Diplomacy*, p. 11.
14. Simmons, "Violent Youth," p. 390.
15. Luce, "The American Century," pp. 170–1.
16. Quoted in Simmons, "Violent Youth," p. 386; emphasis added.
17. "Foreign Relations: Arsenic for the Ambassador," *Time* (23 July 1956), p. 11.
18. "560 Foreign Students Rock 'n' Roll Good-By," *New York Times* (27 July 1957), p. 13.
19. See Nygaard, "The High Priest of Rock and Roll," p. 334.
20. Quoted in Poiger, *Jazz, Rock, and Rebels*, p. 170.
21. Quoted in Ronan, "Rock 'n' Roll Riots," *New York Times* (23 September 1956), p. 188.
22. Quoted in Nygaard, "High Priest of Rock and Roll," p. 340.
23. Blegvad, "Newspapers and Rock and Roll Riots in Copenhagen," p. 152.
24. "Rioters Rock 'n' Roll in Oslo," *New York Times* (24 September 1956), p. 3
25. "33 Arrested in Oslo Rock 'n' Roll Riots," *Washington Post and Times Herald* (24 September 1956), p. 5.
26. Hudson, "Britons Both Approve, Disdain Imported Rock 'n' Roll Craze," *Daily Boston Globe* (9 September 1956), p. B56.
27. Ronan, "Rock 'n' Roll Riots," p. 188.

28. Bragg, *Roots, Radicals, and Rockers*, p. 177.
29. "Rock 'n' Roll Fails to Budge Parisians," *Christian Science Monitor* (17 October 1956), p. 4.
30. Buchwald, "Rock 'n' Roll Leaves 'Em Cold," *Washington Post and Times Herald* (11 November 1956), p. E3.
31. See Pulju, *Women and Mass Consumer Society in Postwar France*.
32. See Briggs, *Sounds French*, chapter 1.
33. Ibid., pp. 19–20, 23, 25–6.
34. "Rock 'n' Roll Adds to Woes in Germany," *Daily Boston Globe* (9 February 1957), p. 13.
35. Ibid.
36. "Europe Rocks 'n' Rolls," *New York Times* (4 November 1956), p. 245.
37. Ingalls, "European Youth Jumps to Rock 'n' Roll Beat," *New York Times* (3 March 1957), p. 170.
38. "Sampling of Rock 'n' Roll for Soviet Union Urged," *New York Times* (12 May 1958), p. 3.
39. Quoted in Zak, *I Don't Sound Like Nobody*, pp. 110–11.
40. See Martin and Segrave, *Anti-Rock*, p. 82.
41. Quoted in Moeller, *West Germany Under Construction*, p. 407.
42. Quoted in Tompkins, "Against 'Pop-Song Poison,'" p. 52.
43. Figure cited in Tsipursky, "Coercion or Consumption."
44. See Tsipursky, "Having Fun," pp. 2–4.
45. See Tompkins, "Against 'Pop-Song Poison'"; Tochka, *Audible States*, pp. 98–100; Vuletic, "Swinging Between East and West."
46. Reproduced in Poiger, "Fear and Fascination," p. 59
47. Stevenson, "The Russians' Big Obsession: You!" *This Week Magazine* (7 December 1958).
48. "Bulgars Cool to Rock 'n' Roll," *New York Times* (26 February 1958), p. 23.
49. "Shepilov Assails Music of the US," *New York Times* (4 April 1957), p. 5.
50. Frankel, "Russia: Unheard, Unseen Enemy," *New York Times* (20 April 1958), p. SM56.
51. Tsipursky, "Fun in the Thaw," pp. 27 and 40–2.
52. Salisbury, "Rock 'n' Roll a Bulgarian Fad Despite Stern Ideological Edicts," *New York Times* (24 September 1957), p. 3.
53. Ball, "Inside Czechoslovakia," *Chicago Daily Tribune* (27 September 1959), pp. 40–1 and 43.
54. Jervis, "Identity and the Cold War," pp. 24–5.
55. "Kuwait Student Digs Rock 'n' Roll," *New York Times* (9 February 1958), p. 4.
56. Gilboy, "Global Report on Rock 'n' Roll," *New York Times* (20 April 1958), p. SM24–25.
57. "Rock 'n' Roll Exported To 4 Corners of Globe," *New York Times* (23 February 1957), p. 12.
58. Pletsch, "The Three Worlds," p. 575.
59. "Malaya Bans Rock 'n' Roll," *Washington Post and Times Herald* (11 May 1959), p. A4.
60. "Cuba Bans Rock 'n' Roll," *New York Times* (14 February 1957), p. 55.
61. "Cuba Restores Rock 'n' Roll," *New York Times* (16 February 1957), p. 13.
62. "Iran Outlaws Rock 'n' Roll," *New York Times* (30 July 1957), p. 20.
63. "Iran Bans Rock 'n' Roll as Threat To Civilization and Dancers' Limbs," *Washington Post and Times Herald* (12 August 1957), p. A1.
64. Gregory, "Youths Studying in U.S. Like Rock 'n' Roll Music," *Daily Boston Globe* (27 July 1958), p. 32.
65. "Rock 'n' Roll Taking Over West Indies," *Daily Boston Globe* (30 May 1957), p. 32.
66. "African Band Has to Learn Rock 'n' Roll for Princess," *Chicago Daily Tribune* (15 October 1956), p. A9.

67. Battelle, "Rock 'n' Roll Music is Tops With Teen-Agers," *Washington Post and Times Herald* (24 June 1956), p. F10.
68. Ibid.
69. "Stritch Calls Rock 'n' Roll 'Throwback to Tribalism,'" *Washington Post and Times Herald* (2 March 1957), p. B7. Marshall, "Rock And Roll Riots Sweep Thru Anglo-Saxon World," *New Journal and Guide* (13 October 1956), p. 14.
70. Altschuler, *All Shook Up*, pp. 48–9.
71. Battelle, "Rock 'n' Roll Beat Irks People the Nation Over," *New Journal and Guide* (30 June 1956), p. 15.
72. Hyams, "Dizzie Gillespie Explains Rock 'n' Roll Craze," *Daily Boston Globe* (3 March 1957), p. A3.
73. Roberts, *Tell Tchaikovsky the News*, p. 121.
74. Reproduced in Roberts, *Tell Tchaikovsky the News*, pp. 139–40.
75. See Foster-Lussier, *Music in America's Cold War Diplomacy*, pp. 79–81.
76. "Segregationist Wants Ban on 'Rock and Roll,'" *New York Times* (30 March 1956), p. 27.
77. Ibid.
78. "Little Rock Deserves Monument for Victory Over Communists," *The Citizens' Council* (August 1958), p. 2.
79. Dobbs, *Red Intrigue and Race Turmoil*.
80. "The Big Sell-Out," *The Citizens' Council* (June 1958), p. 2.
81. "A Fair Exchange" *The Citizens' Council* (July 1957), p. 2.
82. Quoted in Tochka, "My Racist Kentucky Home."
83. Dew, *The Making of a Racist*, p. 43.
84. Ibid., p. 42.
85. Ibid., p. 43.
86. Ward, *Just My Soul Responding*, p. 103.
87. Delmont, *The Nicest Kids in Town*, p. 121.
88. Altschuler, *All Shook Up*, p. 39.
89. Cf. Gerstle, "The Protean Character of American Liberalism," p. 1070.
90. Quoted in Brands, *Strange Death of American Liberalism*, p. 80.
91. Brilliant, "Re-Imagining Racial Liberalism," p. 229.
92. Ibid., pp. 230–1.
93. Myrdal, *An American Dilemma*; cf. Cronan, "Oliver Cromwell Cox and the Capitalist Sources of Racism."
94. Mailer, "The White Negro."
95. Kerouac, *On the Road*.
96. See Lott, *Love and Theft*, and Morrison, "Sound in the Construction of Race."
97. Quoted in Palladino, *Teenager*, p. 129.
98. Did Sam Phillips say this? Probably, at least in some form or another. See Curtis, *Rock Eras*, p. 27, for an early instance in the academic literature.
99. Quoted in Dodge, *Rhythm and Blues Goes Calypso*, p. 204. See The Fabulous McClevertys, "Don't Blame it On Elvis" (1957).
100. Carruthers, *Cold War Captives*, p. 10.
101. Cover blurb from Kohn, *American Nationalism*.
102. Fousek, *To Lead the Free World*, p. 7.
103. Battelle, "Either Like 'Rock 'N Roll' or Forget it," *Chicago Defender* (14 January 1956), p. 15.
104. Stevenson, *What I Think*, pp. 40–1.

Chapter 3

1. Quoted in Sounes, *Notes From the Velvet Underground*, p. 45.
2. Sounes, *Notes From the Velvet Underground*, p. 50.
3. Quoted in Frith, *The Sociology of Rock*, p. 83.
4. White, *The Life and Times of Little Richard*, pp. 90–92.
5. Wilson, "How No-Talent Singers Get 'Talent,'" *New York Times* (21 June 1959), p. 16.
6. Ibid., pp. 16 and 52.
7. Shearer, "Goodbye, Rock 'n' Roll," *Boston Globe* (20 December 1959), p. B8.
8. Pierce and Fulchino quoted in ibid.
9. Cox, "Say Rock 'n' Roll Beat Dying Out," *Daily Defender* (30 November 1959), p. 9.
10. Miller, Fulton, and Steele quoted in "Rock 'n' Roll's On Way Down," *Chicago Daily Tribune* (26 May 1957), p. 16.
11. Interviewed by Lieber, "Down With Rock 'n' Roll!," *Baltimore Sun* (17 May 1959), p. 19.
12. Meerloo, *Rape of the Mind*, p. 47.
13. Quoted in Mosedale, "Rock 'n' Roll Far From Dead," *Boston Globe* (1 September 1958), p. 16.
14. Testimony of Billy Rose, "Monopoly Problems in Regulated Industries," p. 4426.
15. Ibid.
16. "The Voice and Payola," *Time* (9 September 1957), p. 80.
17. "Public First With Pastore Committee," *Billboard* (1 July 1957), p. 29.
18. Quoted in MacNees, "Post Office's 'Rock 'n' Roll' Mailing Subsidy Assailed," *The Sun* (3 March 1957), p. 4.
19. Quoted in "Did Rock 'n' Roll Buy Its Way to the Top?," *Boston Globe* (26 November 1959), p. 83.
20. Quoted in Fisher, *Something in the Air*, p. 85.
21. "The Wages of Spin," *Time* (7 December 1959), p. 47; Gould, "TV: Assessing Effects of Life Under the Table," *New York Times* (20 November 1959), p. 53.
22. Segrave, *Payola*, p. 100.
23. Quoted in Segrave, *Payola*, p. 112.
24. "Freed Sentenced for 'Payola,'" *New York Times* (18 December 1962), p. 3.
25. "Celler Blames Payola for Rise of Rock 'n' Roll," *New York Times* (28 March 1960), p. 17.
26. "The No-Payola Sound of Music," *Variety* (9 December 1959), p. 64.
27. Quoted in Segrave, *Payola*, pp. 115–6.
28. "4 Out to Debunk Payola Lose Disk Jockey Jobs," *New York Times* (26 November 1959), p. 51. Secondary accounts usually misidentify the song as "Pahalacaka," reproducing an error introduced by the Associated Press. The actual song, "Pachalafaka," appears on *Terribly Sophisticated Songs (A Collection Of Unpopular Songs For Popular People)* (Warner Bros. Records, B1210); a wonderful cover version features in *The Muppet Show* (Season 1, Ep. 3).
29. Quoted in Fisher, *Something in the Air*, p. 89.
30. Zausmer, "Mechanical Slaves Bake A Bigger National Pie," *Boston Globe* (14 June 1959), p. A2.
31. Ibid.
32. Jumonville, *Critical Crossings*, p. 158.
33. Quoted in Jumonville, *Critical Crossings*, pp. 164–5. Rosenberg's original remarks can be found in Jacobs, *Culture for the Millions?* and Howe, "A Symposium on TV," *Dissent* (Summer 1960).

34. Rosenberg, *Mass Culture in America*, p. 5.
35. Turner, *The Democratic Surround*, p. 215.
36. Cf. Gendron, "Theodor Adorno Meets the Cadillacs."
37. "Parents Face the Music on Rock 'n' Roll Record," *New York Times* (14 August 1958), p. 20.
38. Zausmer, "Mechanical Slaves Bake A Bigger National Pie," *Boston Globe* (14 June 1959), p. A2.
39. Quoted in Melley, *Empire of Conspiracy*, p. 135.
40. Kellner, *Media Spectacle*, p. 161.
41. See Halberstam, *The Best and the Brightest*.
42. The lyric comes from "A Hard Rain's A-Gonna Fall" (1963); see also Shelton, *No Direction Home*, p. 152.
43. Jeff Roda, "In 79 Days, Innocence Lost, Then Found" *The Atlantic* (22 November 2013).
44. Quoted in Gardner, "The Beatles Invade," *New York Times* (8 February 1964), p. 49.
45. Cameron, "Yeah-Yeah-Yeah," *Life* (21 February 1964), p. 34A.
46. Ibid. p. 34B
47. "The Beatles," Letters to the Editor in *Life* (21 February 1964), p. 22.
48. "A Disaster?," *Life* (28 August 1964), p. 58A.
49. Gould, "It's the Beatles (Yeah, Yeah, Yeah)," *New York Times* (4 January 1964), p. 47.
50. Feron, "Singing Beatles Prepare for US Tour," *New York Times* (5 February 1964), p. 36.
51. Phillips, "Publicitywise," *New York Times* (17 February 1964), p. 1.
52. Alden, "Wild-Eyed Mobs Pursue Beatles," *New York Times* (13 February 1964), p. 26.
53. Osmundsen, "Peoplewise," *New York Times* (17 February 1964), p. 20.
54. "Enjoying Beatles," *New York Times* (15 March 1964), p. SM12.
55. Quoted in Fisher, *Something in the Air*, pp. 67–8.
56. "Beatles Analyzed," *New York Times* (5 April 1965), p. SM10.
57. See "Publicitywise," pp. 1 and 20.
58. Morris, "Clothes Fads Nourish Teen-age Conformity," *New York Times* (16 March 1964), p. 38.
59. Guitar, "Status Seekers, Junior Grade," *New York Times* (16 August 1964), p. SM48; the title is an allusion to Vance Packard's 1959 book *Status Seekers*.
60. "Ticky Tacky," *Time* (28 February 1964), p. 92.
61. Marcus, *Invisible Republic*, p. 21.
62. See Cantwell, *When We Were Good*; Denisoff, *Great Day Coming* and *Sing A Song of Social Significance*; Lieberman, *"My Song Is My Weapon"*; and Weissman, *Which Side Are You On?*.
63. Cantwell, *When We Were Good*, p. 22.
64. Quoted in Thompson, *Hearts of Darkness*, p. 16.
65. Reynolds, "The Gang Meets Here," *Sing Out!* (October-November 1961), p. 6.
66. Avakian, "Folk Music on Major Record Labels," *Sing Out!* (October-November 1961), p. 20.
67. Silber, "Ten Years of Singing," *Sing Out!* (October-November 1961), p. 2.
68. Seeger, "Tradition," *Sing Out!* (October-November 1961), p. 30.
69. Shelton, "City Folk Singers," *New York Times* (8 April 1962), p. X18.
70. Quoted in Hughes, "Allowed To Be Free," p. 48.
71. Shelton, "Bob Dylan: A Distinctive Folk-Song Stylist," *New York Times* (29 September 1961), p. 31.
72. Ibid.; Shelton, "Bob Dylan Sings His Compositions," *New York Times* (13 April 1963), p. 11; Shelton, "Folk Songs Draw Carnegie Cheers," *New York Times* (28 October 1963), p. 22.
73. Quoted in Meehan, "Public Writer No. 1?," *New York Times* (12 December 1965), p. SM44.
74. Ibid., p. 136.

75. Shelton, "Bob Dylan Shows New Maturity in Program of his Folk Songs," *New York Times* (2 November 1964), p. 62.
76. Shelton, "Dylan Conquers Unruly Audience," *New York Times* (30 August 1965), p. 20.
77. Ibid.
78. "Beatles," *Kingsport Tennessee Times* (27 December 1963).
79. Maidenberg, "In Deepest Radioland," *New York Times* (22 January 1965), p. 66.
80. See "Israel Bars Beatles," *New York Times* (18 March 1964), p. 47 and "Beatles Manager Here to Quell Storm Over Remark on Jesus," *New York Times* (6 August 1966), p. 13. Shabecoff, "Beatles Winning in East Germany," *New York Times* (17 April 1966), p. 64.
81. Benjamin, "Official Says Soviet is Ready to Discuss Visit by the Beatles," *New York Times* (18 July 1965), p. 68.
82. See Trumbull, "Tokyo is Girding for the Beatles," *New York Times* (22 May 1966), p. 12, and "Beatles are Booed at Manila Airport," *New York Times* (6 July 1966), p. 38.
83. "Peking Condemns 'Bourgeois Music,'" *New York Times* (18 April 1965), p. 11.
84. Shelton, "Pop Singers and Song Writers Racing Down Bob Dylan's Road," *New York Times* (27 August 1965), p. 17.
85. Shelton, "On Records: The Folk-Rock Rage," *New York Times* (30 January 1966), p. X21.
86. "A Symposium: Is Folk Rock, Really 'White Rock?,'" *New York Times* (20 February 1966), p. X22.
87. Shelton, "On Records: The Folk-Rock Rage," p. X21.
88. Ibid.
89. Frith, "'The Magic That Can Set You Free,'" p. 159.
90. Dallos, "Beatles Strike Serious Note in Press Talk," *New York Times* (23 August 1966), p. 30.
91. "The New Troubadours," *Time* (28 October 1966), p. 92.
92. Ibid.
93. Quoted in Rodriguez, *Revolver*, epigraph to Chapter 6.
94. Quoted in Frontani, *The Beatles: Image and the Media*, p. 145.
95. Sales figure cited in Spitz, *The Beatles*, p. 697.
96. Quoted in Frontani, *The Beatles*, p. 145.
97. Lewisohn, *The Beatles Recording Sessions*, pp. 24–8.
98. Ibid.
99. Quoted in Frontani, *The Beatles*, p. 149.
100. Sullivan, "Beatles: More Than A Mania," *New York Times* (5 March 1967), p. 141.
101. Ibid., p. 94.
102. Quoted in Frontani, *Image and the Media*, p. 130.
103. Maureen Cleave interview with John Lennon, reproduced in Rodriguez, *Revolver*, p. 10.
104. Reproduced in Koestenbaum, *Andy Warhol*, p. 114.
105. Quoted in Leo, "Educators Urged to Heed Beatles," *New York Times* (25 July 1967), p. 29.
106. McAllester, "To Understand Our Children," *New York Times* (1 October 1967), p. 17.
107. Ibid.
108. "The Hippies" (1967), produced and directed by Ken Granger.
109. See Moore, "That Music" (February 1967); Granger, "Lyrics, Artists, Recording Companies, and Other Information for the Analysis of the Big Beat"; Granger and Crow, *Rock Culture Glossary*.
110. Marcus, "Introduction to *The Aesthetics of Rock*" (1970/1987), p. xvii.
111. Meltzer, Foreward to *The Aesthetics of Rock* (1970/1987), p. ix.
112. Sanchez, *SMiLE*, pp. 92–5; the description of Wilson from Tom Nolan's *LA Times* essay, "The Frenzied Frontier of Pop Music" (1966), quoted on p. 93.

Chapter 4

1. Quoted in Fornatale, *Back to the Garden*, p. 21.
2. In Finder, *The 60s: Story of a Decade*, pp. 231–2.
3. *The Beatles Anthology*.
4. Goldstein, *Another Little Piece of My Heart*, p. 53.
5. Cf. Powers, *Writing the Record* and "Rock Criticism's Public Intellectuals."
6. Marsden, *Twilight of the American Enlightenment*, p. 16.
7. Beschloss, *Presidents of War*, pp. 492–3.
8. "Tonkin Gulf Resolution," Public Law 88-408, 88th Congress (7 August 1964). General Records of the United States Government; Record Group 11; National Archives.
9. Savio, "Sit-in Address at the Steps of Sproul Hall."
10. See Gitlin, *The Whole World Is Watching*, chapter 4.
11. Lasch, *New Radicalism in America*, p. 147.
12. Goodman, "Thoughts on Berkeley," *New York Review* (14 January 1965), p. 27.
13. Farber, *The Student as Nigger*, pp. 11 and 51.
14. Cf. Hamilton, *Round About Midnight*, and especially Kramer, *Republic of Rock*.
15. See Laing, *The Divided Self: Sanity, Madness and the Family* and *The Politics of Experience*. See also what was later called the poststructuralist turn in France, especially as characterized by the public lectures of Louis Althusser or Michel Foucault during this period.
16. Quoted in Graebner, *America and the Cold War*, p. 358.
17. Ibid., p. 335.
18. *Montreal Gazette* (23 January 1963). Cf. Fettweis, *Pathologies of Power*, pp. 108–11.
19. Chomsky, *American Power*, p. 353.
20. Goldstein, *Another Little Piece of My Heart*, pp. 52–3.
21. Abraham, "You Are Your Own Alternative," p. 61.
22. Quoted in Turner, *From Counterculture to Cyberculture*, p. 75.
23. Quoted in Joseph, "'My Mind Split Open,'" p. 90.
24. Quoted in Greene, *Rock, Counterculture and the Avant Garde*, p. 147.
25. Quoted in Joseph, "'My Mind Split Open,'" p. 91.
26. McNeil and McCain, "Interview with Moe Tucker," available at https://pleasekillme.com/moe-tucker-velvet-underground/.
27. See Pepin, *Harlem of the West*; Talbot, *Season of the Witch*, chapter 7.
28. Nuttall, *Bomb Culture*, p. 9
29. Turner, *The Democratic Surround*, pp. 1–2.
30. Schechner, "Happenings," p. 230.
31. McLuhan, *The Medium is the Massage*, p. 24.
32. Detroit Annie, "Form Found," *San Francisco Good Times* (28 August 1969), p. 6.
33. Trubee, "Last of the Freaks."
34. Frank, *The Conquest of Cool*.
35. Hill, *San Francisco*, pp. 309–10.
36. "FREAK OUT Hot Spots!" map, *Los Angeles Free Press* (11 November 1966), p. 9.
37. Sally Grossman, quoted in Robertson, *Testimony*, p. 285.
38. In Margotin, *Bob Dylan All the Songs: The Story Behind Every Track*.
39. Marcus, *The Old Weird America*.
40. Chandarlapaty, "*Indian Journals* and Allen Ginsberg's Revival," p. 113.

41. Quoted in Wald, *Global Minstrels*, pp. 222–3.
42. See Calonne, *Conversations with Allen Ginsberg*, p. 158.
43. Timothy Leary Papers, NYPL, "Asoke Fakir" 81.11.
44. Tagore, *The Religion of Man*, p. 207.
45. Capwell, *Sailing on the Sea of Love*, p. 44.
46. Ibid., p. 27.
47. See Baker, *A Blue Hand*, p. 221.
48. Schreiber, "Bauls Dig Provos, Provos Dig Bauls," *Berkeley Barb* (22–28 September 1967), p. 4. The group then traveled to New York City, where they opened for the Paul Butterfield Blues Band at the Cafe Au Go Go before driving upstate; see Capwell, *Sailing on the Sea of Love*, p. xiii.
49. Pearlman, "Patterns and Sounds: The Uses of Raga in Rock," *Crawdaddy!* (December 1966), p. 10.
50. See Gemie, "Cross-Cultural Communication and The Hippy Trail."
51. Rahula, *One Night's Shelter*, p. 138.
52. Wilson, "Kirk Wilson Discusses," *The Rag* (14 November 1966), p. 17.
53. Robertson, *Testimony*, p. 285.
54. Quoted in Zak, "Bob Dylan and Jimi Hendrix," p. 623.
55. Interview with Jann Wenner, "Mick Jagger Remembers," *Rolling Stone* (14 December 1995), available at https://www.rollingstone.com/feature/mick-jagger-remembers-92946/.
56. Goldstein, "The Shaman as Superstar," *New York* (5 August 1968), available at https://thedoors.com/news/the-shaman-as-superstar.
57. Bourne, "Another Turban in the Ring," *Spectator* (13 November 1967), p. 10.
58. Frank, *The Conquest of Cool*, p. 90, advertisement text quoted on p. 105.
59. "Sitarist Packs Them In as C.C.N.Y. Professor," *New York Times* (27 September 1967), p. 49.
60. Quoted in Borgzinner, "His Sitar Sound Rocks the US," *Life* (18 August 1967), p. 40.
61. Goldstein, *Goldstein's Greatest* Hits, p. 84.
62. Liner notes to *Bengali Bauls . . . at Big Pink* (1968).
63. Robertson, *Testimony*.
64. Marcus, *Invisible Republic*, p. xii.
65. Deloria, *Playing Indian*, p. 158.
66. Wolfe, *The Electric Kool-Aid Acid Test*, p. 218; cf. Kramer, *Republic of Rock*, p. 58.
67. Quoted in Thomas, *Did It!*, p. 25.
68. Hinckle, "The Social History of the Hippies," p. 12.
69. From the *VDC Bulletin* (11 October 1965), and quoted in DeGroot, *The Sixties Unplugged*, p. 192.
70. Wolfe, *Electric Kool-Aid Acid Test*, p. 224.
71. Quoted in DeGroot, *Sixties Unplugged*, p. 214.
72. Reproduced in Leary, *The Politics of Ecstasy*, p. 140.
73. Leary and Alpert, "The Subjective After-Effects of Psychedelic Experiences," p. 19.
74. Fisher, "Some Comments Concerning Dosage Levels of Psychedelic Compounds for Psychotherapeutic Experiences," p. 216.
75. Stevens, *Storming Heaven*, p. 149.
76. See Lester, "'Taking A Trip' with Leary," *New York Times* (4 December 1966), pp. X5 and 9. Les Troubadours Du Roi Baudoin, *Missa Luba* (1963/1958), Philips PCC-206.
77. Leary et al., *The Psychedelic Experience*, p. 62.
78. Ibid., p. 104.

79. Wolfe, *Electric Kool-Aid Acid Test*, p. 207.
80. Scully, *Living with the Dead*, p. 12.
81. Ibid., p. 14.
82. Hinckle, "Social History of the Hippies," pp. 18–19.
83. Cottrell, *Sex, Drugs, and Rock 'n' Roll*, p. 101.
84. Scully, *Living with the Dead*, p. 13; cf. Kramer, *Republic of Rock*, pp. 48–9.
85. Scully, *Living with the Dead*, p. 22.
86. Kramer, *Republic of Rock*, p. 48.
87. Hinckle, "Social History of the Hippies," p. 19.
88. DeGroot, *Sixties Unplugged*, p. 247.
89. Dallek, *The Right Moment*, pp. 193–4.
90. Quoted in Rounds, *The Year the Music Died*, p. 291.
91. Quoted in DeGroot, *Sixties Unplugged*, pp. 383–4.
92. Ibid., pp. 209–10.
93. Hoffman quoted in DeGroot, *Sixties Unplugged*, p. 262, Rubin on p. 264.
94. Quoted in DeGroot, *Sixties Unplugged*, p. 264.
95. Hoffman, "Protesters Rehearse for 1968 Democratic Convention in Chicago," *ABC News* (23 August 1968), available at https://youtu.be/LSBTSLtCNcc.
96. Kessler, "Chuck Berry Brings You the Free Speech Movement," p. 141.
97. James Lichtenberg, "Up Against the Amplifier!" *East Village Other* (24 December 1969), p. 6.
98. Christgau, "Rock 'n' Revolution," *Village Voice* (July 1969), pp. 99–100 and 102.
99. Hoyland, "Open Letter to John Lennon," *Black Dwarf* (27 October 1968), p. 4.
100. Reproduced in Neumann, *Up Against the Wall Motherf**er*, p. 64.
101. Quoted in Charone, *Keith Richards*, p. 90.
102. Goldstein, *Another Little Piece of My Heart*, p. 57.
103. Quoted in Kutulas, *After Aquarius Dawned*, p. 60; cf. Frank, *The Conquest of Cool*.
104. Hinckle, "The Social History," pp. 20 and 24.
105. "Street Sweeper," *Berkeley Tribe* (22–28 August 1969), p. 28.
106. Christgau, *Any Old Way You Choose It*, p. 101; see also White, *Panther Stories*.
107. See Brummer, *Vietnam War Song Project (VWSP)* and C. Company feat. Terry Nelson "Battle Hymn of Lt. Calley," available at https://youtu.be/4JoacW7woBY.
108. "Street Sweeper," *Berkeley Tribe* (22–28 August 1969), p. 28.
109. Quoted in Poole, *Grateful Dead's Workingman's Dead*.
110. Rand, "Apollo and Dionysus," Speech at Ford Hall Forum, Boston, MA, available at https://courses.aynrand.org/works/apollo-and-dionysus/.
111. Quoted in Goldstein, *Another Little Piece of My Heart*, p. 184.

Chapter 5

1. See Williams and Edgar, "Up Against the Wall," para. 2.
2. Wenner and Lennon, *Lennon Remembers*, p. 29.
3. See also Moore, "Authenticity as Authentication" and Tochka, "First-Person Music."
4. *Judee Sill* (1971), Asylum Records SD5050.
5. Lewis, "Judee Sill: Soldier of the Heart," *Rolling Stone* (13 April 1972).
6. Brackett, *Interpreting Popular Music*, p. 14.

7. Hagan, *Sticky Fingers*, p. 7.
8. Sam, *Gone Crazy and Back Again*, p. 52.
9. Lydon, "The High Cost of Music and Love," *Rolling Stone* (9 November 1967), p. 1.
10. Hagan, *Sticky Fingers*, p. 8.
11. Quoted in Denisoff, *Solid Gold*, p. 293.
12. See Denisoff, *Tarnished Gold*, pp. 300–1; Gendron, *Between Montmartre and the Mudd Club*, p. 217.
13. Wenner, "Musicians Reject New Political Exploiters," *Rolling Stone* (11 May 1968).
14. "Rock 'n' Roll," *Time* (May 1965), p. 84.
15. Hagan, *Sticky Fingers*, p. 11.
16. Wenner, "John Lennon, Man of the Year," *Rolling Stone* (7 February 1970).
17. *Lennon Remembers*, pp. 100–1.
18. Christgau, "A Man as Good as Janis," *New York Times* (17 August 1969), p. D12.
19. Cawelti, "Notes Toward An Aesthetics of Popular Culture," p. 267.
20. Hagan, *Sticky Fingers*, p. 210.
21. Powers, *Good Booty*, p. 217.
22. Described in Walker, *Laurel Canyon*, pp. 145–6.
23. Interview with Taylor in the documentary film *Troubadours* (2011), dir. Morgan Neville.
24. Bentley, "Los Angeles Troubadours," p. 3.
25. "James Taylor: One Man's Family of Rock," *Time* (1 March 1971).
26. Wolfe, "The 'Me Decade' and the Third Great Awakening," *New York* (23 August 1976).
27. Honneth, "Organized Self-Realization," p. 470.
28. Hoskyns, *Hotel California*, p. 116.
29. Quoted in Walker, *Laurel Canyon*, p. 152.
30. Simpson, "Hit Radio and the Formatting of America in the Early 1970s"; cf. Weisbard, *Top 40 Democracy*.
31. Quoted in Denisoff, *Solid Gold*, p. 9.
32. Simpson, "Hit Radio and the Formatting of America in the Early 1970s," p. 144.
33. Lanza, *Elevator Music*, p. 178
34. Boltanski and Chiapello, *New Spirit of Capitalism*, pp. 35–7.
35. See Biskind, *Easy Riders, Raging Bulls*.
36. Walker, *Laurel Canyon*, p. 210.
37. See Ambrose, *The Wild Blue*, pp. 42–3, and Bagar and Biancolli, "Concert Program," (7 December 1941), Program ID 1637, New York Philharmonic Leon Levy Digital Archives. https://archives.nyphil.org/index.php/artifact/b753cbcd-7915-4435-9a0c-fa13fe7b5309-0.1
38. Orth, "Warren Beatty Sexes Up George McGovern," *Village Voice* (27 April 1972).
39. For an excellent analysis of these events, see Gorzelany-Mostak, "Pre-existing Music in United States Presidential Campaigns." Information here is drawn from the table on p. 57.
40. Orth, "Warren Beatty Sexes Up George McGovern."
41. Thompson, *Fear and Loathing on the Campaign Trail '72*, p. 17.
42. "The American Youth" (1968) campaign advertisement, available at https://youtu.be/20QN5O6XUfM.
43. Thompson, *Fear and Loathing on the Campaign Trail '72*, p. 41.
44. Ginsberg interviewed by Buckley in "The Avant Garde," *Firing Line* (7 May 1968), available at https://digitalcollections.hoover.org/objects/6033.

45. Rodham, "1969 Student Commencement Speech," available at https://www.wellesley.edu/events/commencement/archives/1969commencement/studentspeech.
46. Reich, *The Greening of America*; cover is the Random House 1st ed. 1970.
47. Ibid., p. 120.
48. Reich, *Greening of America*, pp. 21–2.
49. Ibid., p. 24.
50. Ellington, *Music is My Mistress*, p. 424.
51. See Blumenthal, "Children of the Silent Majority: Nixon, New Politics, and the Youth Vote, 1968–1972."
52. According to one recent documentary, Davis Jr. hoped to be forgiven a large federal tax bill. See Peters, *Sammy* (2020).
53. Quoted in Blumenthal, "Children of the Silent Majority," p. 298.
54. Presley, *Elvis and Me*, p. 287.
55. See Orman, *The Politics of Rock Music*, pp. 8–9.
56. Ibid., p. 11.
57. Quoted in Orman, *The Politics of Rock*, p. 12. For the Senate report, see James Buckley, *Congressional Record*, Nov. 21, 1973, vol. 119, no. 180. For the UN report, see *Bulletin on Narcotics*, Dept of Economic and Social Affairs, United Nations, Oct/Dec 1969.
58. Harvey, *A Brief History of Neoliberalism*, chapter 1.
59. Powell, "Attack on American Free Enterprise System."
60. Cf. Hoganson, *The Heartland*.
61. Dunaway and Beer, *Singing Out*, p. 83; cf. pp. 83–87.
62. See Meiman, "What's That I Hear?" and Leonard, *The Folk Singers and the Bureau*.
63. Dutton, *Changing Sources of Power*, p. 50.
64. Frank, *Listen, Liberal*, pp. 48–9.
65. See *Doonesbury* comic strips published on 24 March and 8 April 1977, available at https://www.gocomics.com/doonesbury.
66. Perlstein, *Reaganland*, p. 63.
67. Greenfield, "They Changed Rock," *New York Times* (16 February 1975), p. 12.
68. Didion, *The White Album*, p. 42.
69. Interviewed in Sheff, "John Lennon and Yoko Ono," *Playboy* (January 1981).
70. Bangs, "James Taylor: Marked for Death," *Who Put the Bomp!* (October 1971).

Chapter 6

1. Interview with Eugene in *The Decline of Western Civilization* (1981), dir. Penelope Spheeris.
2. Quoted in Foley, *Dead Kennedys*, pp. 4–5.
3. Wolfe, "The 'Me' Decade," *New York Magazine* (23 August 1976).
4. Quoted in Foley, *Dead Kennedys*, p. 25.
5. Jenkins, *Decade of Nightmares*.
6. See *1991: The Year that Punk Broke* (1992), dir. Dave Markey.
7. See Fields, *My Ramones*.
8. "Ramones Blitz London," *Rock Scene* (November 1976), pp. 23–6.
9. Interview with Danny Fields in *End of the Century: The Story of the Ramones* (2003), dir. Jim Fields and Michael Gramaglia.
10. On the Seventies, see Carroll, *It Seemed Like Nothing Happened* and Schulman, *The Seventies*. My approach especially draws on Jenkins, *Decade of Nightmares*.

11. Cf. Auslander, "Good Old Rock and Roll," pp. 168–9.
12. Bowser's introduction to D2 on *Golden Age of Rock 'n' Roll* (1973).
13. "The Ducktail Syndrome," *Columbia College Today* (Summer 1970), pp. 36–7.
14. Marcus, "Who Put the Bomp in the Bomp De-Bomp De-Bomp?," p. 6.
15. Gewen, "Rock Criticism," *Commentary* (1 June 1970), p. 94.
16. See *Tangled Up with Dylan: The Ballad of AJ Weberman* (2006), dir. James Bluemel and Oliver Ralfe.
17. Marcus, "Who Put the Bomp in the Bomp De-Bomp De-Bomp?," p. 8.
18. Gewen, "Rock Criticism," p. 95.
19. Marcus, *Mystery Train*, p. 175.
20. Miller, Introduction, *Rolling Stone Illustrated History of Rock & Roll*, p. 8.
21. Ibid.
22. Ibid., p. 9.
23. DeRogatis, "A Final Chat with Lester Bangs," *Perfect Sound Forever* (November 1999).
24. DeRogatis, *Let it Blurt*, pp. 94–5.
25. Ward, "The Stooges," *Rolling Stone* (18 October 1969).
26. Quoted in Laing, *One Chord Wonders*, p. 159.
27. Interview with Johnny Ramone in *End of the Century*.
28. From Bangs, "Live at the Paramount," *Creem* (November 1972) and "One Man Dog," *Creem* (February 1973), reproduced in Bangs, *Psychedelic Reactions and Carburetor Dung*, pp. 113 and 114.
29. Riegel, "Lester Bangs: Liberation Critic," *Throat Culture* (1990).
30. See especially Laing, *One-Chord Wonder*, p. 23
31. Bangs, "The Stooges: The Apotheosis Of Every Parental Nightmare," *Stereo Review* (July 1973).
32. Interview with Bayle in *End of the Century*.
33. For a deeper examination of the etymology of the term "heavy metal," see Weinstein, "Just So Stories," pp. 36–51.
34. Saunders, "Exile in Detroit City: A Imaginary Conversation with Lester Bangs," *Brain Damage* (1 June 1974).
35. Marsh, "Punk Attack: 'The Obituary of Rock and Roll,'" *Rolling Stone* (28 June 1979).
36. Saunders, "The Dave Clark Five," *Flash* (1972).
37. Kaye, Liner Notes to *Nuggets* (1972).
38. Bangs "Amon Düül: A Science Fiction Rock Spectacle," sleeve and program notes to Amon Düül II, *Dance of the Lemmings* (1971) United Artists UAD60003/4.
39. Bangs, "Dear Charlie . . . Love, Lester."
40. See Bangs, "Of Pop Pies and Fun: A Program or Mass Liberation in the Form of a Stooges Review, or, Who's the Fool?" reprinted in *Psychotic Reactions and Caburetor Dung by Lester Bangs*, ed. Greil Marcus, pp. 31–52.
41. Safire, "Punk's Horror Show," *New York Times* (30 June 1977), p. 19.
42. Quoted in Mullen et al., *Lexicon Devil*, p. 108.
43. Kukhoff, "Sex, Drugs, and Textbooks," *Los Angeles Magazine* (25 October 2016).
44. Ibid.
45. Quoted in "Drug Abuse: Hearings," Ninety-first Congress, First Session, Parts 1–2 (United States Congress, House Committee on Education and Labor. Select Subcommittee on Education), p. 565.
46. Quoted in Mullen et al., *Lexicon Devil*, p. 16.

47. Interview with O'Grady, "Watch Out Mate! Hitler's On His Way Back," *NME* (August 1975).
48. See Trynka, *Iggy Pop: Open Up and Bleed*, p. 184.
49. Quoted in Waksman, *This Ain't the Summer of Love*, pp. 93–4.
50. Quoted in Doe and DeSavia, *Under the Big Black Sun*.
51. Quoted in Doe and DeSavia, *Under the Big Black Sun*.
52. McNeil and McCain, *Please Kill Me*, p. 300.
53. Al, Editorial, *Flipside* 39 (1983), p. 4.
54. Robert, "Voices of the Reader," *Flipside* 39 (1983), p. 5.
55. Ibid.
56. Gail Butchette, "Voices of the Reader," *Flipside* 39 (1983), p. 7.
57. Al, Editorial, *Flipside* 39 (1983), p. 3.
58. Ibid., p. 4
59. Mattson, *We're Not Here To Entertain*, p. 166.
60. "uni hi punk fag," "Voices of the Reader," *Flipside* 31 (1982), p. 11.
61. Ibid., p. 12.
62. Safire, "Punk's Horror Show."
63. Michelle and Lynn, "Letter," *Maximum Rocknroll* 1 (1982), p. 4.
64. Yohannan, "[Untitled editorial]," *Maximum Rocknroll* 1 (1982), p. 2.
65. Urban, "Know Your Weapon," *Maximum Rocknroll* 1 (1982), p. 13.
66. "Letter," *Maximum Rocknroll* 1 (1982), p. 3.
67. Quoted in Blush, *American Hardcore*, p. 33.
68. For examples, see Worley, *No Future*, Ventsel, *Punks and Skins United*, and Teitelbaum, *Lions of the North*.
69. Erikka, "[Untitled]," *Maximum Rocknroll* 14 (June 1984), p. 19.
70. "Spin, Crash, and Burn," *National Review* (10 August 1984), p. 12.
71. "Pop Music Shift," *National Review* (10 August 1984), p. 17.
72. Jenkins, *Decade of Nightmares*, p. 77.
73. Devorah Ostrov interview with J. Kordosh, "The CREEM Story."

Chapter 7

1. Baez, *And a Voice to Sing With*, p. 357.
2. Freedman, "Live Aid and the Woodstock Nation," *New York Times* (18 July 1985), p. C19.
3. "Watt Changes His Tune!," *LA Times* (7 April 1983), p B1.
4. Skelton, "Watt Changes His Tune on Beach Boys," *LA Times* (8 April 1983), p. 1.
5. "Prouder, Stronger, Better" (1984) campaign advertisement, available at https://youtu.be/m_B2gZCB85c.
6. Quoted in Jenkins, *Against the Grain*, p. 75.
7. See De Dijn, *Freedom*.
8. Grandin, *The End of the Myth*, pp. 217–18.
9. Schonberg, "Reagan Attends 3 Inaugural Concerts Ranging from Opera to Movie Music," *New York Times* (19 January 1981), p. A20.
10. Schonberg, "In the East Room, Horowitz and 2 Surprises," *New York Times* (6 October 1986), pp. A1 and C17.
11. Wiener, "Rockin' with Ron," *The Nation* (6 October 1984), p. 309.
12. Clines, "Reagan Plays His Campaign Song at Country Music's Capital," *New York Times* (14 September 1984), p. A18.

13. Roberts, "Reagan Says Films and Music Must Stop Glorifying Drugs," *New York Times* (20 May 1987), p. A22.
14. Quoted in *The Real Frank Zappa Book*, p. 276.
15. Goldstein, "Rock World Raps Reagan's Drug Stance," *LA Times* (10 August 1986), p. O71. A few musicians did respond with anti-drug songs, and MTV made a series of short spots featuring musicians imploring listeners to "Just Say No"—including the members of hair metal band Cinderella slurring their way through an ad in sunglasses at night.
16. "Beach Boys Return to Washington Celebration," *LA Times* (5 July 1984), p. B4.
17. Hilburn, "Beach Boys Fill Stadium in Wake of Watt Hoopla," *LA Times* (10 May 1983), p. G1.
18. "Music and Drugs," *LA Times* (17 August 1986), p. S115.
19. Morgenthau, "A Wizard Called 'Woz,'" *Newsweek* (20 September 1982), p. 69.
20. Hilburn, "Graham's Really Big on US Festival's 'Big Idea,'" *LA Times* (24 August 1982), pp. G1 and 4.
21. Cummings, "Age of Aquarius Meets Age of the Microchip," *New York Times* (6 September 1982), p. 11.
22. Epstein, "US Festival the Apple of His Eye," *LA Times* (2 August 1982), p. G4.
23. "100,000 at Opening of 3-Day Coast Rock Festival," *New York Times* (4 September 1982), p. 12.
24. Cummings, "Age of Aquarius Meets Age of the Microchip."
25. Morain and Hilburn, "Promoter of US Festival Claims Long-Shot Victory," *LA Times* (6 September 1982), p. 20.
26. Cummings, "Age of Aquarius Meets Age of the Microchip."
27. Epstein, "US Festival the Apple of His Eye," p. G4.
28. Kasem, "US Festival" segment on *America's Top Ten* (5 September 1982). Accessed at https://youtu.be/WtY2nRiguZw.
29. Morain, "Rock'n'roll and 106 Degrees," *LA Times* (4 September 1982), p. 1.
30. Turner, *From Counterculture to Cyberculture*; see also Markoff, *What the Dormouse Said*.
31. Hilburn, "Promoter of US Festival Claims Long-Shot Victory," p. 20. On this broader transformation, see Turner, *From Counterculture to Cyberculture*.
32. See Lomax, *Folk Song Style and Culture*, p. 4.
33. CBS International, "If It's Music, We Speak Your Language," advertisement in *Billboard* (20 April 1974), p. 43.
34. BMI, "BMI," advertisement in *Billboard* (6 November 1976), p. C11.
35. London, "US Festival: Will Biggest Be the Best?" *LA Times* (22 May 1983), p. T57.
36. Ibid.
37. "It is good that they are bringing a little bit of culture to these people," one concertgoer said. "It's a little bizarre, [but] it's good that they're showing us that there are people over there—they live in houses, they drive in cars, they go to parks." Hilburn, "Promoter of US Festival Claims Long-shot Victory," p. 20.
38. Wallace, "US Festival Gives Way to Commercialism," *LA Times* (30 May 1983), p. A3 and 14.
39. Quoted in the clip "US Festival 1983—trailer," by Manmade Pictures, available at https://youtu.be/l7jVNxHpGNw.
40. Hilburn, "US Festival May Mark End of the Megaconcert," *LA Times* (31 May 1983), p. C1.
41. Hackett, "Banding Together for Africa," *Newsweek* (15 July 1985), p. 52.
42. Barol, "Rock Around the World," *Newsweek* (22 July 1985), p. 56.
43. Hackett, "Banding Together for Africa," p. 52.

44. See Human Rights Watch, *Evil Days*.
45. McDougal, "Live Aid feeds the World... and the Ego," *LA Times* (21 July 1985), p. 66.
46. Cocks, Booth, and Holmes, "Rocking the Global Village," *Time* (12 April 1985), p. 66.
47. Ibid.
48. Buckley, "I Confess," *National Review* (6 September 1985), p. 63.
49. "Bangladesh Concert," *The Seed* (1 April 1972), p. 32.
50. Norman, *Shout!*, p. 461.
51. Heckmann, "Bangla Desh: A Legendary Concert," *New York Times* (9 January 1972), p. D28.
52. Drummond, "Funds from Ex-Beatle's Concert Help Drive Wells for Bangladesh," *LA Times* (9 June 1972), p. A17.
53. Hirsch, "Where Have All the Woodstock Flowers Gone?," *New York Times* (16 April 1972), p. D11.
54. Greenspun, "The Screen: Concert for Bangladesh Now a Documentary," *New York Times* (24 March 1972), p. 29.
55. Hirsch, "Where Have All the Woodstock Flowers Gone?"
56. Ibid.
57. Hilburn, "Live Aid: The Good Guys Finish First," *LA Times* (21 July 1985), pp. O58–9.
58. Beck, "A New Spirit of Giving," *Newsweek* (2 June 1986), p. 18.
59. Ibid.
60. Fein, "Reports of Concert Aid Range Up to $50 Million," *New York Times* (15 July 1985), p. C18.
61. Palmer, "Rock Flexed Its Social and Political Muscles," *New York Times* (29 December 1985), p. 23.
62. Miller, with Abramson, McAlevey, Kuflik, "Brother, Can You Spare a Song?," *Newsweek* (28 October 1985), p. 94.
63. Hilburn, "2 Concerts: A Logistics Challenge," *LA Times* (14 June 1985), p. 15.
64. Pareles, "Drums of Rock Music Beat for Different Causes," *New York Times* (21 September 1985), p. 11.
65. Hilburn, "2 Concerts: A Logistics Challenge," p. 15.
66. Podhoretz, "Yes, You Can Fight the Evil Empire," *Washington Post* (11 December 1986), p. A23.
67. Reagan, "Evil Empire Speech (8 June 1982)," *Modern History Sourcebook* available at https://sourcebooks.fordham.edu/mod/1982reagan1.asp.
68. *Linking US Together* (1983), television special available at https://youtu.be/T0jZQq1MOUI.
69. *A Citizens' Summit: US/USSR* (29 December 1985), television special available at https://youtu.be/-GcP-asqXP4.
70. Boomtown Rats, "Rat Trap," *BBC* broadcast of Live Aid (13 July 1985), available at https://youtu.be/BNpsWpxOn4E.
71. Quoted in *Cash Box* (5 July 1986), p. 48.
72. McCormick, "Thriving Underground Scene in Leningrad," *Billboard* (9 August 1986), p. 33.
73. See Yurchak, *Everything Was Forever*, chapter 6.
74. Hilburn, "Rock Star Rises Over Russia: Leningrad Audience Warms Up to Elton John," *LA Times* (23 May 1979), p. G1.
75. Hilburn, "Moscow: 12 Days That Shook a Rock Critic's World," *LA Times* (10 June 1979), p. L3.

76. See Pekacz, "Did Rock Smash the Wall?," Yurchak, *Everything Was Forever*, and Zhuk, *Rock 'n' Roll in the Rocket City*.
77. Vare, "Iron Maiden Pierces Iron Curtain," *Billboard* (13 Oct 1984), p. 48.
78. Jamie Simons and Jon Lapidese, "Reebok Diplomacy: Allan Affeldt of Newport Beach, the Activist: Behind the Peace March on Moscow," *LA Times Magazine* (5 July 1987), L16.
79. Rockwell, "U.S.S.R. Rock Concert," *New York Times* (14 June 1978), p. C23.
80. Bloom, "Is Rock Music Rotting Our Minds?," *Washington Post* (7 June 1987), p. B1; excerpted from Bloom, *The Closing of the American Mind*, p. 77.
81. "Pop Music Shift," *National Review* (10 August 1984), p. 17.
82. Bloom, *The Closing of the American Mind*, pp. 19 and 69.
83. Fukuyama, *The End of History and the Last Man*, p. 72.
84. Cf. De Dijn, *Freedom*, especially the Epilogue.
85. On this argument applied to "human rights" campaigns, see Moyn, *Not Enough*.
86. Hagan, *Sticky Fingers*, p. 118.
87. Rogers, "Random Notes," *Rolling Stone* (11 January 1990), p. 9.
88. O'Rourke, "Berlin Ball," *Rolling Stone* (11 January 1990), p. 39.

Epilogue: Rocking in the Free World

1. Aniftos, "Here's Who Kamala Harris Thinks Is the Best Rapper Alive," *Billboard* (25 September 2020), available at https://www.billboard.com/articles/columns/hip-hop/9455807/kamala-harris-best-rapper-alive.
2. Browne, "Complete Guide to the 2016 Candidates' Favorite Music," *Rolling Stone* (1 February 2016), available at https://www.rollingstone.com/music/music-news/complete-guide-to-the-2016-candidates-favorite-music-240830/.
3. Hu, "If We Voted With Our Music Tastes," *Forbes* (November 2016), available at https://www.forbes.com/sites/cheriehu/2016/11/12/music-tastes-hillary-clinton-election-presidency/?sh=1051db94439a.
4. Kibbe, "No Satisfaction in Socialism," video blog published 18 April 2016, available at https://youtu.be/uNQs8XUrFpw.
5. Barron, "John Lennon's 'Imagine,'" *New York Post* (25 July 2021), available at https://nypost.com/2021/07/25/imagine-blared-at-the-olympics-is-a-totalitarians-anthem/.
6. Levinson, *An Extraordinary Time*.

References

Abraham, Mark. 2014. "'You Are Your Own Alternative': Performance, Pleasure, and the American Counterculture, 1965–1975." PhD Dissertation, Toronto: York University.
Adorno, T. W., Else Frenkel-Brunswik, Daniel Levinson, and Nevitt Sanford. 1950. *The Authoritarian Personality*. New York: Harper & Brothers.
Alden, Robert. 1964. "Wild-Eyed Mobs Pursue Beatles." *New York Times* (13 February), p. 26.
Altschuler, Glenn C. 2003. *All Shook Up: How Rock 'n' Roll Changed America*. New York: Oxford University Press.
Ambrose, Stephen E. 2001. *The Wild Blue: The Men and Boys Who Flew the B-24s Over Germany 1944–1945*. New York: Simon and Schuster.
Anson, Robert Sam. 1981. *Gone Crazy and Back Again: The Rise and Fall of the Rolling Stone Generation*. Garden City, NY: Doubleday.
Arendt, Hannah. 1951. *The Origins of Totalitarianism*. Boston: Houghton Mifflin.
Auslander, Philip. 2003. "Good Old Rock and Roll: Performing the 1950s in the 1970s." *Journal of Popular Music Studies* 15(2):166–94.
Austerlitz, Saul. 2014. "The Pernicious Rise of Poptimism." *New York Times Magazine* (14 April), p. SM48.
Avakian, George. 1961. "Folk Music on Major Record Labels." *Sing Out!* 11:1 (October–November), p. 20.
Baez, Joan. 1987. *And a Voice to Sing With*. New York: Summit Books.
Baker, Deborah. 2008. *A Blue Hand: The Beats in India*. New: York: Penguin Press.
Baruch, Dorothy W. 1953. *How to Live with Your Teen-Ager*. New York: McGraw-Hill Book Company.
Beatles, The. 2000. *The Beatles Anthology*. San Francisco: Chronicle Books.
Beck, Melinda with Michael Reese. 1986. "A New Spirit of Giving." *Newsweek* (2 June), p. 18.
Benedict, Ruth. 1946. *The Chrysanthemum and the Sword: Patterns of Japanese Culture*. Boston: Houghton Mifflin.
Bengali Bauls, The. 1968. *Bengali Bauls . . . at Big Pink*. Buddah Records BDS 5050. LP. Liner Notes.
Benjamin, Philip. 1965. "Official Says Soviet Is Ready to Discuss Visit by the Beatles." *New York Times* (18 July), p. 68.
Bentley, Christa Anne. 2016. "Los Angeles Troubadours: The Politics of the Singer-Songwriter Movement, 1968–1975." PhD Dissertation, Chapel Hill: University of North Carolina.
Beschloss, Michael. 2018. *Presidents of War: The Epic Story, from 1807 to Modern Times*. New York: Crown.
Bettelheim, Bruno. 1943. "Individual and Mass Behavior in Extreme Situations." *Journal of Abnormal and Social Psychology* 34(4):417–51.
Blegvad, Britt-Mari Persson. 1964. "Newspapers and Rock and Roll Riots in Copenhagen." *Acta Sociologica* 7(3):151–78.
Bloom, Allan. 1987. *The Closing of the American Mind*. New York: Simon and Schuster.
Blumenthal, Seth E. 2005. "Children of the Silent Majority: Nixon, New Politics and the Youth Vote, 1968–1972." PhD Dissertation, University of Massachusetts.
Blush, Steven. 2001. *American Hardcore: A Tribal History*. Los Angeles: Feral House.

References

Boltanski, Luc, and Eve Chiapello. 2005. *The New Spirit of Capitalism*. Translated by Gregory Elliott. New York: Verso.

Brackett, David. 1995. *Interpreting Popular Music*. Cambridge: Cambridge University Press.

Bragg, Billy. 2017. *Roots, Radicals and Rockers: How Skiffle Changed the World*. London: Faber and Faber.

Brands, H.W. 2001. *The Strange Death of American Liberalism*. New Haven, CT: Yale University Press.

Briggs, Jonathyne. 2015. *Sounds French: Globalization, Cultural Communities, and Pop Music, 1958–1980*. New York: Oxford University Press.

Brilliant, Mark. 2014. "Re-imagining Racial Liberalism." In *Making the American Century: Essays on the Political Culture of Twentieth Century America*, edited by Bruce J. Schulman, 228–250. New York: Oxford University Press.

Buchwald, Art. 1956. "Rock 'n' Roll Leaves 'Em Cold." *The Washington Post and Times Herald* (11 November), p. E3.

Calonne, David Stephen, ed. 2019. *Conversations with Allen Ginsberg*. Jackson: University Press of Mississippi.

Cameron, Gail. 1964. "Yeah, Yeah, Yeah: Beatlemania Becomes a Part of U.S. History." *Life* (21 February), 34A–34B.

Cantwell, Robert. 1996. *When We Were Good: The Folk Revival*. Cambridge, MA: Harvard University Press.

Capwell, Charles. 2011. *Sailing on the Sea of Love: The Music of the Bauls of Bengal*. New York: Seagull Books.

Carlin, Richard. 2016. *Godfather of the Music Business: Morris Levy*. Jackson: University Press of Mississippi.

Carruthers, Susan L. 2009. *Cold War Captives: Imprisonment, Escape, and Brainwashing*. Berkeley: University of California Press.

Cawelti, John G. 1971. "Notes Toward an Aesthetic of Popular Culture." *Journal of Popular Culture* 5(2):255–67.

Chandarlapaty, Raj. 2011. "Indian Journals and Allen Ginsberg's Revival as Prophet of Social Revolution." *Ariel: A Review of International English Literature* 41(2):113–38.

Charone, Barbara. 1979. *Keith Richards*. London: Futura Publications.

Chomsky, Noam. 1969. *American Power and the New Mandarins*. New York: Pantheon Books.

Christgau, Robert. 1973. *Any Old Way You Choose It: Rock and Other Pop Music, 1967–1973*. Baltimore: Penguin Books.

Clarke, John. 2015. "Stuart Hall and the Theory and Practice of Articulation." *Discourse: Studies in the Cultural Politics of Education* 36(2):275–86.

Cottrell, Robert C. 2015. *Sex, Drugs, and Rock 'n' Roll: The Rise of America's 1960s Counterculture*. Lanham, MD: Rowman and Littlefield.

Cronan, Todd. 2020. "Oliver Cromwell Cox and the Capitalist Sources of Racism." *Jacobin* (5 September). https://www.jacobinmag.com/2020/09/oliver-cromwell-cox-race-class-caste.

Curtis, James M. 1987. *Rock Eras: Interpretations of Music and Society, 1954–1984*. Bowling Green: Bowling Green State University Popular Press.

Dallek, Matthew. 2000. *The Right Moment: Ronald Reagan's First Victory and the Decisive Turning Point in American Politics*. New York: Oxford University Press.

De Djin, Annelien. 2020. *Freedom: An Unruly History*. Cambridge, MA: Harvard University Press.

DeGroot, Gerard J. 2008. *The Sixties Unplugged: A Kaleidoscopic History of a Disorderly Decade*. Cambridge, MA: Harvard University Press.

Delmont, Matthew F. 2012. *The Nicest Kids in Town: American Bandstand, Rock 'n' Roll, and the Struggle for Civil Rights in 1950s Philadelphia*. Berkeley: University of California Press.

Deloria, Philip J. 1998. *Playing Indian*. New Haven, CT: Yale University Press.

Denisoff, R. Serge. 1971. *Great Day Coming: Folk Music and the American Left*. Champaign, IL: University of Illinois Press.

Denisoff, R. Serge. 1972. *Sing A Song of Social Significance*. Bowling Green: Bowling Green University Popular Press.

Denisoff, R. Serge. 1975. *Solid Gold: Popular Record Industry*. New Brunswick, NJ: Transaction Books.

DeRogatis, Jim. 1999. "A Final Chat With Lester Bangs." *Perfect Sound Forever* (November). https://www.furious.com/perfect/lesterbangs.html.

DeRogatis, Jim. 2000. *Let It Blurt: The Life and Times of Lester Bangs, America's Greatest Rock Critic*. New York: Broadway Books.

Dew, Charles B. 2016. *The Making of a Racist: A Southerner Reflects on Family, History, and the Slave Trade*. Charlottesville: University of Virginia Press.

Didion, Joan. 1979. *The White Album*. New York: Simon and Schuster.

Dobbs, Zygmund. 1958. *Red Intrigue and Race Turmoil*. New York: Alliance.

Dodge, Timothy. 2019. *Rhythm and Blues Goes Calypso*. Lanham, MD: Lexington Books.

Doe, John, and Tom DeSavia. 2016. *Under the Big Black Sun: A Personal History of L.A. Punk*. Boston: Da Capo Press.

Dunaway, David King, and Molly Beer. 2010. *Singing Out Oral History of America's Folk Music Revivals*. New York: Oxford University Press.

Eisen, Jonathan. 1969. *The Age of Rock: Sounds of the American Cultural Revolution*. New York: Vintage.

Eisen, Jonathan. 1970. *The Age of Rock 2: Sights and Sounds of the American Cultural Revolution*. New York: Vintage.

Ellington, Duke. 1973. *Music Is My Mistress*. New York: Da Capo Press.

Erikson, Erik. 1950. *Childhood and Society*. New York: Norton

Erikson, Erik. 1942. "Hitler's Imagery and German Youth." *Psychiatry: Interpersonal and Biological Processes* 5:475–93.

Farber, Jenny. 1967. *The Student as Nigger*. Boston: New England Free Press.

Feldman-Barrett, Christine. 2021. *A Women's History of the Beatles*. New York: Bloomsbury Academic.

Fettweis, Christopher J. 2013. *The Pathologies of Power: Fear, Honor, Glory, and Hubris in U.S. Foreign Policy*. Cambridge: Cambridge University Press.

Fields, Jim, and Michael Gramaglia. 2003. *End of the Century*. New York: Magnolia.

Finder, Henry. 2016. *The 60s: Story of a Decade*. New York: Random House.

Fisher, Gary. 1963/4. "Some Comments Concerning Dosage Levels of Psychedelic Compounds For Psychotherapeutic Experiences." *Psychedelic Review* 2(1):208–18.

Fisher, Marc. 2007. *Something in the Air: Radio, Rock, and the Revolution That Shaped a Generation*. New York: Random House.

Foley, Michael Stuart. 2015. *Dead Kennedys: Fresh Fruit for Rotting Vegetables*. London: Bloomsbury Academic.

Foner, Eric. 1998. *The Story of American Freedom*. New York: W.W. Norton.

Fornatale, Pete. 2009. *Back to the Garden: The Story of Woodstock*. New York: Touchstone.

Fosler-Lussier, Danielle. 2015. *Music in America's Cold War Diplomacy*. Berkeley: University of California Press.

Fousek, John. 2000. *To Lead the Free World American Nationalism and the Cultural Roots of the Cold War*. Chapel Hill: University of North Carolina Press.

Frank, Thomas. 1997. *The Conquest of Cool: Business Culture, Counterculture, and the Rise of Hip Consumerism*. Chicago: University of Chicago Press.

Frank, Thomas. 2016. *Listen, Liberal: Or, What Ever Happened to the Party of the People?* Brunswick, VIC: Scribe Publications.

Frith, Simon. 1978. *The Sociology of Rock*. London: Constable.

Frith, Simon. 1981. "'The Magic That Can Set You Free': The Ideology of Folk and the Myth of the Rock Community." *Popular Music* 1:159–68.
Fromm, Erich. 1941. *Escape from Freedom*. New York: Farrar & Rinehart.
Frontani, Michael R. 2007. *The Beatles: Image and the Media*. Jackson: University Press of Mississippi.
Fukuyama, Frances. 1992. *The End of History and the Last Man*. New York: Free Press.
Gemie, Sharif. 2017. "Cross-Cultural Communication and The Hippy Trail 1957–78." *International Journal of Postcolonial Studies* 19(5):666–76.
Gendron, Bernard. 1986. "Theodor Adorno Meets the Cadillacs." In *Studies in Entertainment: Critical Approaches to Mass Culture*, edited by Tania Modleski, 18–38. Bloomington: Indiana University Press.
Gendron, Bernard. 2002. *Between Montmartre and the Mudd Club: Popular Music and the Avant-Garde*. Chicago: University of Chicago Press.
Gerstle, Gary. 1994. "The Protean Character of American Liberalism." *The American Historical Review* 99(4):1043–73.
Gitlin, Todd. 1980. *The Whole World Is Watching: The Making and Unmaking of the New Left*. Berkeley: University of California Press.
Gitlin, Todd. 1987. *The Sixties: Years of Hope, Days of Rage*. New York: Bantam.
Goldstein, Richard. 2015. *Another Little Piece of My Heart: My Life of Rock and Revolution in the '60s*. London: Bloomsbury.
Golub, Adam. 2012. "A Transnational Tale of Teenage Terror: The Blackboard Jungle in Global Perspective." *Red Feather Journal* 3(1):1–10.
Gorzelany-Mostak, Dana C. 2012. "Pre-existing Music in United States Presidential Campaigns, 1972–2012." PhD Dissertation, Montreal: McGill University.
Graebner, Norman A., Richard Dean Burns, and Joseph M. Siracusa. 2010. *America and the Cold War, 1941–1991: A Realist Interpretation*. Santa Barbara: Praeger.
Grandin, Greg. 2019. *The End of the Myth: From the Frontier to the Border Wall in the Mind of America*. New York: Metropolitan Books.
Granger, Ken, and Joseph R. Crow. 1969/70. *Rock Culture Glossary*. Belmont, MA: Movement to Restore Decency.
Greene, Doyle. 2016. *Rock, Counterculture and the Avant-Garde, 1966–1970*. Jefferson, NC: McFarland and Company.
Grogan, Jessica. 2013. *Encountering America: Humanistic Psychology, Sixties Culture & the Shaping of the Modern Self*. New York: Harper Perennial.
Hagan, Joe. 2017. *Sticky Fingers: The Life and Times of Jann Wenner and Rolling Stone Magazine*. New York: Alfred A. Knopf.
Halberstam, David. 1972. *The Best and the Brightest*. New York: Random House.
Halberstam, David. 1979. *The Powers That Be*. New York: Alfred A. Knopf.
Hall, Stuart. 1996. *Stuart Hall: Critical Dialogues in Cultural Studies*. Edited by Kuan-Hsing Chen and David Morley. London: Routledge.
Hamilton, Jack. 2016. *Just Around Midnight: Rock and Roll and the Racial Imagination*. Cambridge, MA: Harvard University Press.
Harvey, David. 2005. *A Brief History of Neoliberalism*. New York: Oxford University Press.
Hill, Sarah. 2015. *San Francisco and the Long 60s*. New York: Bloomsbury.
Hoch, Paul H., and Joseph Zubin eds. 1958. *Problems of Addiction and Habituation*. Proceedings of the Annual Meeting of the 47th American Psychopathological Association 1957. New York: Grune and Stratton.
Hoganson, Kristin L. 2009. *The Heartland: An American History*. New York: Penguin Press.
Honneth, Axel. 2004. "Organized Self-Realization: Some Paradoxes of Individualization." *European Journal of Social Theory* 7(4):463–78.

Hughes, Charles. 2009. "Allowed to Be Free: Bob Dylan and the Civil Rights Movement." In *Highway 61 Revisited: Bob Dylan's Journey from Minnesota to the World*, edited by Colleen J. Sheehy and Thomas Swiss, 44–60. Minneapolis: University of Minnesota Press.

Human Rights Watch. 1991. *Evil Days: Thirty Years of War and Famine in Ethiopia*. New York: Human Rights Watch.

Jacobs, Norman, ed. 1961. *Culture for the Millions? Mass Media in Modern Society*. Boston: Beacon Press.

Jenkins, Philip. 2006. *Decade of Nightmares: The End of the Sixties and the Making of Eighties America*. New York: Oxford University Press.

Jervis, Robert. 2010. "Identity and the Cold War." In *The Cambridge History of the Cold War*, edited by Melvyn P. Leffler and Odd Arne Westad, volume 2:22–43. New York: Cambridge University Press.

Joseph, Branden W. 2002. "'My Mind Split Open': Andy Warhol's Exploding Plastic Inevitable." *Grey Room* 8:80–107.

Jumonville, Neil. 1991. *Critical Crossings: The New York Intellectuals in Postwar America*. Berkeley: University of California Press.

Kellner, Douglas. 2002. *Media Spectacle*. London: Routledge.

Kerouac, Jack. 1957. *On the Road*. New York: Viking Press.

Koestenbaum, Wayne. 2001. *Andy Warhol*. New York: Viking Press.

Kohn, Hans. 1957. *American Nationalism: An Interpretative Essay*. New York: Macmillan.

Kramer, Michael J. 2013. *The Republic of Rock: Music and Citizenship in the Sixties Counterculture*. New York: Oxford University Press.

Kukhoff, David. 2016. "Sex, Drugs, and Textbooks: Inside L.A.'s Most Controversial Educational Experiment." *Los Angeles Magazine* (25 October), https://www.lamag.com/citythinkblog/sex-drugs-textbooks-inside-l-s-controversial-educational-experiment/.

Kutulas, Judy. 2017. *After Aquarius Dawned: How the Revolutions of the Sixties Became the Popular Culture of the Seventies*. Chapel Hill: University of North Carolina Press.

Laing, David. (1985) 2015. *One Chord Wonders: Power and Meaning in Punk Rock*. Milton Keynes: Open University Press.

Laing, R. D. 1960. *The Divided Self: A Study of Sanity and Madness*. London: Tavistock.

Laing, R. D. 1964. *Sanity, Madness, and the Family: Families of Schizophrenics*. New York: Basic Books.

Laing, R. D. 1967. *The Politics of Experience*. New York: Ballantine.

Lanza, Joseph. 1994. *Elevator Music: A Surreal History of Muzak, Easy-Listening and Other Moodsong*. New York: St Martin's Press.

Lasch, Christopher. 1965. *The New Radicalism in America, 1889–1963: The Intellectual as a Social Type*. New York: Alfred A. Knopf.

Lauterbach, Preston. 2011. *The Chitlin' Circuit: And the Road to Rock "n" Roll*. New York: W.W. Norton & Company.

Leary, Timothy, Ralph Metzner, and Ram Dass. 1964. *The Psychedelic Experience: A Manual Based on the Tibetan Book of the Dead*. New York: University Books.

Leary, Timothy. 1968. *The Politics of Ecstasy*. New York: Putnam.

Leary, Timothy, and Richard Alpert. 1963. "The Subjective After-Effects of Psychedelic Experiences: A Summary of Four Recent Questionnaire Studies." *Psychedelic Review* 1(1):18–26.

Leonard, Aaron. 2020. *The Folk Singers and the Bureau: The FBI, the Folk Artists and the Suppression of the Communist Party, USA-1939–1956*. London: Repeater Books.

Levinson, Marc. 2016. *An Extraordinary Time: The End of the Postwar Boom and the Return of the Ordinary Economy*. London: Random House Business Books.

Lewis, Orlando F. 1920. *A Plan for the Reduction of Juvenile Delinquency by Community Effort*. Albany: Lyon Company.

Lewisohn, Mark. 1988. *The Beatles Recording Sessions*. New York: Harmony Books.

Lieberman, Robbie. 1989. *My Song Is My Weapon: People's Songs, American Communism, and the Politics of Culture, 1930–1950*. Urbana: University of Illinois Press.

Lomax, Alan. 1968. *Folk Song Style and Culture*. New Brunswick, NJ: Transaction Publishers.

Lott, Eric. 1993. *Love and Theft: Blackface Minstrelsy and the American Working Class*. New York: Oxford University Press.

Lourie, Reginald S. 1949. "The Role of Rhythmic Patterns in Childhood." *The American Journal of Psychiatry* 105:653–60.

Lydon, Michael. 1968. *Rock Folk: Portraits from the Rock 'n' Roll Pantheon*. New York: Dell.

Mailer, Norman. 1957. "The White Negro: Superficial Reflections on the Hipster." *Dissent* 4(3):276–93.

Marcus, Greil. 1969. "Who Put the Bomp in the Bomp De-Bomp De-Bomp?" In *Rock and Roll Will Stand*, edited by Greil Marcus, 6–27. Boston: Beacon Press.

Marcus, Greil, ed. 1969. *Rock and Roll Will Stand*. Boston: Beacon Press.

Marcus, Greil. 1975. *Mystery Train: Images of America in Rock 'n' Roll Music*. New York: E.P. Dutton.

Marcus, Greil. 1976. "Rock Films." In *The Rolling Stone Illustrated History of Rock & Roll*, edited by Jim Miller, 390–400. New York: Random House.

Marcus, Greil. 1997. *Invisible Republic: Bob Dylan's Basement Tapes*. New York: Henry Holt and Co.

Marcus, Greil. 2000. *The Old, Weird America: The World of Bob Dylan's Basement Tapes*. New York: Picador.

Margotin, Philippe, and Jean-Michel Guesdon. 2015. *Bob Dylan All the Songs: The Story Behind Every Track*. New York: Black Dog and Leventhal.

Markoff, John. 2005. *What the Dormouse Said: How the Sixties Counterculture Shaped the Personal Computer Industry*. New York: Viking.

Marsden, George. 2014. *The Twilight of the American Enlightenment: The 1950s and the Crisis of Liberal Belief*. New York: Basic Books.

Marten, James. 2018. *The History of Childhood: A Very Short Introduction*. New York: Oxford University Press.

Martin, Linda, and Kerry Segrave. 1988. *Anti-Rock: The Opposition to Rock "n" Roll*. Hamden, CT: Archon Books.

Maslow, Abraham H. 1943. "A Theory of Human Motivation." *Psychological Review* 50(4):70–396.

Mattson, Kevin. 2020. *We're Not Here to Entertain: Punk Rock, Ronald Reagan, and the Real Culture War of 1980s America*. New York: Oxford University Press.

McLuhan, Marshall, and Quentin Fiore. 1967. *The Medium Is the Massage: An Inventory of Effects*. London: Penguin.

McNeil, Legs, and Gillian McCain. 1996. *Please Kill Me: The Uncensored Oral History of Punk*. New York: Grove Press.

Mead, Margaret. 1942. *And Keep Your Powder Dry: An Anthropologist Looks at America*. New York: William Morrow & Co.

Means, Genevieve. 1920. *Economic Conditions of Juvenile Delinquency*. Bloomington, IN: Indiana University Press.

Medovoi, Leerom. 2005. *Rebels: Youth and the Cold War Origins of Identity*. Durham, NC: Duke University Press.

Meerloo, Joost A. M. 1956. *The Rape of the Mind: The Psychology of Thought Control, Menticide, and Brainwashing*. Cleveland: World Publishing Company.

Meerloo, Joost A. M. 1962. *Dance Craze and Sacred Dance*. London: Peter Owen.

Meiman, Kathryn L. 2007. "What's That I Hear?: Domestic Surveillance and Counterintelligence on Antiwar Musicians in the 1960s." MA thesis, Lehigh University.

Melley, Timothy. 2000. *Empire of Conspiracy: The Culture of Paranoia in Postwar America.* Ithaca: Cornell University Press.

Melley, Timothy. 2002. "Agency Panic and the Culture of Conspiracy." In *Conspiracy Nation: The Politics of Paranoia in Postwar America*, edited by Peter Knight, 57–81. New York: New York University Press.

Melley, Timothy. 2008. "Brainwashed! Conspiracy Theory and Ideology in the Postwar United States." *New German Critique* 103:145–64.

Meltzer, Richard. (1970) 1987. *The Aesthetics of Rock.* New York: Da Capo Press.

Mennel, Robert M. 1969. "Attitudes and Policies Towards Juvenile Delinquency in the United States, 1825–1935." PhD Dissertation, Ohio State University.

Miller, Jim, ed. 1976. *The Rolling Stone Illustrated History of Rock & Roll.* New York: Random House.

Moeller, Robert G. 1997. *West Germany Under Construction: Politics, Society, and Culture in the Adenauer Era.* Ann Arbor: University of Michigan Press.

Moore, Allan. 2002. "Authenticity as Authentication." *Popular Music* 21(2):209–23.

Morgan, Robin, and Ariel Leve. 2013. *1963: The Year of the Revolution.* New York: It Books.

Morrison, Matthew. 2014. "Sound in the Construction of Race: From Blackface to Blacksound in Nineteenth-Century America." PhD Dissertation, New York: Columbia University.

Moyn, Samuel. 2018. *Not Enough: Human Rights in an Unequal World.* Cambridge, MA: Harvard University Press.

Mullen, Brendan, Don Bolles, and Adam Parfrey. 2002. *Lexicon Devil: The Fast Times and Short Life of Darby Crash and the Germs.* Los Angeles: Feral House.

Myrdal, Gunnar. 1944. *An American Dilemma: The Negro Problem and Modern Democracy.* New York: Harper and Brothers.

Neumann, Osha. 2008. *Up Against the Wall Motherf**ker: A Memoir of the '60s, with Notes for Next Time.* New York: Seven Stories Press.

Neville, Morgan. 2011. *Troubadours: The Rise of the Singer-Songwriter.* Beverly Hills: Hear Music.

Norman, Philip. 1981. *Shout! The Beatles in Their Generation.* New York: Schuster and Schuster.

Nuttall, Jeff. 1968. *Bomb Culture.* New York: Delacorte Press.

Nygaard, Bertel. 2019. "The High Priest of Rock and Roll: The Reception of Elvis Presley in Denmark, 1956–1960." *Popular Music and Society* 42(3):330–47.

Orman, John M. 1984. *The Politics of Rock Music.* Chicago: Nelson-Hall.

Palladino, Grace. 1996. *Teenagers: An American History.* New York: Basic Books.

Pekacz, Jolanta. 1994. "Did Rock Smash the Wall? The Role of Rock in Political Transition." *Popular Music* 13(1):41–9.

Pepin, Elizabeth, and Lewis Watts. 2006. *Harlem of the West: The San Francisco Fillmore Jazz Era.* San Francisco: Chronicle Books.

Perlstein, Daniel. 2000. "Imagined Authority: Blackboard Jungle and the Project of Educational Liberalism." *Paedagogica Historica* 36(1):407–24.

Perlstein, Rick. 2020. *Reaganland: America's Right Turn 1976–1980.* New York: Simon and Schuster.

Peterson, Richard A. 1990. "Why 1955? Explaining the Advent of Rock Music." *Popular Music* 9(1):97–116.

Pletsch, Carl E. 1981. "The Three Worlds, or the Division of Social Scientific Labor, Circa 1950–1975." *Comparative Studies in Society and History* 23(4):565–90.

Poiger, Uta G. 2000. *Jazz, Rock, and Rebels: Cold War Politics and American Culture in a Divided Germany.* Berkeley: University of California Press.

Poiger, Uta G. 2003. "Fear and Fascination: American Popular Culture in a Divided Germany, 1945–1968." In *Kazaaam! Splat! Ploof!: The American Impact on European Popular Culture Since 1945*, edited by Sabrina P. Ramet and Gordana Crnkovic, 55–68. Lanham MD: Rowman and Littlefield.

216 References

Poole, Buzz. 2016. *Grateful Dead's Workingman's Dead*. New York: Bloomsbury.

Powell, Lewis F. Jr. 1971. "Attack on American Free Enterprise System." Snail Darter Documents. Paper 79. http://lawdigitalcommons.bc.edu/darter_materials/79.

Powers, Ann. 2017. *Good Booty: Love and Sex, Black and White, Body and Soul in American Music*. New York: Dey St. Books.

Powers, Devon. 2010. "Rock Criticism's Public Intellectuals." *Popular Music and Society* 33(4):533–48.

Powers, Devon. 2013. *Writing the Record: The Village Voice and the Birth of Rock Criticism*. Amherst: University of Massachusetts Press.

Presley, Priscilla Beaulieu. 1985. *Elvis and Me*. New York: Putnam.

Price, David H. 2008. *Anthropological Intelligence: The Deployment and Neglect of American Anthropology in the Second World War*. Durham, NC: Duke University Press.

Price, David H. 2016. *Cold War Anthropology: The CIA, the Pentagon, and the Growth of Dual Use Anthropology*. Durham, NC: Duke University Press.

Pulju, Rebecca J. 2011. *Women and Mass Consumer Society in Postwar France*. New York: Cambridge University Press.

Rahula, Bhikkhu Yogavacara. 1985. *One Night's Shelter (from Home to Homelessness): The Autobiography of an American Buddhist Monk*. Colombo: Public Trustee of Sri Lanka.

Reich, Charles A. 1970. *The Greening of America*. New York: Random House.

Remmers, H. H., and D. H. Radler. 1957. *The American Teenager*. Indianapolis: Bobbs-Merrill.

Reynolds, Simon. 2016. *Shock and Awe: Glam Rock and Its Legacy, from the Seventies to the Twenty-First Century*. London: Faber & Faber.

Roberts, Michael James. 2014. *Tell Tchaikovsky the News: Rock 'n' Roll, the Labor Question, and the Musicians' Union, 1942–1968*. Durham, NC: Duke University Press.

Robertson, Robbie. 2016. *Testimony*. New York: Crown Archetype.

Rodriguez, Robert. 2012. *Revolver: How the Beatles Re-Imagined Rock "n" Roll*. Montclair, NJ: Backbeat Books.

Rogers, Carl R. 1951. *Client-Centered Therapy: Its Current Practice, Implications and Theory*. Boston: Houghton Mifflin.

Rosenberg, Bernard, and David Manning White, eds. 1957. *Mass Culture: The Popular Arts in America*. Glencoe: The Free Press.

Rounds, Dwight. 2005. *The Year the Music Died*. Austin, TX: 1st World Library.

Sanchez, Luis. 2014. *SMiLE*. New York: Bloomsbury.

Sargant, Walter W. (1957) 1985. *Battle for the Mind: A Physiology of Conversion and Brainwashing*. Chicago: University of Chicago Press.

Savage, Jon. 2007. *Teenage: The Creation of Youth Culture*. London: Chatto & Windus.

Schechner, Richard. 1965. "Happenings." *The Tulane Drama Review* 10(2):229–32.

Schlesinger, Arthur M. 1949. *The Vital Center: The Politics of Freedom*. Boston: Houghton Mifflin.

Scully, Rock, and David Dalton. 1995. *Living with the Dead: Twenty Years on the Bus with Garcia and the Grateful Dead*. New York: Little Brown and Co.

Sears, Fred F. 1956. *Don't Knock the Rock*. Columbia Pictures.

Segrave, Kerry. 1994. *Payola in the Music Industry: A History, 1880–1991*. Jefferson, NC: McFarland and Company.

Segrave, Kerry. 2002. *Jukebox: An American Social History*. Jefferson, NC: McFarland and Company.

Simmons, Jerold. 2008. "Violent Youth: The Censoring and Public Reception of The Wild One and The Blackboard Jungle." *Film History* 20:381–91.

Simpson, Kim Jefferson. 2005. "Hit Radio and the Formatting of America in the Early 1970s." PhD Dissertation: University of Texas at Austin.

Smolko, Tim, and Joanna Smolko. 2021. *Atomic Tunes: The Cold War in American and British Popular Music*. Bloomington, IN: Indiana University Press.
Sounes, Howard. 2015. *Notes from the Velvet Underground: The Life of Lou Reed*. London: Doubleday.
Spitz, Bob. 2005. *The Beatles: The Biography*. New York: Little, Brown and Company.
Springsteen, Bruce. 2016. *Born to Run*. New York: Simon and Schuster.
Stevens, Jay. 1987. *Storming Heaven: LSD and the American Dream*. New York: Atlantic Monthly Press.
Stevenson, Adlai E. 1956. *What I Think*. New York: Harper and Brothers.
Talbot, David. 2012. *Season of the Witch: Enchantment, Terror, and Deliverance in the City of Love*. New York: Free Press.
Teitelbaum, Benjamin. 2017. *Lions of the North: Sounds of the New Nordic Radical Nationalism*. New York: Oxford University Press.
Thomas, Patrick. 2017. *Did It!: From Yippie to Yuppie: Jerry Rubin, an American Revolutionary*. Seattle: Fantagraphic Books.
Thompson, Dave. 2012. *Hearts of Darkness: James Taylor, Jackson Browne, Cat Stevens, and the Unlikely Rise of the Singer-Songwriter*. Milwaukee, WI: Backbeat Books.
Thompson, Hunter S. 1973. *Fear and Loathing on the Campaign Trail '72*. San Francisco: Straight Arrow Books.
Tochka, Nicholas. 2014. "Voicing Freedom, Sounding Dissent: Popular Music, Simulation and Citizenship in Democratizing Albania, 1991–1997." *European Journal of Cultural Studies* 17(3):298–315.
Tochka, Nicholas. 2016. *Audible States*. New York: Oxford University Press.
Tochka, Nicholas. 2018. "The Battle Over 'America's Troubadour.'" *Van Magazine*. https://van-magazine.com/mag/my-racist-kentucky-home/.
Tochka, Nicholas. 2020. "John Lennon's Plastic Ono Band as 'First-Person Music': Notes on the Politics of Self-Expression in Rock Music Since 1970." *Popular Music* 39(3–4):504–22.
Tompkins, David G. 2014. "Against 'Pop-Song Poison' from the West: Early Cold War Attempts to Develop a Socialist Popular Music in Poland and the GDR." In *Youth and Rock in the Soviet Bloc: Youth Cultures, Music, and the State in Russia and Eastern Europe*, edited by William Risch, 43–54. Lanham, MD: Lexington Books.
Trynka, Paul. 2008. *Iggy Pop: Open Up and Bleed*. New York: Broadway Books.
Tsipursky, Gleb. 2012. "Having Fun in the Thaw: Youth Initiative Clubs in the Post- Stalin Years." *The Carl Beck Papers in Russian and East European Studies* 2201:1–68. https://carlbeckkpapers.pitt.edu/ojs/index.php/cbp/article/view/172.
Tsipursky, Gleb. 2013. "Coercion and Consumption: The Khrushchev Leadership's Ruling Style in the Campaign Against 'Westernized' Youth, 1954–64." In *The Socialist Beat in the Soviet Bloc*, edited by W. J. Risch and K. Transchel, 82–126. Lanham, MD: Lexington Books.
Tunstall, Jeremy. 1977. *The Media Are American: Anglo-American Media in the World*. London: Constable.
Turner, Fred. 2006. *From Counterculture to Cyberculture: Stewart Brand, the Whole Earth Network, and the Rise of Digital Utopianism*. Chicago: University of Chicago Press.
Turner, Fred. 2013. *The Democratic Surround: Multimedia and American Liberalism from World War II to the Psychedelic Sixties*. Chicago: University of Chicago Press.
Ventsel, Aimar. 2020. *Punks and Skins United: Identity, Class and the Economics of an Eastern German Subculture*. London: Berghahn.
Vuletic, Dean. 2015. "Swinging between East and West: Yugoslav Communism and the Dilemmas of Popular Music." In *Youth and Rock in the Soviet Bloc: Youth Cultures, Music, and the State in Russia and Eastern Europe*, edited by William Risch, 25–41. Lanham MD: Lexington Books.

References

Waksman, Steve. 2009. *This Ain't the Summer of Love: Conflict and Crossover in Heavy Metal and Punk*. Berkeley: University of California Press.

Wald, Elijah. 2007. *Global Minstrels: Voices of World Music*. New York: Routledge.

Wald, Elijah. 2009. *How the Beatles Destroyed Rock and Roll*. New York: Oxford University Press.

Walker, Michael. 2006. *Laurel Canyon: The Inside Story of Rock-and-Roll's Legendary Neighborhood*. New York: Faber and Faber.

Ward, Brian. 1998. *Just My Soul Responding: Rhythm and Blues, Black Consciousness and Race Relations*. London: UCL Press.

Weinstein, Deena. 2014. "Just So Stories: How Heavy Metal Got Its Name—A Cautionary Tale." *Rock Music Studies* 1(1):36–51.

Weisbard, Eric. 2014. *Top 40 Democracy: The Rival Mainstreams of American Music*. Chicago: University of Chicago Press.

Weisbard, Eric. 2021. *Songbooks: The Literature of American Popular Music*. Durham, NC: Duke University Press.

Weissman, Dick. 2005. *Which Side Are You On?: An Inside History of the Folk Music Revival in America*. New York: Continuum.

Wenner, Jann. 1995. "Mick Jagger Remembers." *Rolling Stone* (14 December). Available at https://www.rollingstone.com/feature/mick-jagger-remembers-92946/.

Wenner, Jann S., and John Lennon. 1971. *Lennon Remembers: The Rolling Stone Interviews*. San Francisco: Straight Arrow Books.

White, Charles. 1984. *The Life and Times of Little Richard: The Quasar of Rock*. New York: Harmony Books.

White, Monica M. 1998. "Panther Stories: A Gendered Analysis of the Autobiographies of Former Black Panther Members." PhD Dissertation, Western Michigan University.

White, Timothy. 1984. *Rock Stars*. New York: Stewart, Tabori and Chang.

Whitfield, Steven. 1991. *The Culture of the Cold War*. Baltimore: John Hopkins University Press.

Williams, Paul, and Brian Edgar. 2008. "Up Against the Wall: Primal Therapy and 'the Sixties.'" *European Journal of American Studies* 3(2). https://doi.org/10.4000/ejas.3022.

Winner, Langdon. 1969. "The Strange Death of Rock and Roll." In *Rock and Roll Will Stand*, edited by Greil Marcus, 38–55. Boston: Beacon Press.

Wolfe, Tom. 1968. *The Electric Kool-Aid Acid Test*. New York: Farrar, Straus & Giroux.

Worley, Matthew. 2017. *No Future: Punk, Politics and British Youth Culture, 1976–1984*. Cambridge: Cambridge University Press.

Yarrow, Andrew L. 2010. *Measuring America: How Economic Growth Came to Define American Greatness in the Late Twentieth Century*. Amherst: University of Massachusetts Press.

Yurchak, Alexei. 2005. *Everything Was Forever, Until It Was No More: The Last Soviet Generation*. Princeton: Princeton University Press.

Zak, Albin. 2004. "Bob Dylan and Jimi Hendrix: Juxtaposition and Transformation in 'All Along the Watchtower.'" *Journal of the American Musicological Society* 57(3):599–644.

Zak, Albin. 2010. *I Don't Sound Like Nobody: Remaking Music in 1950s America*. Ann Arbor: University of Michigan Press.

Zappa, Frank, and Peter Occhiogrosso. 1989. *The Real Frank Zappa Book*. New York: Poseidon Press.

Zhuk, Sergei I. 2010. *Rock and Roll in the Rocket City: The West, Identity, and Ideology in Soviet Dniepropetrovsk, 1960–1985*. Baltimore: John Hopkins University Press.

Index

For the benefit of digital users, indexed terms that span two pages (e.g., 52-53) may, on occasion, appear on only one of those pages.

? And the Mysterians, 141–42, 143
13th Floor Elevators, 142

Acuff, Roy, 161
Adorno, Theodor, 14
Alice Cooper, 115–16, 146
Alpert, Richard (Ram Dass), 93–94
Altamont, 104, 105, 128–29, 144, 155, 163, 170
the Amboy Dukes, 142
the American Century, 35, 46–47, 178, 181
"American music," claims about, 10, 21, 31, 53, 58, 144, 165
Amnesty International, 1–2, 169, 180
  Secret Policeman's Other Ball: The Music (1981), 169
Anger, Kenneth, 73–74
Angry Samoans, 144, 151
  "Get Off The Air" (1980), 151
Anka, Paul, 38, 132–33
Anthony, Richard, 38
anthropology and anthropologists, 13–14
anxieties
  communism, 3, 14, 75 (*see also* the Three Worlds)
  conformism, 14, 17, 66, 125
  consumption and mass culture, 3, 15, 46, 54–55, 58–59
  juvenile delinquency, 13, 19–20, 32–33, 140
  nuclear war, 23, 25–26, 176–77
  personality or identity, 13–15, 17–18, 121
  race, 22, 49, 60–61
  social change, 40, 97, 134, 185
  teenagers, 8, 10–11, 13–14, 18–19, 21, 22–23, 27–28, 39–40, 65, 97
Arendt, Hannah, 18
ASCAP, 57–59
assassinations (real or imagined), 64, 72, 103, 104, 119, 127, 128–29, 130, 132–34, 149, 150, 152–53
astrology, 108, 158

Asylum Records, 115, 169
Auden, W. H., 69
Avakian, George, 56, 60, 67
Avalon Ballroom, 84
Avtograf, 173, 176

the B-52s, 162–63
Baez, Joan, 66, 80, 92, 95–96, 156–57
the Band, 89, 137–38
  Danko, Rick, 91
  Music from Big Pink (1968), 91, 134–35
  Robertson, Robbie, 91
Bangs, Lester, 130, 139–44
Baraka, Amiri, 101
the Barbarians, 142
Baruch, Dorothy, 8
basements
  necking in, 34
  recording in, 91
the Bauls, 86–89
  Bengali Bauls . . . at Big Pink (1968), 91
the Beach Boys, 1, 54, 76, 156, 158, 162
  Love, Mike, 158
  SMiLE, 76
  "Surfin' USA" (1962), 63
  Wilson, Brian, 62–63, 76, 103
  Wilson, Carl, 122–23
  Wilson, Dennis, 103, 121
  Wilson, Murry, 62–63
the Beatles, 1, 17–18, 53, 64–66, 69–71, 72, 73, 74, 75, 92, 93, 95–96, 103, 104, 107, 123, 128, 165, 175
  Abbey Road (1969), 103
  "All You Need Is Love" (1967), 165
  Apple Corps, 105, 113–14
  "Back in the USSR" (1968), 176
  Beatle George, 88–89, 103
    "Here Comes The Sun" (1969), 165
  Beatle John, 53, 69–71, 72–73, 100–1, 103, 109–10
    "Come Together" (1969), 103

the Beatles (cont.)
    How I Won The War (1967), 109–10
    "You've Got To Hide Your Love Away" (1965), 69–70
  Beatle Paul, 74, 103, 123–24
  Beatle Ringo, 103
  Beatlemania, 64–66, 70, 92–93
  The Beatles Anthology (1995), 78
  Help! (1965), 88–89
  Let It Be (1970, film), 107
  Martin, George (producer), 165
  and nostalgia, 135, 140, 168
  reunion rumors, 166
  Revolver (1966), 72–73
  Sgt Pepper's Lonely Hearts Club Band, 72–73
  and the Soviet Union, 70, 175
the Beats, 51, 81, 89–90, 93
Beatty, Warren, 119–20
Bernstein, Leonard, 74–76
Berry, Chuck, 7, 24, 55, 63, 100, 112, 142, 165
  "Johnny B. Goode" (1958), 165
  "Sweet Little Sixteen" (1958), 24, 63
  "You Can't Catch Me" (1956), 134–35
Biafra, Jello, 131, 149–50, 154
  Alternative Tentacles (label), 152
  Dead Kennedys, 131
  East Bay Ray, 152
  "Holiday in Cambodia" (1980), 149–50
the Big Beat Club, 94–96
Bingenheimer, Rodney, 146, 151
birds, 54–55, 75, 78–79, 92, 96, 115, 131, 144, 176–77. *See also* the Byrds
Black Dwarf, 100–1
Black Panther Party, 81–82, 99, 151
Black Sabbath, 115–16, 139
Blackboard Jungle (1955), 9, 25, 32–34, 35–37, 38
BMI, 57–59, 165
bombs (literal and figurative), 8, 23, 25, 37–38, 50–51, 70, 84–85, 101, 118–19, 150, 164
bondage and domination, fantasies of, 73–74, 84, 89–90, 95–96, 146
Boothe Luce, Clare, 32, 35–36, 93
the Bosstown Sound, 102
Bowie, David, 37, 145–46, 156
Boy George, 178–79
Brando, Marlon, 104
the Brill Building, 54–55
Brotherhood of Light, 84
Browne, Jackson, 112, 113, 115, 138, 162–63
  "Late for the Sky" (1974), 134

Buffalo Springfield, 81, 85, 112–13
Buffet, Jimmy, 162–63
the Byrds, 70–71, 81, 83, 85, 88, 140
  "Ballad of Easy Rider" (1969), 129
  "Eight Miles High" (1966), 88–89
  "I Wasn't Born To Follow" (1968), 105
  McGuinn, Roger, 75–76, 129

Cale, John, 54
Callas, Maria, 164–65
Canned Heat, 139
the Cars, 162–63
Casals, Pablo, 57
CBGB, 133, 141
Celler, Emanuel, 57–58
Chicago Democratic National Convention protests, 98–99, 101, 110, 131
civil rights, 47–48, 50, 68, 69, 80, 82, 121, 127
Clapton, Eric, 169–70
  Cream, 139
Clark, Dick, 60, 151
  American Bandstand, 134, 151
the Clash (and Joe Strummer), 166
classical music, 9, 33, 37–38, 41, 56, 57, 59, 60, 119, 122, 160, 162, 179
Cleese, John, 169
Cochran, Eddie, 23–24
the Coffee Gallery, 81
Cold War. *See* the Three Worlds
Cole, Nat King, 50
Collective Vision, 176, 179–80
Collins, Judy, 119–20
Collins, Phil, 156
conspiracies (real or imagined), 64, 75, 102, 103, 125–26, 143, 159
Cooke, Sam
  "A Change Is Gonna Come" (1964), 68
Cording, Henry (and His Original Rock and Roll Boys), 38
Count Five, 141–42
  Psychotic Reaction (1966), 143
the counterculture, 80, 84, 85, 89–90, 96–97, 99, 102, 104–5, 109, 114–15, 117–18, 123–24, 135, 150–51, 164
criticism and histories of rock, 28
  books
    The Aesthetics of Rock, 75
    The Age of Rock: Sounds of the American Revolution (1969/1970), 112, 136
    Please Kill Me (1996), 146–47
    Rock Folk: Portraits from the Rock 'n' Roll Pantheon (1968), 112

Index

Rock and Roll Will Stand (1969), 3–4, 136
Rolling Stone Illustrated History of Rock and Roll (1975), v, 138–39
The Story of Rock (1970), 137
magazines and zines, 139–40 (*see also* Rolling Stone [magazine])
   Broadside, 68
   Crawdaddy, 78–79, 110
   Creem, 139–40, 155
   Flipside, 147, 148
   Maximumrocknroll, 150–51
   Punk, 146–47
   Sing Out, 67
   Slash, 151
rockism, xii–xiii, 108
writers and key commentators (*see also entries for* Bangs, Lester; Marcus, Greil; *and* Wenner, Jann)
   Belz, Carl, 136, 137
   Christgau, Robert, 28, 72–73, 100–1, 111–12
   Gillett, Charles, 143
   Goldstein, Richard, 72–73, 78–79, 82, 90–91, 101–2
   Hilburn, Robert, 162, 164, 166–67, 171, 172, 174–75
   Landau, Jon, 110, 112, 140
   Loder, Kurt, 2
   McNeil, Legs, 146–47
   Marsh, Dave, 141
   Meltzer, Richard, 75, 144
   Miller, Jim, v, 138
   Saunders, Metal Mike, 144
   Shelton, Robert, 68–69, 70–71
   Ward, Ed, 140
   Williams, Paul, 78–79, 110
   Winner, Langdon, 4, 110
   Yohannon, Tim, 149, 150–51
Crosby, Stills, Nash, and Young, 116–17, 156, 181
   "Long Time Coming" (1969), 181
   "Teach Your Children" (1970), 160
the Crucifucks, 132, 153

the Dave Clark Five, 141–42
Dead Kennedys. *See* Biafra, Jello
Dean, James, 32, 38, 68–69
Deep Purple, 174
Def Leppard, 127
Delacourt, Duane (*Doonesbury* character), 127–28

Denver, John, 161
the Dicks, 152
Diddley, Bo, 50
Didion, Joan, 128–29
the Diggers, 104
disco, xii–xiii, 127, 147, 148
Dog Day Afternoon (1975), 134
Domino, Fats, 22–23
Don't Knock the Rock (1957), 9, 44–45
Donahue, Phil, 173
Donegan, Lonny, 37
Donovan, 72, 169
doo wop, 56, 63, 134, 135
the Doors, xii, 81, 89
   "The End" (1966), 81
   Morrison, Jim, 79–80, 89–90
Dylan, Bob. *See* Hammond's Folly
Dzidzornu, Rocky, 89–90

the Eagles, 115, 131
Easy Rider (1969), 116–18, 129
the Ed Sullivan Show, 51, 64
Elektra Records, 88, 132–33, 142
Elephant's Memory, 126
Ellington, Duke, 122
Ellis, Peter, 163, 166
The Exploding Plastic Inevitable, 74, 83–84

Fakir, Asoke, 87–88
Faulkner, William, 69
Feinstein, Dianne, 149
Ferlinghetti, Lawrence, 150
Fields, Danny, 132, 133
the Fillmore, 84, 85, 88, 129–30, 170
Fischer, Wild Man, 102, 103
Fleetwood Mac, 162–63
folk music, 66–69, 70–71, 72–73, 126
   folk revival, 66–67
   folkies, 80, 143, 171
   folk rock, 70–71, 112–13
Fonda, Peter, 116–17, 129
Ford, Glenn, 25, 32, 33
Frampton, Peter, 131
Franzoni, Carl, 83, 85, 102
freaks, 83–84, 86
Freed, Alan, 7, 9–11, 57, 60
Friedman, Thomas, 157
Fromm, Erich, 18
Fromme, Squeaky, 133–34
the Fugs, xii, 94
   Kupferberg, Tuli, 93

Index

Fulbright, William F., 43
the Funk Brothers, 62–63
Furnier, Vince, 146

Geffen, David, 115
Geldof, Bob, 156, 168, 171, 173
the Germs, 145, 151
  Crash, Darby (Paul Beahm) 145–46
  Smear, Pat (Georg Ruthenberg), 145–46
Gillespie, Dizzy, 48
Ginsberg, Allen, 86–87, 94, 121, 125–26, 138
Gleason, Ralph, 109–10, 140
Goodman, Paul, 80–81
Gorbachev, Mikhail, 174
government agencies, committees, foundations (United States), 34–35, 39–40, 57–59, 73–74, 123–24, 145, 161
Graham, Bill (Wulf Wolodia Grajonca), 2, 84, 102, 156, 162–63, 164, 168, 171, 176
the Grateful Dead, 84, 94, 102, 112, 139, 162–63
  Anthem of the Sun (1968), 139
  Garcia, Jerry, 4, 96, 110, 120, 164
Great Society (band). *See* Jefferson Airplane
The Great Society (government programs), 82–83, 97
Grossman, Albert, 68, 86–87, 88, 89
Grossman, Sally, 86, 88
the Guess Who, 140
Guthrie, Woody, 55, 68, 126

hair, 8, 41, 51–52, 56, 74, 83, 88, 96, 134, 142–43, 157
Haley, Bill and His Comets, 25, 35, 50, 56, 134
  "Rock Around The Clock" (1954), 25, 33, 37–38, 42, 47
Hallyday, Johnny, 38
Hamilton, Roy, 22
Hammond, John, 68, 75
Hammond's Folly, xii, 1, 2, 31, 66, 67–71, 74, 75, 86–88, 89–91, 95, 100, 110, 112, 127, 134–35, 136–37, 138, 139, 140, 157, 168–70, 171
  "A Hard Rain's a–Gonna Fall" (1963), 64, 68, 69
  as "an American Baul," 87–88
  "Ballad of a Thin Man" (1965), 95
  "Blowin' in the Wind" (1963), 68
  Bob Dylan (1962)

Bringing It All Back Home (1965), 89–90
  "Chimes of Freedom" (1964), 1–2, 177, 187
Dinkytown, 66
  The Freewheelin' Bob Dylan (1963), 68
  "I Shall Be Released" (1967), 2, 180
  "I Threw It All Away" (1969), 137–38
  "I Want You" (1966), 86
  John Wesley Harding (1967), 86
  "Like A Rolling Stone" (1965), 1
  Nashville Skyline (1969), 137–38
  "Subterranean Homesick Blues" (1965), 101
  as Yevtushenko, 68–69
Happy Birthday, America! (1976), 132–33
Harrison, George (solo), 1, 119, 169–70. *See also* the Beatles
  "Bangla Desh" (1971, single), 169
  Concert for Bangla Desh (concert and album), 169–70
Havens, Richie, 77
Hays Code, 161
heavy metal, 127, 141, 159–60, 166, 175–76
Hells Angels, 96, 128–29
Helms, Chet, 84
Hendrix, Jimi, xii, 135
hippies (or hippy), 75, 83, 89, 90–91, 92, 95, 96, 102, 104, 118–19, 134–35, 150, 159, 164, 182
The Hippies (filmstrip), 75
Hoffman, Abbie, 99–103
Hofstadter, Richard, 75
Holly, Buddy, 7, 38, 55, 60, 63–64
Hopper, Dennis, 116–18, 129
Horowitz, Vladimir, 160
Humble Pie, 141
Hurt, Mississippi John, 92

Inside Pop: The Rock Revolution (1967), 74
Interrupted Melody (1955), 9
Iron Maiden, 175–76

Jackson, Janet
  "Nasty" (1986), 182–83
jazz, 48, 56, 77–78, 144, 149–50, 182
jeans (blue), 17, 29, 36, 41–42, 63–64, 96, 101–2, 127–28, 174, 176, 181
Jefferson Airplane, 81, 84, 100
  Balin, Marty, 100
  Slick, Grace, 81, 100
  Surrealistic Pillow (1967), 100
  "Volunteers" (1969), 100

jelly
    babies, 72
    beans, 152
John Birch Society, 75
John, Elton, 113, 174–75
    To Russia... With Elton (1979), 174
Johnson, Robert, 89–90, 137–38

Kasem, Casey, 164
Kaufman, Murray ("Murray the K"), 39–40, 69
Kaye, Lenny, 142–43
    Nuggets: Original Artyfacts from the First Psychedelic Era (1972), 142
KC and the Sunshine Band, 132–33
Kerouac, Jack
    On The Road (1957), 51
Kesey, Ken, 92–93, 94–95, 125–26
    his Merry Pranksters, 92, 95–96
    "Home on the Range," 92–93
    One Flew Over the Cuckoo's Nest (1962), 81–82
Khan, Ali Akbar, 169–70
King, Carole, 54–55, 119
    Goffin and King, 62–63, 105
    Tapestry (1971), 114
Kookie (Edward Byrnes), 56–57
Kraus, Peter ("the German Elvis"), 39
Kustom Kar Kommandos (1964), 73–74

Lasch, Christopher, 80
Lauren, Rod (Roger Strunk), 32
LDM Spiritual Band, 88
Leary, Timothy, 88, 93–94, 95–96, 97, 103
    League for Spiritual Development, 94
    The Psychedelic Experience (1964), 93–94
Leigh, Mickey, 144
Lennon, John (solo), 107–8, 111, 112–13, 123–24, 126–27, 128–29, 134–35, 142, 169–70, 183. See also the Beatles
    "Give Peace a Chance" (1969), 103
    "Imagine" (1971), 183
    Lennon Remembers (1971), 111
    Plastic Ono Band (1970), 107, 128–29
    "Power to the People" (1971), 126
    Rock and Roll (1975), 134–35
    Some Time In New York City (1972), 126
    "Woman is the Nigger of the World" (1972), 126
Levy, Morris, 9, 134–35
Lewis, Jerry Lee, 7, 55, 135

Lewter Jr., Cleve, 29, 52
Lewy, Henry (Heinz), 114
Lieber and Stoller, 62–63
    "Yakety Yak" (1958), 63
Light Sound Dimension, 84
Lippman, Walter, 26
Little Eva, 54–55, 76
    "The Loco-Motion" (1962), 54–55
Little Steven, 178–79
    "I Am A Patriot" (1986), 179–80
Live Aid, 156–57, 167–69, 171, 173
Lodge, Henry Cabot, 50
Lord Baltimore, 141
Love (band), 81
    Lee, Arthur, 103
Lowell, Robert, 69
LSD, 86, 93–94, 103, 123–24, 125–26
Luce, Henry, 35. See also the American Century
Lymon, Frankie, 7, 60

MacAllester, David, 74
MacDonald, Country Joe, 105
Mailer, Norman
    "The White Negro" (1957), 50–51
Malanga, Gerard, 83–84, 95–96
the Mamas and the Papas, 72
    Elliott, Cass, 113
    "San Francisco (Be Sure To Wear Flowers In Your Hair)" (song by John Phillips), 89–90
Manson, Charles, 103, 104, 133–34
Marcus, Greil, 3–4, 33, 67, 75, 86–87, 91, 110, 136, 137, 142–43
Marcuse, Herbert, 78–79
    One-Dimensional Man (1964), 97
the Masque, 146, 147
Mayall, John
    Blues from Laurel Canyon (1968), 113
Maysles, Albert, 104
MC5, xii, 99
    Sinclair, John, 102
McCarthy, Joseph, 20
McCartney, Paul (solo), 1, 156, 171. See also the Beatles
    McCartney (1970), 112
McGuire, Barry, 70–71
McLuhan, Marshall, 83–84, 85, 157
MDC (aka, Millions of Dead Cops), 152, 153
    "John Wayne Was A Nazi" (1982), 153
Me Decade, 114–15, 131, 163

Me Generation, 108, 162–63
Mellencamp, John Cougar, 166, 171
metaphorical language about society, 3–4, 79
    Amerikkka, 143, 149
    invasion, 63–64, 81, 132–33
    the Plastic Society, 79, 89, 145–46
    sickness and health, 8, 11, 12–13, 14–15, 27–28, 45–46, 81–82, 95, 97–98, 105, 114, 179
    the System, 79–80, 147–48, 150–51
Metzner, Ralph, 93–94
Milk, Harvey, 149
Miller, Glenn, 42, 60–61
Miller, Mitch, 15–16, 57
Miller, Steve, 139
mind control and brainwashing, 3, 14, 69–70, 140–41, 146
    and "Itsy Bitsy Teenie Weenie Yellow Polka Dot Bikini" (1961), 62
    Meerloo, Joost A. M., 18
    MKUltra, 125–26
    Sargant, William, 17–18
Mingus, Charles, 48
Minutemen, 131
Mitchell, Joni, 119–20
    Ladies of the Canyon (1970), 113
the Monkees, 74
Moscone, George, 149
Motown, 53, 85

Nelson, Paul, 71
Nelson, Willie, 171
New Hollywood, 117–18
Newport Folk Festival, 69–70
Nicholson, Jack, 117–18, 119, 168–69
Nico
    The Marble Index (1978), 139
nightmares
    decade of, 131–32, 150
    Oedipal, 81
the Now Generation, 108, 127–28, 133

Ochs, Phil, 98–99, 100, 112, 126
Oingo Boingo, 162–63
Ono, Yoko, 103, 107, 126, 129
O'Rourke, P. J., 181
Orwell, George, 26
Osbourne, Ozzy, 166
Owsley, Stanley, 94

Packard, Vance
    The Hidden Persuaders (1957), 62

Page, Jimmy, 37
Paramount Theater, 9, 44–45
Parents Music Resource Center (PMRC), 159, 161
Paulekas, Vito, 83–84
payola, 59–61
    "Pachalafaka" (1958), 60
Peebles, Ann, 112–13
Peter and Conny, 39
Peter and Gordon, 80
Peter, Paul, and Mary, 68, 80, 119–20
    Travers, Mary, 171
Picasso, Pablo, 71, 73, 164–65
Pickwick City Records, 54–55, 74
political labels, ideologies, and -isms, 1–2, 5, 181
    anarchism, 5, 7–8, 9, 40, 128, 147, 148, 149, 178
    anti-communism, 35, 39–40, 48, 50, 51, 172
    antifascism, 148, 154
    democratic, xi, 5–6, 12–13, 14–15, 33, 49, 55, 61–62, 83–85, 95–96, 132, 138, 144–45, 148, 172, 179–80
    Democrats (political party), 99–100, 119, 121, 127–28, 149, 154, 159, 182, 184–85
    evangelicism, 153, 158, 159
        Chick, Jack ("Chick tracts"), 159
        Falwell, Jerry, 154, 159
    fascism, 11, 12, 14, 16–17, 18, 49, 85, 92, 144–45, 148, 151, 153
    humanitarianism and human rights, 2, 157, 169, 180 (*see also* Live Aid)
    individualism, xii–xiii, 5, 14, 17, 36–37, 63, 66, 68–69, 90, 92–93, 96, 108, 112–13, 114–15, 129, 147, 150–51, 154–55, 162–63, 178–79, 185
    liberalism, 50–51, 80–81, 99–100, 116–17, 120, 122–23, 145–46, 149–50, 154, 168
        and identification with marginalised groups, 67, 80–81, 99
    liberation, 3, 77–78, 81–82, 86–87, 89–90, 93, 99, 110, 121, 143–44, 154–55, 180 (*see also* bondage and domination, fantasies of)
    libertarianism, 2, 104, 183
    nationalism (United States), 52–53, 125, 157
    Nazism, 129, 130, 146, 153, 154
    neoliberalism, 116, 124–25

New Left, 74–75, 77–78, 79, 92, 96, 99, 125, 131, 150
Old Left, 71, 140
one-world-ism and globalization, 157, 165
   Our World broadcast (1967), 164–65
   "We Are The World" (1985), 168
racism, 21–23, 37, 48–49, 50, 82, 111, 123, 148
radicalism, 80
Republicans, 96, 99–100, 119–20, 121, 127, 153–54
Thatcherism, 133
totalitarianism, 18, 26, 27–28, 61–62, 172, 173
utopianism, 83–85, 94, 95, 105, 164–66
Porter, Cole, 58
positionality and biases (author's), xii, 4–5, 132, 137
   The Chipmunks Sing the Beatles Hits (1964), 114
   favorite bands (*see* Angry Samoans; the Guess Who, *and* Sha Na Na)
   put-ons and shucks, 63, 93, 106, 139, 187
Powell Memorandum, 124–25
Pozner, Vladimir, 173
presidential candidates (United States)
   campaigns' use of rock music, 4, 182–83
   Clinton, Hillary Rodham, 121, 182–83
   Goldwater, Barry, 121, 159
   Harris, Kamala, 182
   Kennedy, Robert F., 119
   McGovern, George, 119–21, 122–23, 128
   Mondale, Walter, 2, 160, 161
   Pig, Pigasus J., 98–100
   Sanders, Bernie, 182
   Stevenson, Adlai, 41
   Wallace, George, 49, 99–100, 121
presidents (United States)
   Brown, Jerry (imaginary), 154
   Bush, George H. W., 182
   Carter, Jimmy, 127–28, 154, 158
   Clinton, Bill, 121, 182
   Ford, Gerald, 133–34
   Humphrey, Hubert, 99–100
   Kennedy Jr., John F., 64, 65, 127, 156
   Nixon, Richard, 4–5, 99–100, 120, 124–25, 126–27, 161, 169–70
      and dirty tricks, 123
      and Elvis, 123
      and Sammy Davis Jr, 122
   Obama, Barack, 31, 182

Reagan, Ronald, 97, 119–20, 150, 152–53, 154, 158–62, 172, 174, 185
Truman, Harry, 21
Trump, Donald, 182–83
Presley, Elvis, 19, 36, 38, 39, 40–41, 45–46, 51–52, 55, 59, 65, 123, 134, 137–38, 140, 174
press and commentary, consensus mainstream, 110
   Battelle, Phyllis, 27, 28, 47–48
   Life magazine, 12, 26, 35, 64, 93
   Newsweek, 96, 162, 167, 171
   Time magazine, 1–2, 66, 72, 110
   Salisbury, Harrison, 15–16, 19–20, 42–43, 64
   Samuels, Gertrude, 16–17
   Zausmer, Otto, 61, 63–64
press and commentary, conservative
   Bloom, Allan, 178–79
   Buckley, William F., 121, 153–54, 168–69
   Commentary, 23, 136
   Fukuyama, Frances, 157
   Goldman, Stuart, 178–79
   National Review, 2, 153–54, 168–69, 178–79
   Rand, Ayn, 104
   Safire, William, 123–24, 144–45, 148–49
   Sokolsky, George, 20
press and commentary, liberal and progressive
   Berkeley Barb, 88
   Chomsky, Noam, 82
   East Village Other, 100
   MTV, 160–61, 167, 173
   The Nation, 2, 160–61
   Ramparts, 92, 95, 109–10
   Schlesinger Jr., Arthur, 26
   Thompson, Hunter S., 120–21
   The Village Voice, 72–74, 90–91, 119–20
   Wolfe, Tom, 93, 94, 114–15, 131
Preston, Billy, 169–70
psy-disciplines, psychiatrists, and psychologists, 8, 13–15, 18–19, 50–51. *See also* the entry for Leary, Timothy
   American Psychopathological Association, 10–11
   Erikson, Erik, 15
   est (Erhard Seminars Training), 145, 164
   Janov, Arthur (and *The Primal Scream* [1970]), 107

psy-disciplines, psychiatrists, and psychologists (*cont.*)
   Laing, R. D., 81–82
   Maslow, Abraham, 18–19
   psychological integrity, 14, 17, 18–19, 27, 37, 62, 65
   psychological warfare, 75–76, 79–80, 125–26 (*see also* mind control and brainwashing)
   Rogers, Carl, 18–19
   self-actualization, 18–19, 97–98

The Quarrymen, 23

Raitt, Bonnie, 176
the Ramones, xii, 132–33, 140, 141
Ravi Shankar, 88–89, 90–91, 169–70
   raga rock, 89, 90
Reagan, Nancy, 158
Reed, Lou, xii, 54–55
   "Cycle Annie" (1963), 54
   "The Ostrich" (1964), 54
Reynolds, Malvina, 67
   "Little Boxes" (1962), 66
Richard, Cliff
   "Power To All Our Friends" (1973), 174
Richard, Little, 1, 55, 59, 66
Richie, Lionel, 168
Ricker, Dorothy, 19
Riesman, David
   The Lonely Crowd (1950), 62, 101–2
Robbins, Jerome, 83
Rock Against Reagan, 152–53
Rock and Roll Hall of Fame, xiii, 1
Rock Liberation Front, 136–37
rock music
   antinuclear proliferation movement, 169
   as art, v, 54, 57, 72–74, 75, 111–12, 141, 143, 178
   government bans or control, 45–46, 48, 52, 60, 123–24, 126–27, 158, 159, 162
   gut feelings about, v, 2, 3, 113, 137, 139, 141
   and hip capitalism, 66, 81, 86, 90, 171
   humanitarianism and fundraising, 51, 168, 169–70
   in the liberal imagination, 126–27, 128, 138
   material conditions influencing reception of, 21, 24, 26, 28, 53, 97, 116, 124–25, 133–34, 186–87
   multimedia surrounds (Happenings), 83–86, 92, 109
   real ("not bullshit"), 1, 111, 131
   as revolutionary, 74, 76, 77, 82–83, 93, 95–96, 97–98, 100–2, 103, 105, 110, 128, 138, 146–47, 170
   as self-expression, 100, 111–12, 113, 114, 115
   as social message, 72, 74, 100, 110, 115–16, 160, 165, 171
   studio recording, 68, 111
rock 'n' roll
   evolution to "rock," 71, 142
   fads, 30–31, 39, 46–47, 52, 54–55, 57, 65, 90
   as a release valve for pent-up energies, 10, 19, 27, 28, 30–31, 39
   riots, 7, 20, 22–23, 36–37, 38, 39–40, 47–48
   teen-age clubs (teen canteens), 11–13
Rock 'n' Roll Summit television program (1986), 179–80
Rodgers and Hammerstein, 58, 122
Rolling Stone (magazine), xi, 108–10, 111–12, 114–15, 120, 137, 139, 140, 181
the Rolling Stones, 70, 112, 154, 174, 183
   Gimme Shelter (1970), 104
   Jagger, Mick
      as "a fake moneybags revolutionary," 143
      as Shango, 89–90
   "Paint It Black" (1966), 88–89
   "Street Fighting Man" (1968), 101
Ronstadt, Linda, 131, 154
Rose, Billy, 58
Rotolo, Suze, 68
Rubin, Jerry, 92, 97–99, 131
Run DMC, 168
Rush, Tom, 67

Santana, 162–64
Schaeffer, Pierre, 73
Scully, Vince, 94–95, 96
SDS (Students for a Democratic Society), 80, 96, 101, 163
Savio, Marco, 80
Seeger, Pete, 67, 74, 126
Sellers, Peter, 73
Sex Pistols
   "God Save the Queen" (1977), 133
Sha Na Na, 134–10, 140
Shostakovich, Dmitri, 67, 119
Shurlock, Geoffrey, 33–34

Silber, Irwin, 67, 71, 72
Sill, Judee, 108–9, 114, 115
the Silver Beetles, 63–64
Simon and Garfunkel, 72, 73, 119–20
Simon, Carly
  No Secrets (1972), 116
Simone, Nina, 48
Sinatra, Frank, 58–59, 60, 64
singer–songwriters, xii–xiii, 70–71, 109, 113, 119–20, 140
skiffle, 37
Sly Stone, 137–38
soft rock, 115–16, 131, 134, 162–63
Solanas, Valerie, 101
Spheeris, Penelope
  The Decline of Western Civilization (1981), 131, 155
Springsteen, Bruce, xii–xiii, 1–2, 11, 112, 160–61, 171, 172, 177
  "Born in the USA" (1984), 182
  "Springsteenian integrity," 171
Sri Satchidananda, 77
the Standells, 141–42
Starr, Ringo (solo), 1, 158, 166, 169–70. See *also* the Beatles
Steppenwolf
  "Born to be Wild" (1968), 116–17
  "The Pusher" (1968), 116–17
Stevens, Connie, 32
Stevenson, John Fell, 41–42
Stingray, Joanna
  Red Wave (1986), 173
the Stooges, 132–33, 140–41, 143–44
  Asheton, Ron, 146
  Fun House (1969), 144
  Pop, Iggy, 140–41, 143, 146
Straya, 9, 55, 156
Streisand, Barbara, 119
Sunset Strip, 77, 81, 83, 85, 113, 117–18
SUNY-Stony Brook, 75
Symbionese Liberation Army, 133–34

Taxi Driver (1976), 134
Taylor, James, 63, 113, 119, 130, 131, 140, 176–77
  James Taylor (1969), 105–6
  Sweet Baby James (1970), 113–14
Thompson, Dickie, 22–26
the Three Worlds, xi–xii, 2, 31, 42, 43–44, 46, 48–49, 50, 63–64, 165, 173
  cultural diplomacy, 29–30, 34, 48, 174

the First World, 2, 39, 43
  France, 37–39
  Italy, 34, 35–36
  West Germany, 38–39, 51–52, 138–39, 156
freedoms, 27–28, 61, 62, 96, 97, 108, 159–60, 172, 179, 184, 185
the Second World ("the communist world"), 38–43, 51, 58, 62, 138, 172, 174–75 (see *also* Vietnam)
  Albania, xi–xii, 46
  Berlin Wall, 1, 2, 4, 145, 178–79, 181
  Bulgaria, 41–42
  China, 20, 70, 145, 165, 173
  Cuba, 45, 46–47, 86–87, 162, 183
  Czechoslovakia, 42–43, 86–87, 172
  East Germany, 40–41, 162
  Hungary, 48–49, 51, 175–76
  North Korea, 143
  Poland, 138, 174, 175–76, 178–79
  the Soviet Union (or USSR), 15–16, 34, 40–42, 43, 50, 70, 104, 160, 166, 172–77
  Yugoslavia, 156, 174
the Third World ("the developing world"), 47, 52, 125–26, 133–34, 168
  Egypt, 29–30, 52
  India, 86–89, 165
  Indonesia, 44–45
  Iran, 45–46
  Kuwait, 44
  Nepal, 89
  Nicaragua, 177
  Palestine, 151
  Philippines, 70
  Singapore, 45
  Tanzania (Tanganyika), 47
the Trashmen, 75, 78–79, 179
the Troggs, 141–42
the Troubadour, 112–14, 115
Turner, Tina, 119–20

U2, 180
Unuson, 162–63, 164, 173
US Festival, 162–64, 166–67
USA For Africa, 168

Van Halen, 166
the Velvet Underground, 74, 83–84, 144. See *also* Reed, Lou
  White Light/White Heat (1968), 139

Index

Vietnam, 72, 79–80, 82, 99–100, 103, 125–26, 133–34, 146, 163–64, 181, 182
   the Vietcong, 95–96, 143
   Vietnam Day Committee, 92–93
Vollmer, Jurgen, 134–35
VOM, 144
voting
   spite, out of, 121
   youth, 121, 127, 158, 160–61, 185
Voyager Golden Records, 165

Warhol, Andy, 54, 73–74, 84, 101, 105, 141
Warwick, Dionne, 119–20
Waters, Muddy, 89, 160–61
Watt, James, 158, 162
Weathermen, 101
Weberman, A. J., 136–37
Wenner, Jann, 107, 109–11, 112, 139, 181
White, Dan, 149, 150

White, Josh, 67
The Wild One (1954), 33–34, 35
Willis, Betty Jean, 76
Woodstock, 77–78, 104, 156, 163–64, 166–67
   Woodstock (film), 170
Wozniak, Stephen ("Woz"), 162–63, 164, 166
Wrecking Crew, 62–63

X
   Cervenka, Exene, 146

Yippies (Youth International Party), 99
Young, Neil, 103, 113, 114, 171
   "Rockin' in the Free World" (1989), 182

Zappa, Frank, xii, 24, 75–76, 83, 161
   Freak Out! (1966), 86
   "Trouble Every Day" (1966), 82–83
   We're Only In It For The Money (1968), 102